Happy Birthday,
Jesse.

April 29, 2007

With love,

THE GOLFER'S BOOK OF DAILY INSPIRATION

A Year of Motivation, Revelation, and Instruction

KEVIN NELSON

CONTEMPORARY BOOKS

A TRIBUNE COMPANY

Library of Congress Cataloging-in-Publication Data

Nelson, Kevin, 1953–
    The golfer's book of daily inspiration : a year of
motivation, revelation, and instruction / Kevin Nelson.
        p.   cm.
    ISBN 0-8092-3213-8
    1. Golf—Quotations, maxims, etc.   2. Golf—
Calendars.   I. Title.
GV967.N45   1996
796.352'02—dc20   95-51318
                                                        CIP

Interior design by Kim Bartko

Copyright © 1996 by Kevin Nelson
All rights reserved
Published by Contemporary Books, Inc.
Two Prudential Plaza, Chicago, Illinois 60601-6790
Manufactured in the United States of America
International Standard Book Number: 0-8092-3213-8
10   9   8   7   6   5   4   3   2   1

To Annie,
my 365-days-a-year inspiration

A Word from the Author

This is a golfing book of days. Its sole purpose is to help you play better and enjoy the game more. I believe that if you do the latter, the former will surely follow.

Of all sports, golf lends itself most readily to a book of this kind because it is a game that you can play every day. That is one of the great things about it. It is a year-round game that is played in the summer, fall, winter, and spring. Golf can still be a part of your everyday life even when your local course is buried under snow.

My aim in writing this book is to encourage you to trust yourself and your swing. I want you to think positive thoughts and eliminate distractions. I want you to relax when you play. I want you to try different practice techniques and set motivational goals that will improve your game. I want you to learn how to prepare mentally for a round and increase your concentration over 18 holes. I want you to make more putts and sink chips off the green. I want you to boost your game off the tee and send balls rocketing down the fairway. I want to share colorful bits of golf lore with you. I want you to laugh about your game and keep it in perspective. Always, I want you to feel good about yourself as a golfer and confident about your abilities.

Mainly, though, I want to inspire you to go out and play. I believe that good things will happen when you play.

Put another way: You will *make* good things happen when you play.

Each day in this golfing book of days is divided into three parts: quote, message, and resolution. The intent of each part singly, and all the parts taken together, is to inspire you to play better golf. Nobody knows more about your golf game than you. You are your own best expert. Therefore, the first step in learning how to play better golf is agreeing to listen to yourself. Listening to yourself will help you achieve lasting success in the game and increase your enjoyment tenfold.

The quotes at the top of each page are from a variety of people—everybody from Epictetus to Ralph Waldo Emerson to Yogi Berra. Though these people may never have played the game, what they say has great relevance for golfers. That is another one of the great things about this game. So many of the challenges we face in a round of golf are like the challenges in our everyday lives. And we can apply the lessons we learn to both.

There are, of course, many golf quotes. Some of these are from greats like Nicklaus, Norman, and Bobby Jones. Others are from golf pros and teachers. Still others are from people who, while they may have achieved great success in business, government, the arts, and other fields, struggle like the rest of us on the golf course.

For this book I also drew from athletic success stories outside the world of golf—great athletes like George Foreman, Joe Montana, and Florence Griffith Joyner, and coaches like John Wooden. I have taken their motivational techniques and applied them to golf.

Tommy Armour, one of the greatest of all golf teachers, said that golfers should think about only one or two things when they play. This has served as my guide in writing each message for the day. The underlying theme of every message is simplicity. Get rid of what is not important. Concentrate on what you do best. A daily message may contain many separate thoughts, but I have tried to funnel all these thoughts into one simple swing key.

The resolution that concludes each message is really just a swing key. But it is probably the most important part of each message, for that is what each golfer takes onto the course that day. My writing style at times reminds me of a preacher repeating the most important elements of his sermon to the congregation. Most athletes would say, however, that repetition is a vital element in establishing rhythm and tempo, which, of course, are crucial to playing successful golf.

Find a simple message for yourself each day, a message that works for you. Carry that message onto the course with you, and use it to play better golf.

A note about the structure of the book. In general, I follow the seasons. The winter, when we play less, contains lots of material about the mental game of golf. The spring focuses on more practical advice. In the summer, tournament season begins, and I delve into the competitive elements of the game—how to play and win. In the fall, when the days become shorter and cooler, I talk more about the contemplative side of golf.

But this is only a broad outline. The art of putting is discussed year-round. So are chipping and driving the ball and hitting approaches. People can read this book each day and progress through the year with it. Or, what is more likely, they can refer to it when they are going out onto the course and find something that might be useful to them. The most inspiring thought to me as a writer is that in these pages people will grab a handful of stardust that will truly motivate them to go out and play their very best.

January 1

"Most golfers spend their whole lives trying to develop a repeating swing, as if mechanics alone will make them good players. I learned early on there is more to golf than that."
—Phil Mickelson

A round of golf is a journey. It is a journey through a green land of unforeseen challenges, difficulties, and terrors. A person needs both pluck and luck to complete this journey successfully.

The people who undertake this journey learn valuable lessons about themselves and their world. They feel sorrow, joy, pity, laughter, rage, ecstasy, pain, disappointment, and hope. They share their experiences with friends and strangers who, like them, have embarked on this odyssey that begins at home (the clubhouse) and works its way back home again.

This is the first day of a new year, the beginning of what promises to be the best year of your golfing life. This is the start of a journey that will travel over days and months and through the seasons. On this journey we will learn about the practical, mechanical side of golf, its physical component. But we will also teach ourselves considerably about the emotional and mental sides of the game, which ultimately determine one's success in golf.

We begin our journey today with a commitment—a firm, quiet commitment to ourselves. It is not one of those New Year's resolutions that people forget after a few weeks. We are sticking to it.

Today is day one. The best year of our golfing lives.

Resolved: I make this the best year of my golfing life.

January 2

"The man who thoroughly enjoys what he reads or does, or even what he says, or simply what he dreams or imagines, profits to the full."

—Henry Miller

Every golf book worth its salt needs a philosophy, and these are the basic tenets of *The Golfer's Book of Daily Inspiration*:

Trust yourself.

Play with confidence.

Have fun.

A fourth tenet—or four through six, for all the sticklers in the audience—is borrowed from the ancient Greeks, who did not play golf but who nevertheless had many outstanding qualities.

It is: Simplicity, simplicity, simplicity.

There are, of course, many corollary points to be drawn from these basic principles. But one fundamental rule of this book is that golf is already way too crowded with rules and regulations and we do not want to make the situation any worse by adding more.

Recite these principles like a mantra:

Trust yourself.

Play with confidence.

Have fun.

Make them the foundation stones of your game—along with that simplicity stuff—and you *will* have the best year of your golfing life.

Resolved: I trust myself, I play with confidence, and I have fun.

January 3

"The body ceases to grow in a few years; but the mind, if we will let it, may grow almost as long as life lasts."

—Sir John Lubbock

Keep growing. Keep an open mind.

Be open to everything that is potentially useful to you, even if the source is unusual or strange.

Sam Snead tells about watching a baseball game on TV. The announcer commented that a hitter wasn't extending his arms enough, that his arms were too close to his body for him to make good contact with the ball. "That's what I'm doing wrong," thought Snead, and the next day he went out on the range and practiced extending his arms more. The day after that he shot a 60, the best round of his life.

Watch a baseball game. Shoot a 60. Anything is possible if you keep your mind open.

Be open to it all. Wisdom can come from anywhere. A slurred utterance from a wino on the street may tell you more about your game than a golf pro with all his experience and skills.

Take a golf tip from a wino. Now, *there* is some advice for you.

Nevertheless, remaining open to suggestions from winos— or as the case may be, golf pros—does not necessarily mean *taking* them. Be a ruthless editor. Reject all that does not meet your rigorous standards. But always, always, always keep your mind open. Because you never know: A masterpiece may come over the transom, from out of nowhere, in today's mail.

Resolved: I keep an open mind.

January 4

"So when you are listening to somebody, completely, attentively, then you are listening not only to the words, but also to the feeling of what is being conveyed, to the whole of it, not part of it."

—J. Krishnamurti

Listen to yourself. Listen inwardly. This is the true and lasting way to become a good golfer.

So many words are spewed in the guise of helping people improve their golf games. Most of these words are of the same type:

Tell, tell, tell.

Books tell you what to do. Magazine articles tell you what to do. Videos tell you what to do. Teaching pros tell you what to do. Even your dang playing partners who don't know any better tell you what to do.

The truth is, being told by others what to do will not make you a better golfer. You are the only person who can do that, and you start by listening to yourself. Listening inwardly will teach you more about golf than you will ever learn from someone telling you what to do.

This book will talk about lots of things. There will be lots of advice, lots of sentences filled with imperatives. But we really don't want to *tell* you anything. Listen to the sense of what is being conveyed, as much as to the words themselves, and you will better understand what this book is all about.

To the extent that such a thing is possible in a book, let's open up a dialogue, a dialogue intended to make you a better golfer and enjoy the game more.

Resolved: I open up a golfing dialogue.

January 5

"I had no notion that I could possibly get anything less than a birdie. The image I had of myself was so positive that all negative reality was blocked out."

—Colman McCarthy, on a hot streak

Listen to your positive self. Not just on a hot streak, but always. Block out the negative.

A voice within you will chirp, "Wrong club. Wrong choice."

Ignore it. Listen to your positive self. Listen to the voice that says "All right. I like this club. This is *my* club."

The negative and positive are always in conflict in a golfer's mind. Give power to the positive side. Stuff the negative in a closet, lock the door, and render its obnoxious little chirpings impotent.

Make your positive side strong by listening to it. Then act upon its sweet whisperings.

Imagine your mind as a street. Walk on its sunny side. You will get where you are going quicker if you do. You will feel looser in the sunlight as you stretch your limbs. You will have more fun.

Negative thoughts are like those white-robed religious zealots who try to talk to you at the airport. Pay them no heed. Detour to the bathroom if you must. Just dodge them.

Listen to your positive side, the side that wants you to make shots, score pars, win championships. You may have ignored it for so long that you have come to doubt its strength, its efficacy. Never doubt its power. It is plenty strong. And it will work for you.

Just listen to it. As it grows stronger, you grow stronger.

Resolved: I listen to my positive self.

January 6

Today (in honor of Nancy), play happy.

Forget about what you were doing before your round. Play happy.

Forget about what you will be doing after. Play happy.

Give yourself plenty of time. Play happy.

Commit yourself totally to the game while you are doing it. Play happy.

Forget that last shot. Forget that last hole. Play happy.

Enjoy the company of your friends, the beauty of the setting. Play happy.

Is this approach too Goody Two-shoes for you? Oh, you'd rather be like that grumpy New Zealand pro golfer from a few years back? "He has only done three things wrong in his life," his peers on the tour said about him. "Get born, come to America—and stay."

Better to go the Nancy Lopez way. It worked out all right for her, didn't it? She won a few tournaments in her day, made the LPGA Hall of Fame, has a beautiful family, and is rich to boot. Playing happy did not hurt her competitive fire, her toughness, her ability to withstand pressure.

On the contrary, it helped. Look at any kid playing competitive sports. When she is having fun she is learning and growing. When the fun stops, so does the learning. Never let the fun stop. Play happy.

Resolved: I play happy.

January 7

*"When I was first learning to play, I always used to see the
trouble. Then a very smart man told me that to be a good
player I must see only the good. You must always be positive,
because your body can only do what your brain sees."*

—Chi Chi Rodriguez

Instead of trouble, I see opportunity.

Instead of the negative, I see the positive.

Instead of the bad, I see the good.

Instead of "can't," I say "I can."

Instead of "I hope," I say "I will."

Instead of self-doubt, I feel self-confident.

Instead of second-guessing myself, I trust myself.

Instead of dwelling on my mistakes, I accept them and move ahead.

Instead of kicking myself for my last shot, I think about my next shot.

Instead of worrying about what could go wrong, I focus on what I do right.

Instead of being self-critical, I give myself the benefit of the doubt.

Instead of pondering my weaknesses, I assert my strengths.

Instead of thinking of the player I am not, I think of the player I am.

Resolved: I see opportunity instead of trouble.

January 8

"When you are hitting a golf shot, a negative shot is pure poison."

—Harv Penick

For Harv Penick, one of the greatest of all golf teachers, words mattered. He put as much thought into how he said a thing as what he said. For this reason he banished negative words and imagery from his Austin golfing realm.

Words have power, he knew. Negative words can cause negative thoughts to form, and allow expression for those negative thoughts. Better to be positive, said Harv. Better to think positive thoughts, say positive things.

Penick never used the words "never" and "don't" when working with his students. It's a good rule to institute in your own game. Here are a few more words we could all do with less of in golf:

Can't.
Not.
Should.
Shouldn't.
Bad.
Fault.
Blame.

Eliminate these words from your golfing vocabulary, and you will instantly become a better golfer.

Resolved: I eliminate "can't" from my golfing vocabulary.

January 9

"Anything can happen to anybody in this country, so long as they're daring in their defeats and outsized in victory. The world will always belong to those who swing from the heels."

—Richard Hoffer

Damn the consequences! Swing from your heels.

Grab for the world, as much of it as your fist can hold. Swing from your heels.

Be daring in defeat. Be outsized in victory. Swing from your heels.

The Miss Grundys of golf will tell you it is foolish, unwise, imprudent. Do not listen. Turn your ear to the song that sings inside you. Swing from your heels.

Walk up to the tee with a swagger. Then swing from your heels.

And if the ball goes into a fairway other than the one you are playing? Hit it from *there*, and swing from your heels when you do.

A person who swings from the heels cares only about today, this moment, this shot. Who controls his own destiny? Only a fool thinks he can. A person who swings from the heels is going to get his licks in, no matter what. He or she is going to give destiny a run.

Throw away the book. *Burn the book*. Let the ball land where it may. Swing from your heels.

Resolved: I swing from my heels.

January 10

"It wasn't a miracle. They just did it."

—Tom Hanks as Jim Lovell in *Apollo 13*, explaining how the
United States put men on the moon

We can wish, hope, dream, imagine, visualize, picture, envision, want, desire, yearn for, pray. These are critical elements of success, their importance not to be diminished.

But, ultimately, it comes down to this:

We act. We transform our dreams into deeds.

If you want to become a better golfer—if you want to become a better anything—this simple truism must obtain practical force. You have to take your game out of the realm of what can be and put it in the realm of what is.

This takes guts. This takes sweat and hard work. The old-fashioned virtues.

Nor is it something that will happen overnight. Persistence—staying with it, long after everybody else has gone home for the night—is the uncredited star of every success story.

You have made up your mind. That is no longer an issue. Now start. Do it. It won't take a miracle.

Self-esteem follows achievement as surely as the children danced to the tune played by the pied piper. Think how merry you will be when you can say "I did it! I did the thing I dreamed of doing!"

Resolved: I do it! I transform my golfing ambitions into action.

January 11

"Confidence is everything. From there, it's a small step to winning."

—Craig Stadler

Craig Stadler has been to the top of the golf mountain, fallen down, and climbed back up again.

Stadler won the Masters in 1982. Four years later he was struggling to make the cut on Fridays. His confidence eroding, he knew he needed to make changes. This is what he did:

He lost weight. John Garrity once said of Orville Moody, "His very presence on a fairway gives it the look of an unmade bed." The same is true of Stadler.

He changed his swing. A natural "fader," Stadler wanted to learn how to draw the ball because he felt his inability to hit from right to left when he needed to cost him some tournaments.

Interestingly, these changes produced only mixed results. After winning the Byron Nelson Classic, he soon regained the weight he lost. He continues to struggle with it. Learning to draw the ball took a long time, and while he was doing it he forgot how to hit the fade.

Finally, he hit on the solution: setting goals for himself. This provided motivation—"a target to shoot for"—and eased the pressure. "If you have a long-term goal in mind, you don't try to force things," Stadler says. "You figure if you don't do it this week, you still have another week or two to meet that goal."

Stadler did not achieve all his goals. But he achieved some and came close on others, and revived his confidence.

Resolved: I build my confidence over time.

January 12

"Thinking always ahead, thinking always of trying to do more, brings a state of mind in which nothing seems impossible."

—Henry Ford

Every business operates under a plan, whether it's Microsoft or Mike and Tina's Fish Market. Every business has to know where it is going and how it expects to get there.

Golfers are the same. Whether you're Greg Norman or just trying to break 100, it helps to have a plan.

A plan enables you to think ahead, to do more than you expected, to dream the impossible (such as break 100).

Whether your goals are short-term or long-term, planning pays. If you are playing a round today, plan it mentally ahead of time. See each hole in your mind and envision how you will play it. It would be insanity to write a business plan without foreseeing potential losses or unanticipated contingencies. So, in your golf game, expect mistakes. When they come (if they do) they will land with a softer impact because you have anticipated them in your plan.

Use the same approach if you are writing a golf plan—and writing it down is a good idea—for the coming month, or six months, or the entire year. Expect times when you are too busy to play. Expect periods of low energy or interest. Planning for the doldrums will take you more easily through them into the realm of high-spirited play that certainly and abundantly lies ahead.

Planning will not take away the joy you feel when you play golf. It will increase the opportunities you have to experience the joy.

Resolved: I adopt a golf strategy for the year.

January 13

Try this one on for size: You are the best expert you know.

Jack Nicklaus plays better golf.

Fred Couples plays better golf.

Heck, the guy on the stool at the end of the bar may play better golf than you.

But nobody knows more about your golf game than you. You are best expert on your golf game. You are the top teaching pro. As such, you have a responsibility to yourself.

You have a responsibility as teacher to treat with dignity and respect the part of you that is still a student, the part that is still learning. What happens when a teacher is overly strict and harsh? The student retreats and hides within himself or herself. Growth suffers, even stops.

The teacher has a responsibility to promote, encourage, support, and nurture the student. Learning flourishes in an atmosphere of love and trust.

This is no small thing. We would all buy a better golf game if it were possible to do so. We would all seek out the pro who could magically turn it around for us. But the only answers that count come from the only expert who does: you. And the only answers that last and have meaning are the ones we find ourselves.

Resolved: I treat the part of me that is still learning with dignity and respect.

January 14

"Confidence as an outgoing act is directness and courage in meeting the facts of life, trusting them to bring instruction and support to a developing self."

—John Dewey

Expect good things to happen.

The pessimists will say "No, no, expect the worst. Then you will be pleasantly surprised when something good occurs." If you view life optimistically, goes this reasoning, you will only be disappointed.

The pessimists have obviously never won a championship or competed at the highest levels of sport.

Listen to the talk that emanates from a winning team. "We are confident," they say. "Winning breeds confidence, and we go out there expecting to win." They expect good things to happen. They are confident they can overcome every obstacle they face.

It is a little bit different in golf. You cannot expect help from your teammates to boost you up. You have to do it yourself. You have to summon the attitude on your own.

But otherwise it is the same. You must walk onto the tee with the attitude that you are going to make good things happen. You must know that you have the wherewithal to surmount any and all obstacles. You must say these words to yourself, not unlike the little train engine in the children's story, and you must believe them with every molecule of your being:

I can.

I will.

Resolved: I make good things happen on a golf course.

January 15

For many people, history is lifeless and dry, a subject they hated in school. This attitude will only deprive you of the many pleasures the game affords. An appreciation of history deepens your understanding of the rich 80 percent of the game that holds golf's true meaning and appeal.

You make history every time you step onto a golf course. No reporters or cameras are there to record the event, but you are doing it all the same. You have a personal history with the golf courses you play. The good players recognize this. They constantly update their histories and refer to them as needed. They know the hidden (and not so hidden) traps in a course, where to play the second shot on 5, what to watch out for, when to be conservative, and when they can shoot for all the marbles.

Every golf course has its own personality. Each one presents its own unique challenges and difficulties. Your history with a golf course makes you more attuned to its individual rhythms, moods, and idiosyncrasies.

Who can truly know another person without knowing his or her past? It is the same with golf. Knowing the past will render the present all the more vivid.

Resolved: I learn more about the game's history.

January 16

"Golf's a hard game to figure. One day you'll go out and slice it and shank it, hit into all the traps and miss every green. The next day you go out and for no reason at all you really stink."

—Bob Hope

Golf is a hard game to figure. Some days, despite our best efforts, we really do stink. So what's to do?

Well, we can stomp around and throw our clubs and act like a professional tennis star. Or we can laugh about it, like Bob Hope.

Psychologists say that humor is a form of control. After a sensational murder or a cataclysmic event like an earthquake or a hurricane, people around the country almost immediately begin swapping jokes about it. Humor is a natural human response to restore normalcy to what are, at bottom, profoundly disturbing events.

Murder. Cataclysm. Earthquake. Profoundly disturbing. Sounds like your typical golf match to me.

Humor is a way of keeping things in perspective in golf. A bad round is not the end of the world, though it may feel like it. Golf is a diversion. A thing we do to make ourselves feel good for when we tackle the real problems of life. Bob Hope first began playing as a young man and has lived into his nineties—as rich and full a life as a person can have. He is a good person to keep in mind when we begin to take ourselves too seriously on the golf course.

Resolved: I smile in the face of golf.

January 17

Make time for what is important. Golf is important. Make time for it.

Easier said than done, you say? What with kids, spouse, job, house, other commitments . . .

Here is a suggestion: Schedule it. Schedule golf as you would an important meeting with a client. You wouldn't break that; why break golf?

Put it on the schedule and make it part of your routine. It is a way of saying, to yourself and to others, "This is what I am doing. I am taking the time to do it." Let others deal with it. Let them work around your schedule.

Golf can be a daily, weekly, monthly feature of your schedule. That part is up to you. But put it on the schedule and then zealously guard against all intrusions. Guard your golf time like the Marines defending a beachhead. You will find there is much less conflict about your playing golf when you do. Putting it on the schedule is another way of saying "It's done."

Write it down. Make sure it is in your appointment book. Writing things down has a concreteness to it that a mere verbal commitment does not.

Often when a friend or business associate says "Let's get together and play one of these days," one of these days takes forever to roll around, if it comes at all. Putting it in the schedule fastens it like a nail.

Resolved: I make golf a regular part of my schedule.

January 18

"Don't think about it. Just make it happen."

—Florence Griffith Joyner

Florence Griffith Joyner (or "Flo-Jo," as she is called) won four sprint medals at the 1988 Seoul Olympics. Later she retired. Known for her long, powerful stride and her long painted fingernails, she decided to make a comeback and try to compete again for the U.S. team in the 1996 Games in Atlanta.

Her training regimen consisted of 75 miles of running a week (including sprint and hill work) and lots of hours in the weight room. Ever the modern woman, she juggled her workout schedule with commitments to her husband, daughter, and professional career.

One of Flo-Jo's motivational techniques consisted of writing her goal down on pieces of paper—"One more Olympic Games!"—and posting them in visible places around her house. The bathroom, bedroom, kitchen—her goal appeared wherever she did. These acted as daily reminders of why she was working so hard and what she was striving for.

Think about doing something similar for your golf. Write your goal down—"Break 80!"—on a piece of paper and post it where you can see it, perhaps above your desk at work or on a bulletin board at home. Summarize your goal in three or four words at most. Make it short and pithy. Cut to the essence of your goal and what you truly want. Seeing this summation every day in a prominent place will remind you of how important it is to you and will spur you on to achieving it.

Resolved: I write my golfing goals down and post them in a visible place.

January 19

"Most people say that as you get old, you have to give up things. I think you get old because you give up things."
—Theodore Green, U.S. senator, age 87

Here is a challenge for the older golfer: Shoot your age.

Sam Snead did it. In a PGA tournament, no less. He shot a 67 at age 67 in the opening round of the Quad Cities Open. Two days later, he did himself one better with a 66. As Sam got older he shot his age or better many times.

Some of the older hands on the Senior Tour shoot their ages as well. But one need not be a professional to do it, merely be professionally persistent. Many golfers in their 70s and 80s show such persistence. One such fellow was Jimmy Drake, an amateur golfer who always set the bar higher for himself and never regretted it a day. He said it was "no challenge" to shoot your age. "The challenge is to better it," said Jimmy. At 89 he regularly shot in the 80s.

In this manner (and in so many others!), the older golfer can inspire the younger. "Look at me," he seems to say. "In the time of my life I am living, still grabbing for everything I can. How 'bout you?"

The conventional view of the aging process is spun dizzy by the older golfer in lusty pursuit of his goals. Every birthday is a joyous occasion for him, for it gives him another stroke's allowance and brings him closer to shooting his age.

What's that you say, old-timer? You say you'd trade it all in a heartbeat to be 27 again? Wouldn't we all!

Resolved: I shoot my age or better.

January 20

There are times when it seems as if your round is hanging in the balance. It could go either way, up or down. You have reached a turning point, the proverbial fork in the road.

In the words of the ever-wise Yogi, take it. Do not delay. Charge on through.

Sink that putt and make your round go. Get up and down out of the sand. Knock that 7-iron stiff to the pin. Sting that tee ball like there's no tomorrow.

There *is* no tomorrow. The future is today. Go out and make your break . . . *now*.

Take this approach off the golf course, too. Are you waiting for the perfect moment to learn to play? To start playing a lot? To become really good?

Have you been dreaming about taking a golf vacation? Joining the PGA/LPGA/Senior/Nike Tour? Buying a home along the seventh fairway? Chucking it all and becoming a golf bum? Traveling around the country playing the best courses?

Your dreams *are* doable. But you have to do them.

If you wait for the perfect time or the perfect situation or the perfect opportunity, that is what you will do: wait. Waiting breeds more waiting. And tomorrow never comes.

Carpe diem. Go out and make your break. When it comes to the fork in the road, take it!

Resolved: I make my breaks on and off the golf course.

January 21

"A true knowledge of ourselves is knowledge of our power."
— Mark Rutherford

Through belief comes power.

Everybody has faith in themselves when the putts are dropping. The trick is to keep those internal fires burning when they are not.

There is a wonderful story told by Tom Weiskopf about the unshakable faith that Jack Nicklaus—Happy Birthday, Jack!—had in himself. Jack needed to hole a 10-foot putt to keep the lead in a tournament. After studying the putt for a long time (as Jack is wont to do), he tapped the ball to the edge of the cup.

The ball was afraid of heights. It got to the rim, looked down, and said, "Not me."

Jack did not blink. For him it was as good as a make. "I don't care if the ball didn't drop," he muttered. "I hit it in the hole."

Sometimes you *will* hit the ball in the hole, but, like Jack's ball, it just won't go in.

You did the right thing. You did everything you could. You hit the ball on the nose. Still, it refused to cooperate. That's golf for you.

Have faith in yourself, and the balls will drop.

Resolved: I draw power from my faith in myself.

January 22

"Slow is long, fast is short."

—Don January

This is one of the most valuable maxims in golf. It bears repeating over and over.

Bring the club back slow, the ball goes far. Bring the club back fast, the ball falls short.

Now let's add a pair of concepts to this thought:

Acceleration.

Explosion.

Golf would seem on the surface to have little in common with weight lifting. But it shares these twin concepts.

A person lifting a large stationary weight must use speed and explosive force, the same as a golfer. He accelerates to get the bar up to his shoulders, bringing his feet underneath him so his legs and body—not just his arms—can hold the weight. Then he explodes upward to extend his arms fully and raise the weight above his head.

A weight-lifting clean-and-jerk may be divided into segments. But it is really one continuous act. The same is true of the golf swing.

Keep your swing simple and uncluttered, like your life.

Bring it back slowly, extend fully but comfortably, then accelerate and explode into the ball.

Resolved: I accelerate and explode into the ball.

January 23

"Great is the art of beginning, but greater the art is of ending."
— Henry Wadsworth Longfellow

Most of us hardly need pumping up when we place the tee in the ground, set the ball upon it, and prepare for our first drive of the day. If anything, we need the opposite instruction: Chill, man.

It is impossible to overstate the importance of the first drive and the first hole in setting the tone for our day. But that is precisely the problem. We make too much of it. A good first hole sends us soaring. A bad first hole sends our spirits plummeting. Why? Neither event conclusively determines anything. They total the score at the end of 18, not at the end of one.

Better to take the long view when it comes to that first hole. It is only one of 18. The influence it has on our round stems from the inflated emphasis we give it in our mind. Similarly, that tee ball on 1 is only one of many tee balls to come, and likely long forgotten by day's end.

Take the long view on the first hole. Take the long view on *every* hole. This attitude will contribute to a relaxed state of mind, and improve your performance.

Resolved: I take the long view on the first hole.

January 24

"There are very few truths in putting. You get the ball in the hole, and it doesn't matter how."

—Arnold Palmer

Putting is one of the game's great mysteries. But it was no mystery to Arnold Palmer in his prime. You just get it in the hole.

"Don't hope," Palmer adds. "Don't try and don't second-guess your vision of line and speed." Don't do anything but get it in the hole.

Of course, even Palmer's strong-willed approach—in the hole, or else!—does not work all the time. Nothing works all the time. This understanding may be central to becoming a good putter. What works today may not work tomorrow. You stay flexible, alert, sensitive to mood. You discover what is working, and you do it.

Second-guessing is second nature in putting. What do you do when things go really, really bad? Do what Palmer did. Spend a couple of hours making one-foot putts.

That's right: measly little one-footers. One after another, just to renew your confidence, just to get back in the habit of getting the ball in the hole. It worked for Arnold.

This may be another key to good putting. Humble yourself. The golfing gods may take pity on you if you show the proper humility and respect. You may also want to consider animal sacrifices.

In putting there is only one rule: Do whatever it takes. Just get it in the hole.

Resolved: I get it in the hole.

January 25

"Hit the shot you know you can hit, not the one you think you should."

—Bob Rotella, teaching pro

Should schmould. That's our message for the day.

We've said it before, we'll say it again: "Should" has no place in your golf game. It only causes headaches.

You do what you do. Accept it. Move on. You'll be a better player with this attitude.

Heavy reliance on the should concept is a form of excuse-making. The implied message of every should sentence is: If I did what I "should" have—used a different club, kept my eye on the ball, laid it up, etc.—I would have hit a much better golf shot.

Well, maybe you would have and maybe you wouldn't have. We'll never know. You played the shot you did and that's that.

Should thinking leads to looking back. The best golfers are scoped into the present. If you are looking back you are in the past and always playing catch-up.

Don't think twice, it's all right. You're a golfer; you've got everything you need.

Forget the should shots. Play the shot you can make. You've got the goods. Have confidence in yourself and the tools at your disposal. Look ahead, not back. Accept the reality you create for yourself, and move forward with courage.

Resolved: I hit the shot I know I can hit.

January 26

"If I had only one more round of golf to play, I would choose to play it at Pebble Beach."

—Jack Nicklaus

There are a handful of golf courses every golfer must play, and one of them is Pebble Beach.

Ken Venturi said that Pebble Beach was as close to paradise on earth as he ever expected to find. Designed by California State Amateur champion Jack Neville and built in 1919, it brings into harmonious relation the four essentials of life: earth, water, sky, and golf.

Pebble is a public institution, like the Lincoln Monument and Central Park. Like every great golf course, it is a place of history. Young Johnny Goodman rode a freight train from Nebraska to California and beat Bobby Jones in the 1929 U.S. Amateur there. Jack Nicklaus hit a searing 1-iron into the wind on 17 to set up a birdie and clinch one of his U.S. Open titles. The 209-yard par-3 17th points straight at the ocean— what Nicklaus calls "the world's biggest water hazard." Tom Watson deprived Nicklaus of yet another Open title with a chip from the rough on 17 in 1982. The improbable birdie made Watson champion. Tom Kite won his Open at Pebble in gale-force winds.

There are few things in this life more sublime than to sit on the balcony of the Pebble Beach Lodge overlooking the 18th green and fairway. The grass sweeps across to the cliff. The ocean stretches out as far as a person can see. If there is contentment to be found anywhere, this is it.

Resolved: I play Pebble at least once in my life.

January 27

Sandy Tatum tells a nice story about his friend and longtime pro-am partner, Tom Watson. One year Watson had a terrible tournament at Pebble Beach. Laboring under the flu and a 100-plus fever, Tom managed only a few holes of practice on Wednesday.

On Thursday, it showed. Still battling the flu, he played poorly and missed the cut.

Late in the day on Saturday, the two men had lunch. Tatum expected his friend to be gloomy over his poor showing, but Watson was surprisingly chipper. He had recovered from the flu and felt like himself again. As they were leaving, Tatum asked what time it was and Watson said, "It's 4:30. I think we have time to play a few holes."

Tatum was flabbergasted. The wind had come up along the Pacific and it was cold. It was nearly dark.

Tom borrowed a sweater. They dug up some shoes for him. He played out of Sandy's bag. They reached the tee before 5 P.M. and sneaked in six spirited holes.

Take a cue from Tom. There is *always* time to get in a few holes. Even if you are tired or disappointed, even if the light is fading fast, even if there are no shoes to be found. Summon the energy and the obstacles will disappear. Summon the energy and you will find the time.

The energy *is* there. You have it. And it will surge back into you like a river once you get on the course.

Resolved: When someone asks "Play?", I say "Yes!"

January 28

"A diamond is a chunk of coal that made good under pressure."
—Saying

One of the best stories about handling pressure involves one of the athletes who did it best—Joe Montana, in Super Bowl XXIII.

Unlike most Super Bowls, this one—between Montana's San Francisco 49ers and the Cincinnati Bengals—was actually a close game, with the Bengals leading 16–13 late in the fourth quarter.

Following a punt, the 49ers got the ball back deep in their own territory. There was less than a minute left. The fans at Joe Robbie Stadium were going nuts. The TV announcers were engaged in hyperbole. The tension was so thick—well, you know the program.

Meanwhile, what was Joe Montana doing? He was on the sidelines, pulling a teammate over and pointing out a celebrity he had spotted in the stands.

"Do you know who that is?" Joe asked. "That's John Candy."

His teammate looked over with him, and together they marveled at the sight of a real-life Hollywood celebrity in their midst. Then Joe trotted on the field and won the game for his team.

Which is an excellent formula for handling the pressure you face during a round of golf:

Find ways to take your mind off the situation, while sticking to the business at hand.

Resolved: I find ways to take my mind off the pressure in golf.

January 29

"Golf is a game whose aim is to hit a very small ball into an even smaller hole, with weapons singularly ill-designed for that purpose."

—Winston Churchill

Tommy Armour had an interesting take on this famous saying by Churchill. He wondered whether Winston's clubs were the right size for him.

Armour, who was to a previous generation of golfers what Harv Penick is to this one, was downright dogmatic on the subject of using clubs of the proper weight and length. He felt that many of the problems experienced by weekend golfers stemmed from ill-fitting clubs—clubs that were too long or too short, too heavy or too light, too stiff or too wobbly.

Imagine trying to play in shoes that pinch your feet or a shirt whose sleeves hang over your hands. It is the same when we play with clubs that do not suit us.

It is too late for Winston, but not too late for you. Stop by a pro shop and get your clubs checked out.

Resolved: I check to see how my weapons fit me.

January 30

"Nothing can be more useful to a man than a determination not to be hurried."

—Henry David Thoreau

A good round of golf begins well before the first tee. It begins with a determination not to be hurried.

Sam Snead knew this. He knew that hurrying to the course—and worse, a hurried state of mind—caused problems, especially on the opening holes. On the days he played (which was almost always), his motto was: Nice 'n' easy does it.

One trick he used to slow himself down was to hold the steering wheel lightly in his hands as he drove to the course. Drive time was critical to Sam. He used this time to prepare himself mentally, relax, slow down, get himself in the mood to play. The light grip on the wheel was like a swing trigger. It helped him ease up and back off. It commenced his pre-round driving meditations. And it reminded him of how to hold a club: with the same lightness of touch.

Think of Sam the next time you drive to the course, and use that time to get yourself in the mood to play.

Resolved: I hold the steering wheel lightly when I drive to the course.

January 31

"When we are full of life, we take chances, risk great odds, love, laugh, dance, write poems, paint pictures, romp with children; in short, we play. It is only the impotent who do not play. The people who play are the creators."

—Holbrook Jackson

Everything gets better when you play. Nothing gets better until you play.

This is the answer for what ails you: Play. This is the answer when you are in no need of answers: Play. The answers are all found in the playing.

Dedicate yourself to play. "Dedicate" is too stodgy a word for what is intended here. Play golf, as opposed to working at it, and your game will instantly leap forward.

Golf is creative. Good players are creative players. The more we play at the game, the more creative we will be.

If you are "working" when you go to the driving range, get off the range. If you work when you are on the practice green, get off the green. Go out and play.

Or, better still, when you are on the practice green or driving range, find a way to turn that time into play. Your practice will leap forward too.

Psychologists say the basic elements of a child's personality are formed by the age of three, if not before. And how does a kid that age spend her time? She plays, she sucks (and eats), she squawks, she sleeps.

Make that a model for your golfing personality. Play, squawk, suck on a beer after, get some shut-eye, and then do it all over again the next day. But most of all, play!

Resolved: I play a whole bunch more in February.

February I

"I don't care what becomes of me so long as it's a change for the better."

—William Feather

You want to be a better golfer but you are not sure how. Here is a simple strategy: Invest in your golf the way you would invest your money. To wit:

Invest over the long term. Except possibly at the beginning, golf is not a game that lends itself to the "get rich quick" syndrome. Progress comes over time. Be in it for the long haul.

Invest regularly. Play and practice, practice and play. Do this on a routine basis. It is impossible to sustain your improvements by playing every now and then.

Diversify your portfolio. Play at different courses from time to time. Test yourself on a new track and see how your game measures up.

Be wary of "hot tips." Many a golfer has been led astray by the game's legion of unpaid consultants. While golfers may not be able to fix what's wrong with their game, they can advise you on yours. Listen to them at your peril.

Seek periodic investment advice to review the status of your portfolio. Every now and then it pays to see a golf pro for a tune-up on your swing.

Reinvest your dividends. Commit time and resources to your golf. Buy some new sticks. Get some sharp-looking duds. Join a club.

Start today. It's never too late to begin a sound golf investment program, and the best time to do it is now.

Resolved: I begin a golf investment program today.

February 2

"Snow is what you are up to your neck in when people send you postcards from Florida saying they wish you were there, and I wish they might sit on a burr."

—Ogden Nash

It ain't fair. While parts of the United States and Canada are up to their mashies in snow, plagued by arctic storms and icy cold weather, people in places like Florida and Arizona and California play golf all year long.

It is more than not fair. It's criminal, is what it is.

Occasionally those blond and tan denizens of the Sun Belt must sit out a day or two because of an untimely wet spell, but all that does is wash their cars for them.

Ah, but those Sun Belters do not know what they are missing. For truly one of the unappreciated pleasures of golf is the pleasure of anticipation. Anticipating the game—thinking about it, imagining, preparing, conceiving, talking, dreaming—is as good as playing it.

Well, almost as good.

Okay, half as good.

All right. Better than nothing. What the hell else are people supposed to do when the snow is up above the windows and you can't see out?

Winter is an especially fruitful time for working on one's visualization skills. Visualize a golf getaway to Florida, where all those people live who send those irritating postcards.

Enough visualization. Let's play. Today is Groundhog Day. What did Punxsutawney Phil say? Did he see his shadow?

Resolved: Spring is around the corner. Golf is on its way. I will be ready!

February 3

"Ninety percent of this game is half mental."

—Jim Wohlford

Golf is a mental game. Ben Hogan said that you can learn the physical game of golf in about six months, but learning the mental game takes the rest of your life. How true.

Unlike in baseball or football or tennis or most other ball sports, the ball is a stationary object in the field of play. You do not react to the movement of the ball and in turn set your body in motion, as you do in those other sports. One person, swinging a stick, initiates the action. This fact alone makes you think harder about what you are going to do and how to do it.

There is also so much more time to think about things in golf, and so the cerebral inclination of the game is heightened even further.

Make a commitment to understand the mental game of golf and make it work for you.

Ideally, golf is a mind-body partnership. A golf game at its best is an expression of this partnership. The physical and mental sides of your game act as one. Your swing becomes one unified fluid motion. The club becomes an extension of your arm, and they move in tandem.

Vision translates into reality. You see the shot before you hit it. Then the ball conforms to your vision. This is the ideal we all seek and sometimes attain.

Mind-body partnership. That is what we are aiming for.

Resolved: I learn the mental game and make it work for me.

February 4

"It won't help to tell yourself, 'Don't hit it in the water.' Your mind will only hear water."

—Bob Rotella, teaching pro

Researchers at the University of California conducted tests on the causes of stress and how to minimize its effects. What they found is of value to golfers in our constant battle against the negative voices we hear in our head.

Researchers learned that "the presence of positive factors in life, rather than merely a lack of negative factors, was most important in reducing stress," according to the report. "Too much emphasis," it goes on, "has been given to eliminating negative experiences and not enough to teaching people to develop positive aspects of life."

In other words, to borrow from a somewhat lighter text, it is not enough to eliminate the negative. One has to accentuate the positive.

This is most certainly true in this game. Visualize a positive result. Create positive visualizations.

In golf, as anyone who has ever tried to sidle past a water hazard will testify, telling yourself "Don't hit it in the water" is a surefire way to make your ball swim with the fishes. Fill up your head with positive images and thoughts.

The ball bouncing down the center of the fairway.

The ball skipping onto the green.

Holing it out of the sand.

The ball rolling across the green into the cup.

Aren't those pretty pictures? Fill your head up with them.

Resolved: I create positive visualizations when I play.

February 5

"The ball went miles and miles and miles."

—Alan Shepard, admiring his golf shot on the moon

An intergalactic day in the history of golf: February 5, 1971. Alan Shepard hits a golf ball on the moon.

The story goes like this: Shepard, who in 1961 became the first American to be launched into space, was a golf nut. As commander of the Apollo 14 Lunar Landing Mission ten years later, he sneaked a cut-down 6-iron and two golf balls into the spacecraft with him.

They blasted off January 31 and landed on the moon six days later. Shepard became the fifth man to walk on the moon, and while he was out there he decided to play a little golf.

Shepard's club was actually four pieces of attached aluminum that he rigged up from the device used to gather lunar dust samples. Because of his Michelin man spacesuit, he could only swing with one hand. Nor was his lie too good. "The moon," as one writer said, "is one big sand trap."

Shepard chili-dipped the first ball. On earth it might have gone 30 yards. In the moon's reduced-gravity atmosphere it traveled 200 yards. According to Bob Hope, Shepard shanked his second shot—"and tossed his club into the Sea of Tranquility."

Hope had an even better line about what Shepard saw on his way back to the spacecraft: "Something lying in the dust caught his eye. It was another golf ball, with Jerry Ford's name on it."

Resolved: Like Alan Shepard, I carry my golf clubs when I travel.

February 6

"Now, usually conventional ideas are right, but not always. When they're wrong and you go in new directions, then you make progress."

—Martin Perl, Nobel Prize winner in physics

Sometimes conventional wisdom is right. But sometimes it is wrong. This is as true in golf as it is in science.

Conventional wisdom says keep your head still when you swing. Yet you may move your head slightly. But you know this is "wrong" and you try to stop from doing it. This results in neck and body tension that would not be there if you permitted yourself a variation from conventional teaching and recognized the truth of your own swing.

The same applies for holding the left elbow straight, the overlapping grip, and the many other conventional notions of golf that may work for some but certainly do not work for all. Look at the swings of the greats. Some elements are the same, but there are many, many variations among them, variations that frequently divert from the path of conventional wisdom. Every great golfer finds the truth of his own swing.

Whether you seek championships or simple respectability, the message is the same: Find the truth of your own swing.

When you divert from the common path and go out on your own, you make progress. How to make real progress in golf? Find the truth of your swing.

Resolved: I find the truth of my own swing.

February 7

"I've never played a perfect 18 holes. There is no such thing. I expect to make at least seven mistakes a round. Therefore, when I make a bad shot, I don't worry about it. It's just one of the seven."

—Walter Hagen

Walter Hagen was one of the best golfers and possibly the best match player of all time. He won a collection of Grand Slam titles and captained the American Ryder Cup team six times.

Since one of the greatest golfers of all time allowed himself at least seven mistakes a round, is it unreasonable to give yourself double that number—say, 14? Perhaps you are an excellent player striving for better. Allow yourself 10, then. Or maybe you are without illusions or pretensions. Give yourself 18.

Whatever the actual number, the point is, allow yourself *some*. There ain't no such animal as a perfect round of golf. Give yourself permission to make mistakes.

Most golfers would respond that they hardly need permission to make mistakes; they do it quite freely and openly of their own accord. But what is your attitude when mistakes occur? Do you regard them with tolerance or impatience?

Of all of life's pursuits, golf is least susceptible to perfection. We are going to make mistakes. That is not a fatalistic or negative view. It is instead a very tolerant and understanding one. A person who is making mistakes is frequently a person who is testing his or her limits, expanding his or her range. Be generous of spirit toward that person, especially if that person is you.

Resolved: I allow myself a certain number of mistakes per round.

February 8

Learn from your mistakes. But never let them keep you from moving forward.

There is a limit to what you can learn from your mistakes. Never let your mistakes get too big for their britches. Keep 'em in their place.

There is no single cause for a mistake in golf. A golf swing is, as Ben Hogan says, "a chain reaction. Each correct movement is linked with and sets up the next ensuing movement."

The links are very subtle. It is impossible to see where one stops and another begins. These links are both physical and mental. They encompass more than the physical act of the swing itself or even the moment you took the swing. They stretch back to before you ever stepped onto the first tee. You may not be rotating enough in the turn because you slept funny the night before. You may have had an argument with your wife and that is why you skulled that iron.

The golf swing is ultimately a mysterious act. If we knew how we did it the way we did it when we hit it so well, we would do it that way every time. But we don't.

Analysis will provide only partial answers. Nobody, not even you, understands how all the links of the chain fit together.

In any case, always move forward. Accept the limits of analysis and keep playing.

Resolved: I never let my "mistakes" stop me from moving forward.

February 9

"Before you begin a thing remind yourself that difficulties and delays quite impossible to foresee are ahead. You can see only one thing clearly and that is your goal. Form a mental vision of that and cling to it through thick and thin."

—Kathleen Norris, writer

Live your goals.

If you want to compete on a high level as a golfer—if you want to compete and win—you must live your goals every day you live. This is the minimum you must do.

Have submarine vision. Fix your target in your sights and never let it go. Follow it, track it, hunt it down. Even if you cannot immediately do the thing you want to do, if life or events conspire to push you away from your target, drop below the surface and stay close.

Living your goals means persevering. This is what it means above all. Difficulties and delays occur, impossible to foresee. But the person who is living his goals will outlast them all.

Today, next month, a year from tomorrow. Everything changes except your steadfast commitment to your heart's deepest longings.

David Mamet, the playwright, said that other people must realize that you simply will not go away. You are there and you are going to stay there until you get what you want, even if they see you as a righteous pain in the neck. Living your goals means being a pain in the neck if you have to be. Nothing is going to drive you away. And if you do have to leave, people must know that you will be back again the next morning, and the morning after, and the morning after that.

Resolved: I live my goals. I make a steadfast commitment to my heart's deepest longings.

February 10

"Golf, like art, is a goddess whom we woo in early youth if we would win her."

—H. Rider Haggard

It's never too early to start. It's never too early to dream.

Bobby Jones began at age five. Four years later he won his first junior golf title, beating a 16-year-old.

At age 10 Jack Nicklaus shot a 51 in the first nine holes he ever played. At 13, he won three matches in the National Junior Championship. He won the Ohio State Open when he was 16.

At age five Tiger Woods had already appeared on national TV showing off his golf prowess. His early promise foreshadowed excellence as a teenager. At 15 he played in a PGA Tour event, the youngest ever. At age 19 he won the U.S. Amateur, just as Nicklaus (two times) and Jones (five times) before him.

These three were prodigies. There is no guarantee that early success in golf or anything else will translate into success as an adult. Then again, it *may*. No one can say for sure.

A few things we can say for sure:

You have to start sometime. It's almost always better to start early than late. It all starts with a dream.

The author William Bagley has noted that older people tend to look on the advice they give to young people as "something that should disillusion them." But is this so wise?

Young people: Pursue your dreams whatever your age. Start today. Parents: Lend a hand.

Resolved: I never let someone talk me out of a dream.

February 11

"Nothing happens unless first a dream."

—Carl Sandburg

When he was a struggling actor trying to make it in Hollywood, Jim Carrey read "every self-help book you could ever conceive of." One of the cornerstones of self-help literature is the belief that people can make their dreams come true.

First, you must know what your dream actually is. So you write it down. This is an essential step in making it real.

Jim Carrey did that. He wrote a check to himself for "acting services rendered" and postdated it Thanksgiving 1995. The amount of the check was for $10 million.

The rest is the stuff of movie legend (as they say). The man with the elastic face and body bounced between minor parts in movies before landing a steady gig on TV's *In Living Color*. This led to the starring role in the then-unheralded *Ace Ventura: Pet Detective*, which astonished observers by making millions of dollars and actually being funny, too. One Carrey celluloid triumph followed another, and in 1995 he signed to do a movie for $20 million—double what he had fantasized as a young actor and months ahead of his personal schedule.

Why not adapt the Carrey technique to golf? (Asking for $10 million would be nice, but probably not realistic.) Take a scorecard from your home course (or one that you find challenging) and record your dream score. Put down the strokes for each hole with the appropriate 2s, 3s, 4s, and 5s and total it up. What is it—69? 72? 80? Date the scorecard and store it in a drawer for safekeeping. Then go out and make your dream happen.

Resolved: I write down my dream score and aim for it.

February 12

"Though it may not be realistic, there is nothing wrong with imagining yourself birdieing every hole."

—Don Green, teaching pro

Jack Nicklaus, the most famous golf visualizer of all, likened his techniques to watching movies in his head. Seeing the shot before he did it was a means of making reality conform to his imagination.

You can do the same thing. But like anything else, it takes practice. Mental practice.

Where are you right now? In bed? In a soft chair in the living room? Those are both good places to watch a movie.

Put down this book and give it a try. It won't take long— 10 or 15 minutes. Play a round in your head, all 18 holes.

It might be wise to get in the mood first. See yourself on the road to the course, feeling relaxed, with an old Marvin Gaye tune on the radio. See yourself pulling on the spikes, loosening up. This is when the opening credits are rolling.

You step up. The movie begins in earnest. You hit a drive as pure as anything Nicklaus ever did. (Why not? It's your movie.) Then you go on. Shot by shot by shot. Hole after hole.

If something doesn't go quite as you envisioned, rewind the tape. Erase the part you didn't like and substitute the shot you know you are capable of.

Have goals in your mental practice, just as you would in the physical kind. Practice your putting. Make those balls behave the way they never do in real life. But that's the point, isn't it? Harnessing the power of your mind to put real life on the run.

Resolved: I play a mental round of golf—or at least a few holes.

February 13

"But, if one should guide his life by true principles, man's greatest wealth is to live on a little with a contented mind; for a little is never lacking."

—Lucretius

Okay, so you're frustrated. You didn't play yesterday (except in your head). You're not playing today (you don't even have time to play in your *head* today). Tomorrow looks bad too.

This weekend? Not so good either. The in-laws are coming to town. June and Harry hate golf. What about the week after? Nah. That's even worse. The boss thinks he's running a diamond mine and you're one of the slaves. There's no way you'll be able to play then either.

Listen. Cheer up. Not about work. Or the in-laws. They both sound pretty bad. About golf. There's hope yet. First, realize you're not alone. There are plenty of other people just like you who never get to play as much as they'd like. Now this may sound Pollyannaish, but what you need to do is turn your attitude around. Look at your situation from a different point of view. Stand it on its head.

Instead of being frustrated by a seeming lack of time on the course, cherish the time you have. A little can be a lot if you pour yourself fully into the moment. Concentrate not on what you lack but what you have. It is way, way better than no time at all. Try to parlay a little time now into more time later. Make the most of your time now, and when your schedule changes and you can play more, you will be ready to seize fully the opportunity.

Resolved: I am happy to play a little—until I can play more.

February 14

Here is the best Valentine's Day gift you could give to your spouse: Leave your game at the course. (That, and flowers.)

Share a good day on the links. That is bringing home good news.

But a bad day? Leave it where it lies. Better still, toss it in the trash can in the parking lot.

Who needs all that grief? Not your spouse or family. It's like coming home and dumping on everybody because you had a bad day at the office. They deserve better.

It is in your self-interest to treat a bad day like roadkill. Take a quick peek in the rearview mirror and keep right on going. Let someone else deal with it.

Treat a bad shot the same way. If you are still castigating yourself for your miscue when you step up to hit your next ball, you are a goner and you know it.

A bad day is like an earthquake. It is an act of nature. It happened—and sitting in your chair sulking about it will not change a thing.

Let it go. Leave it behind. You will be a much more pleasant person to be around, and a more pleasant golfer as well.

Resolved: Today I come home with flowers—and a good attitude.

February 15

"Work consists of whatever a body is obliged to do. Play consists of whatever a body is not obliged to do."

—Mark Twain

Golf is play. Golf is not work. It may be time for a break if it is beginning to feel like something you are obligated to do.

Or perhaps it is merely time for an Attitude Adjustment. Sample Attitude Adjustment techniques are:

Putt left-handed.

Play in your barefeet.

Drive from on your knees.

Use only one club on a hole.

Play an entire round with only one club or two.

Practice trick shots.

What, you don't like these ideas? Make up your own, then.

Golf costs so much and it is so hard to make time for that people tend not to want to be frivolous when they finally do play. They want to make every minute count. They want to do their best, and play well.

But being silly can be a very productive use of time. Frivolous play is not so frivolous. Sometimes the best thing you can do for your game is loosen up about it. The more relaxed you are, generally speaking, the better you play. Unbutton that top collar button, loosen the tie. Dedicate yourself to frivolity. Practice your trick shots today.

Resolved: I loosen up a little.

February 16

"Things almost always turn out otherwise than one anticipates."
—Maurice Hulst

In golf as in life, things almost always turn out otherwise than one anticipates.

We set a date to play golf. We look ahead eagerly. We count the days. The day finally arrives, and it turns out nothing like we expected. We are crushed, and blame it on golf.

We hit a good shot. We move up quickly to the ball and anticipate our next one. The shot goes a different way than we envisioned, and once more we blame golf.

When we anticipate we jump ahead to results, ignoring process. When you are in a good golf groove you are immersed in process—the doing of the thing—unconcerned with results. Anticipation is an enemy of this sort of bliss. It creates a kind of mirage where we think we see something that is not actually there.

Stay in the moment—which in golf means *this shot, this swing*—and let the future unfold as it may. And if an event unfolds otherwise than anticipated, absolve yourself and others and the world at large of blame. You will find that things always have a way of working out. There is an unseen benevolent pattern to events. Frequently a thing that appears terrible at first glance turns out to be the best thing that could have happened. That putter that you broke after three-putting 13 prompted you to get a new one, and with that trusty new licking stick you entered the club tournament and became champion.

Resolved: I concentrate on the ball at my feet.

February 17

"Good chippers are scramblers, and off the course they usually live carefree lives, worrying as little as possible. They commit all the sins of golf save one: despair. They know that with one happy shot, disaster can be turned around."

—Colman McCarthy

Oh, to be a scrambler, a scrambler—and nothing more!

Lee Trevino and Seve Ballesteros are prototypical scramblers. If they had been captains of the *Titanic* they would have said, "What's a little water? Gives us a chance to try out our lifeboats."

Scramblers thwart disaster at every turn. One does not know how they do the things they do (*they* may not even know). Still, they do them. Somehow they extricate themselves from the pickles they get into with ease to spare. A scrambler is like Indiana Jones: dashing, unafraid, ever resourceful, with a hang-the-consequences ability to scramble up the rope ladder away from the pit of vipers just in the nick of time.

What are the characteristics of these Indiana Joneses of golf?

They listen to themselves and trust their instincts.

They know they have the ability and fortitude to overcome all hazards, pot bunkers and knee-high rough included.

They do not fret if their plans go awry; they formulate new plans, and act on *them*.

They put faith in the improbable. For they know that in golf, perhaps more so than in any other sporting pastime, the improbable is probable.

Resolved: I maintain a scrambler's faith in the improbable.

February 18

"It is in this very way that a player should approach every shot on the course or even the practice tee. Let him always decide first upon the result he wants to produce; second, upon the precise manner in which to strike the ball; and then let him place himself before the ball in such position that he knows he will be able to deliver the blow in this manner."

—Bobby Jones

One, two, three.

The genius of Bobby Jones as a writer and golfer reveals itself in this simple instruction.

The subject is a person's approach to making a golf shot. Jones's message is implicit in the structure of the second sentence. This sentence contains a certain structure, just as there is a structure underlying every golf shot.

The pattern advocated by one of the greatest golfers who ever lived is this:

One, two, three.

The first clause (and the most important part of every golf shot) has to do with making up your mind; the second concerns the how of it; and the third, putting yourself in position to achieve what your mind and body seek to do.

But the movements are not separate. They are bound to one another like the links in a chain (to use the image of another great golfer-teacher, Ben Hogan). The movements are simple, routine, and possess an elementary structure upon which every golfer can build his or her game.

One, two, three.

Resolved: I make my setup as simple as one, two, three.

February 19

"It's not hard to find Gerald Ford on a golf course. Just follow the wounded."

—Bob Hope

Many of our presidents have played golf, but none worse than Gerald Ford.

Ford beaned a spectator on the first hole of the very first charity golf tournament he entered after becoming president in 1974. Thus began a head-hunting trend that continued well after Ford left office three years later.

Ford was a favorite target of Bob Hope. "There are over forty golf courses in Palm Springs," said Hope, "and nobody knows which one Ford is playing until after he hits his tee shot." "You could tell which cart Ford was driving; it was the one with the Red Cross insignia on top." "Ford's gallery doesn't come out to watch him play," Hope added, "they come to play chicken with his tee shots."

Ford took the ribbing in stride, making jokes about his golf—"During my last game I hit an eagle, a birdie, an elk, and a moose"—in his good-natured way.

This may be an approach worth imitating. Everyone gets kidded about their game, everyone gets razzed by their friends. Does it do any good to react defensively? To get mad? To lash back or sulk in silence? Naw. Just take it in stride and laugh along with the others. *Their* time will come.

And remember to apologize to your victim if, like Gerald Ford, you do happen to bop an unsuspecting person with a tee shot.

Resolved: I take kidding about my golf game in stride.

February 20

"Love and putting are mysteries for the philosophers to solve."
—Tommy Armour

Putting is only one of the many mysteries in this mysterious game, not the least of which is: Why?

Why do we play? Why does it so completely command our attention? Why is hitting a ball into a hole with a stick such an endlessly fascinating exercise? What makes us do it? Even those who have spent 50 or 60 years playing golf cannot fully say why.

The cartoonist Charles Schulz suggests an answer: "It's probably the best sport man has invented, because you never conquer it, and because of the beauty of the surroundings. Every shot is different, every hole is different. For some idiotic reason we all like the challenge."

For some idiotic reason, we all like the challenge. That's a pretty good answer. The writer John Updike says we play golf "because it rests the overused parts of ourselves and tests some neglected aspects—the distance-gauging eye and the obscure rhythmic connection between feet and hands."

The distance-gauging eye. That's good too. In this way, and in so many others, golf resembles life. Why are we here? There are lots of possible answers to *that* one too. Mystery is central to both life and golf. So is hope. And joy.

Today, take a moment to ponder the mystery that is golf. Then go out and put a dent in that little ball.

Resolved: I accept this idiotic challenge. I put a dent in the ball.

February 21

"Swing tempo has been the most important factor in my career. It relieves the pressure and stress of the game."

—Nick Faldo

Ever watch pro basketball players shoot free throws? The good ones who make 80, 85 percent of their attempts?

It's all rhythm, all tempo. Each has his own rhythm, his own routine prior to the shot. Deep breath, bounce, shoot. Three quick bounces, pause, shoot. Bounce, spin ball, shoot. Each shooter's routine is distinctly his own, as individual as a fingerprint.

A basketball free throw is somewhat analogous to a golf shot. The shooter is at a stop. He must manufacture his own rhythm; it is not supplied by the pace of the game. His preshot routine is an attempt to establish tempo, or rhythm. Watch someone like Shaquille O'Neal clank free throws off the rim and you see a player whose rhythm is just *off*.

You would do well to keep this in mind the next time you go out to the course or practice range. Tempo is all. It relieves stress and pressure. Lacking tempo, a technically sound swing is like a machine without oil, just a lot of gears grinding.

Be the mechanic of your golf swing. Lubricate it freely. Find a rhythm that works for you.

Resolved: I get into a swing tempo that works for me.

February 22

"Wind, hole design, your lie and a hundred other factors in golf mean that you never hit the same shot two times in a row."

—Phil Mickelson

Let's assume that you have been playing golf for ten years. You are a person of regular habits and you have faithfully played once a week during this span, rain or shine.

This means that you have played golf 52 times a year for 10 years, or 520 times. On these 520 outings, let's say, you averaged 100 strokes per round. Therefore, over the past 10 years, you have hit roughly 52,000 shots, give or take a mulligan or two.

Not one of those shots was the same as any other.

Let's go even further. Say you are a twice-a-week player with the same average score. But you have been playing 70 of your 76 years. That computes to 3,640,000 strokes over an extremely well spent lifetime.

That is definitely a lot of golf shots, but it still adds up to the same: no two alike.

You may not consider yourself a creative person, but if you play golf, you most certainly are. After shooting a 64 one year in the British Open, Greg Norman compared the round to "painting a beautiful picture." The comparison is apt. Golf is a creative process. You need to enter into a round of golf with the spirit of an artist.

Now, then. The canvas is the course. Your clubs are the brushes. Go paint a beautiful picture.

Resolved: I paint a beautiful picture today.

February 23

"I never did any real amount of winning until I learned to adjust my ambitions to more reasonable prospects. In a season's play I could perform at my best rate for not over a half-dozen rounds. In any one of these best rounds I would not strike more than six shots, other than putts, exactly as I intended."

—Bobby Jones

Set realistic goals. A realistic goal is a limited goal. Make it an "achievable" goal if limited sounds too negative.

You must be able to realize your goals in golf, whatever they are, especially in the beginning. Setting grand goals and then falling short of them is a recipe for disappointment.

Look at Bobby Jones, one of the greatest ever. He figured he only played his best on six occasions over an entire season. Adjust your prospects accordingly. Set realistic goals for yourself, and work to achieve them.

A psychologist might say that establishing too lofty a goal is a subconscious effort to defeat yourself. You want to fail on some level, and thus you make unreasonable requests of yourself that you cannot fulfill.

You must be vigilant against this. Oppose all efforts to subvert your hopes and dreams, especially those engineered by your own self.

When you achieve the goal you have set for yourself, move on to the next one. You will find when you do this that you have improved your view of reality. Your next set of realistic goals will be more ambitious than your previous set. By taking small steps at first, you will soon find that you are making forceful, powerful, assertive strides ahead.

Resolved: I set achievable goals.

February 24

*"My own favorite key for slowing down the swing is just to think
of Sam Snead swinging a club. All I have to do is picture his
nice flowing action and my swing gets smoother."*

—Tom Watson

Since the sweet-swinging Snead is no longer active, you might
want to picture Fred Couples at the tee or Ernie Els. See if
either of them puts you in the mood to swing.

The idea is not to imitate these golfers. Imitation is the sin-
cerest form of bad golf. The idea is to create a positive mental image that helps you create a positive reality. Watson did
not copy Snead's swing; the picture he formed in his mind
helped relax him even as it provided a motivational boost.

Another Watson tip: Swing every club with the same easy
rhythm. Weekenders tend to think that when they've got a
driver in their hands they need to kill the ball. Again, next
time out, picture Fred Couples. Does he ever look as if he's
killing the ball? And yet the ball flies and flies when he hits.

Think of Fred Couples. Draw a nice, easy mental picture
of yourself hitting a nice, easy ball.

Resolved: I picture the swing of Fred Couples when I step
up to the tee.

February 25

"You'll never increase your driving distance without a positive mental attitude. Confidence is vital."

—Greg Norman

You will also never increase your driving distance by trying to always hit it down the middle.

The middle of the fairway is good. It is almost always a good place to be on a golf course. It is a very worthy location to park your ball.

However.

The drive is only your first shot on the hole. Others will follow. You can whack the ball way the hell over there and still recover. Still make a good score on the hole.

Look at Seve Ballesteros and Ben Crenshaw. They do it. They both make a nice living in the professional game by hitting less-than-perfect drives. Lee Trevino once joked that Crenshaw could get a much better suntan if he ever hit the ball in the fairway.

Of course, Seve and Ben (and Lee, too) have great short games. Seve and Lee are terrific scramblers and chippers. Crenshaw wields the putter the way Zorro wielded a sword. In some ways, their game begins after their tee ball, on their second or third shot.

There are a variety of ways to play a golf hole and still have success. Other avenues exist than going straight down the center of the fairway. Realize that you have a shot after your tee shot, and shots after that, and walk up and pulverize the ball.

Resolved: I pulverize the ball.

February 26

"The ball's scared of him. He'll get it in the hole if he has to scare it in."

—Bob Rosburg, on Arnold Palmer's putting style

When it comes to putting, take a page from Arnold Palmer's book: Scare the ball into the hole.

You think we're kidding? Forget those wimpy extra-long putters or Bernhard Langer's hands-twisted-up-like-the-gnarled-root-of-a-tree grip. We're talking attitude now, serious attitude.

Some of us adopt a passive approach to putting, whether we are conscious of it or not. We feel as if somehow the act is slightly out of our control. We get nervous and rush. Or we get nervous and slow down. Our anxieties take over, and we yip the ball.

The best putters are aggressive. They do what they do, and it's done. Their confidence shows in the assertive nature of their play. They don't make a putt so much as pull the trigger on it. They treat the ball the way Clint Eastwood treated that weasely little bad guy in the movie. "Go ahead," said Eastwood, holding him dead in his sights with his gun. "Make my day." The ball rolls up to the hole and, frightened of the consequences if it does not obey, it drops in.

Make your own day. Become more aggressive on the greens.

Resolved: I become more aggressive on the greens.

February 27

"It's been my experience, since I was a kid learning to play, that if you try to sink a chip shot you will get closer to the hole. And occasionally make one."

—Tom Watson

Today, try to sink it.

Forget about the rest of it. Try to sink it.

This simple yet profound thought is as much about having confidence in yourself as it is about chipping. If you chip just to get close, you are selling yourself short. You are saying, in effect, "I can't make it. So I'll do the best I can." That's not realistic; it's defeatist. It is settling for second best.

Get rid of these thoughts. Strike them from your shot-making process.

Have the confidence of Tom Watson as a kid. Know you can make it. Know that you will get it close. Go for the hole. Go for it all. People make their chips all the time. You can too.

Try to sink it. Then sink it.

Resolved: I shoot for the hole when I chip.

February 28

Every golf course has one or two very difficult holes—or
"Train Wreck Holes," as they're called. These trouble holes
can derail a player and wreck his round.

Golf pro Steve Caulkins offers a few tips on how to
approach these holes:

Rely on your favorite clubs. Play these holes with the clubs
you feel most comfortable with.

Use a fairway wood or a long iron off the tee. Leave the
driver in the bag.

Fix your attention elsewhere. Look beyond the trouble, or
around it. Like those who looked upon Medusa in ancient
myth, you may become fixated and turn to stone.

Concentrate on what you are about and what you do well.
Your swing; your favorite swing key, if you have one.

Be positive. A worrisome frame of mind—looking ahead,
imagining disaster, as golfers are wont to do—can make these
holes seem harder than they are. There is no sense worrying
about a calamity until it comes. But take a positive approach.
Have faith in your ability to captain your golfing ship through
these passages into placid, sunny seas.

Resolved: I face the trouble holes with confidence.

February 29

"What do I like about golf? It's the scenery and the fact that you can get away from everything, especially phones. Between holes 2 and 17 it's a lot of fun."

—Huey Lewis, rock singer

Today is a good day to get away from everything. Today is a good day to play golf.

It's February 29, Leap Day. It's like a free day. What better way to spend a free day than playing golf?

A Leap Year occurs every four years. The past three years were not Leap Years, nor will the next three years be Leap Years. A Leap Day is so rare they ought to declare it a national holiday. You'd play golf on a holiday wouldn't you? Take the day off. It's Leap Day.

You probably can't even remember what you were doing last Leap Day. Make *this* one memorable. Play golf.

A Leap Day is taken every four years to adjust the calendar. Apparently our way of calculating the days and years is so wacky that they need to take it into the shop every now and then. While they're working on the calendar, you play golf.

What, the calendar needs adjusting? We'll tell you what needs adjusting. My swing needs adjusting; my putting stroke needs adjusting.

You *can* get away from everything in golf, and what better day to do it than today?

Resolved: It's Leap Day. I'm playing golf!

March I

"To know oneself, one should assert oneself."

—Albert Camus

Use who you are. Whoever you are, whatever you do best, use it. Assert it.

Use your energy and drive if you are a young player. Use your experience and your coolness under fire if you are a more mature player. Whatever you bring to the golf course, use it.

Rely on your game off the tee if you play long. Use it to intimidate and discourage those around you; *their* ball never travels as far. But if you are a short-game player, use *that* to your advantage. Watch the expression on the faces of those big hitters when you get up and down.

All of us have a unique life experience that we bring to the things we do. We have individual abilities and particular talents. We cannot use another person's abilities to do the things we do, nor would we want to. Using our abilities, our gifts, our experience, our knowledge, our talents, our energy, our emotion, our *essence*—that is how we achieve true success, true progress, in our lives.

Golf is the same. We all have certain talents, certain things we do well. We know what these talents are and we know that they are different from our friends'. They have their own strengths. Are they equal in nature? Naw, that's not the way the world works. Some possess gifts that are truly great.

Assert who you are. It is the most powerful tool you have in golf. In asserting yourself you will find out more about yourself, about who you are, and through this knowledge you will continue to grow in power.

Resolved: I assert who I am in golf.

March 2

*"In trying to get better, I monkeyed with my swing. I played
poorly for so long that I lost all confidence. I found out it takes
a long time to overcome all the negative thoughts."*

—Bob Tway

Every golfer can sympathize with Bob Tway. What happened
to him can happen to anybody.

The year 1986 was his golden year. The winner of four
titles, including the PGA (on a miracle shot out of the bunker
on the 72nd hole), he appeared to be one of the rising stars
of the Tour. Appearances proved deceiving. After that year he
fell into a funk that slowly robbed him of his confidence.

In the beginning when things started to go bad for him,
Tway thought that all he needed was a little tinkering with
his swing. So he sought the advice of a pro. Then, when more
problems arose, he talked to another pro. And another. And
another.

Finally, Tway gave up listening to what other people
thought was wrong with his swing. That just fueled his doubts
and made him overly conscious of mechanics. He returned to
what he was most comfortable with and what had worked for
him in the past—and in the process resurrected his game. In
1995 he won his first PGA tournament in years, and he con-
tended until the final holes of that year's U.S. Open.

Monkeying with your swing seldom produces the results
you seek. Feeling confident about yourself always does. Trust
your swing, trust your game.

Resolved: I trust my swing.

March 3

"There is one word in baseball that says it all, and that one word is: 'You never know.'"

—Joaquin Andujar

You never know in golf either, although plenty of people think they do. Shine 'em on.

The know-it-alls in golf and life are just negative people. They think they know everything, and really they know nothing.

The people who know would have counted out one kid. He hailed from a small town in a rural state. He wasn't a country-club kid. He learned golf on his own. He learned by hitting a ball over a backstop on the baseball field near his house.

That is no way to learn a golf game, say the people who know. You need expensive clubs, lessons, country-club membership, and a privileged upbringing.

This boy didn't have any of that. His dad drank too much. So did he. He was a teenager who drank a six-pack of beer and whiskey shooters for breakfast. He was a wild kid who was going nowhere with his life, said the people who know.

Well, John Daly fooled them. And the British Open and PGA champion continues to fool them. People keep counting him out, but he never counts himself out. That is the important thing.

You never know. Nobody ever knows, least of all the people who think they know. People may count you out. Do not let yourself be one of them. Never count yourself out.

×

Resolved: I never count myself out.

March 4

"A few strong instincts, and a few plain rules."

—William Wordsworth

Observe a few strong instincts in golf and a few plain rules. Everything else is clutter.

Here is one of those few plain rules: Get positive on each shot.

Before you step up to hit, get positive. Get positive that this is the shot you want to make with the club you want to use. Get positive each and every time you swing.

Your ball is 125 yards from the green. The pin is tucked into the right side of the green in front of a bunker. It is a tricky shot because normally you like to play the ball from left to right. But the pin placement is going to make that type of shot very difficult.

Take your time, that's the first thing. Take as much time as you need.

See the shot before you hit it. Make a movie of it in your mind, the way Nicklaus does.

Think about the club you'll need to make that mental picture come true. Trust your instincts. Choose the club you feel good with.

Step up when you're ready. Hit the shot you want, when you want. This is a rule for which there are no exceptions. Do it every time.

When you get positive on every shot, you will produce better shots and fewer shots.

Resolved: I get positive on every shot.

March 5

"An angry golfer is a loser. If he can't control himself he can't control his shots."

—Sam Snead

A dad we know sat down and had this talk with his golf-playing son:

"Listen, you are sixteen. You're a heckuva player for someone your age. You have a ton of talent. If I was your age and had your abilities—well, that's another story.

"I'm not just another old coot trying to hand you a line. It's right there for everyone to see. I'm not making this up: Your attitude is killing you.

"Golf isn't like tennis. You can't act like a spoiled brat and expect to do anything in this game. Pouting, lipping off, sulking after a mishit, blaming others for your mistakes, tyranically demanding perfection with every swing and then erupting in a rage if you do not meet the impossibly high standards you have set—these are the characteristics of an immature golfer, a golfer who will never achieve his maximum potential until he grows up or changes his attitude, or both.

"Sorry to pull rank on you there. But I have lived considerably longer than you, and while I don't know everything I do know that nobody likes a kid with a chip on his shoulder.

"Look at Tiger Woods. Do you think when he was your age he flew off the handle every time something didn't go his way?

"I love you. I care about you. I want the best for you. That is why I am talking to you like this. You will never be the player—or person—you can be until you stop fighting yourself and everyone around you."

Resolved: I control my temper on a golf course.

March 6

"Praise youth and it will prosper."

—Irish proverb

This is the saddest of all sights on a golf course:

A child is out playing, hitting balls, having a grand time. And playing very well, too. Relaxed, confident, a fledgling testing its wings.

Then Dad joins him. (The drama almost always consists of a father and son, though moms and daughters may take on roles as well.) Dad watches, while the child hits.

Immediately the criticism begins. Don't do that, says Dad. You're doing it wrong, says Dad. Aren't you listening to me, says Dad. What's wrong with you, says Dad.

The child, who was hitting like Tiger Woods before, no longer can do anything right. Whatever he does isn't good enough. He withdraws, goes into a shell. And the criticisms increase. Before long the child, turned sullen and inward, quits the game because it isn't fun.

Some advice: Give your kid a break. Your constant niggling criticisms, however well-intended, are only hurting the individual you seek to bolster. All your child hears is that he or she is being criticized, even if your advice is technically sound.

Err on the side of generosity. Err on the side of praise. A child will be far more receptive to your suggestions if they are given in an atmosphere of love, support, and trust. Think of how strong your father's words were to you as a child (even the mildest of utterances) and think of how deeply in your being they resonate still. And if your father was a harsh taskmaster, was that so good for you?

Resolved: I love and support my kid in his efforts to play golf.

March 7

"Give me good clubs, fresh air and a beautiful partner, and you can keep my clubs and the fresh air."

—Jack Benny

Enjoy the blessings of life and golf. Find a partner to join you.

You will play more often and more regularly with a partner. He will convince you to play on days when your energy is low, just as you will stir him into action.

Preferably your partner will be equal in ability or even a shade better. For he will push you to improve your game even as you are pushing him to improve his.

A partner knows your game. He may see something that can be of help. A good partner also knows when to keep his advice to himself.

A partner will share costs and the driving. He will let you play a club from his bag. He will pick up the drink tab half of the time. He will bring you up when you are feeling down.

A partner will motivate and catalyze. Each time out will be a scene of friendly competition. This will bring out the best in both of you. Perhaps he is long off the tee and you are a genius around the greens. There is always a rough parity in the best partnerships. If one person beats the other every time, the partnership will not last long. But a good partner will push himself to catch up, because he does not want his mate to beat him for long.

Finding a steady golf partner whose schedule matches yours may require some doing. But that's no reason not to try. Pick up the phone, see who's available. Who knows? You may get lucky and find someone beautiful.

Resolved: I find a steady partner.

March 8

"If a five-year-old can learn to swing, there is no reason why you cannot."

—Ernest Jones

On March 8, 1968, Tommy Moore stepped up to the tee of a par 3 at Woodbrier Golf Course in Hagerstown, Maryland and hit the ball in the hole. Tommy was six years old, the youngest person ever to strike a hole-in-one.

Writing half a century earlier in his classic golf instructional, *Swing the Clubhead*, Ernest Jones had this to say about what older people can learn from young golfers: "All you need to do is repeat the action of that child [in Jones's case, a five-year-old girl]. Her mind was not cluttered by the endless don'ts that fill the air whenever people talk golf. She merely took the club as it should be taken, in her two hands, and did with it what comes naturally. She swung."

Unclutter your mind of don'ts. Take the club in your two hands, and swing.

Jones's naturalistic philosophy is not an argument against technique or experience. These are important to a point. He was instead advocating a frame of mind for golfers: more instinctual, less analytical and intellectual, relying on touch and feel the way a young child would do it—the way *you* can do it too, if you let yourself.

Let today be your day! Step up to the tee like Tommy Moore, and give it a ride.

Resolved: I take the club in my two hands, and I swing.

March 9

"Perfection never exists in reality but only in our dreams. But the notion of perfection is very real and has tremendous power in disparaging whatever is actually at hand."

—Rudolf Dreikurs

Are you happy with your golf game? If you are like most golfers your reply will be an untranslatable guttural snort that sounds something like "harrumph!"

But why? Why the discontent? Because it is not perfect? Whose is—Nick Faldo's? If it is perfect, why does he tinker with it so?

Okay, you are willing to concede the point. Nobody's game is perfect. Still, you say, your game could stand improvement. Again, whose couldn't?

A revolutionary thought: being happy with your golf game as it exists today.

You can accomplish more with a positive feeling about your game than you can with a self-critical one. Some golfers say, "I won't be satisfied until . . ." or "I can't be happy unless . . ." Avoid this self-critical trap as if it is Hell Bunker.

The traditional notion of self-improvement is that it stems from a personal lack or character flaw. This simply is not true. The most motivated people are the ones who feel good about themselves and want to feel better, who have accomplished something and want to do more.

The best thing you can do for your golf game is feel good about it.

Resolved: I feel good about my game.

March 10

"When in doubt, risk it."

—Holbrook Jackson

Here is a radical thought, suggested by Jan Goben: Let your doubts live.

Doubts are not necessarily a bad thing. They suggest problems in your golf game, but they also point the way toward possible solutions.

Be confident of yourself. Have confidence in your game. These are essential to good golf.

But doubt, within reason, has a place in your golf bag too. A truly confident golfer is not one who has denied or tried to obliterate his or her doubts. A confident golfer is one who sees his doubts for what they are. He analyzes and examines them at the proper time, then leaves them behind in the locker room when he enters the field of play.

Be aware of your doubts. If you slam the door shut on your doubts, you close off the potential for advancement. Seen in a more positive light, a doubt is but the first inkling of the yearning for self-improvement. Ignore your doubts and you are ignoring your better self.

Explore your doubts. But do not magnify them beyond what they are. See them in the context of your whole game. See how small they are, how trifling, compared to the solid assurances you receive from the game.

As golfers, we tend to overstate our imperfections. Our doubts get blown up proportionally. Letting our doubts live— letting them play themselves out—reduces their size and potency.

Resolved: I let my doubts live.

March 11

"You're always learning in this game. The moment you stop improving, you start to regress."

—Dale Douglas

Learn one new thing every time you play.

Learn about the course. Learn about your partners. Learn about yourself. The lessons are there if you are willing to keep our eyes and ears open to them.

Learn one thing every time you hit a bucket of balls. Learn one thing every time you step on a putting green.

Was your round a "disaster"? It is only a disaster if you do not learn from it. Take one thing away from a failure and it is no longer a failure.

Take at least one thing away from your successes, too.

You can learn something from every situation, every experience, every person, every round of golf. One thing plus one thing plus one thing adds up to a whole bunch of things over time—a veritable *Encyclopaedia Britannica* of knowledge about your game and you.

Resolved: I learn one new thing every time I play.

March 12

"Most people live, whether physically, intellectually or morally, in a very restricted circle of their potential being."

—William James

Break out of the circle. Play to your fullest potential.

Only a gifted few can play as well as Norman or Nicklaus. But everyone, whatever their level of skill, can realize their abilities to the fullest.

"Realizing your potential" is such an abstract concept. How do you actually *do* it? Some thoughts:

Have fun. A player who is maximizing his or her abilities is having a good time.

Work hard. Playing to your potential means having fun *and* working hard.

Focus. Get the most from the game that you possibly can while you are playing. Commit to it.

What is interesting about these three simple ideas is that you can put them all into practice today. Not tomorrow or on some hazy date in the future—*today*.

Realize your potential. Have fun, work hard, and focus. Get everything you can out of this day. Wring the cloth dry.

Golf is like anything else. The love you take is equal to the love you make. Give yourself fully to the game. Break out of the circle and realize your full potential as a player.

Resolved: I play to my fullest potential.

March 13

"Always factor in your strengths and weaknesses before deciding on strategy. A hole may be ideally played with a fade, but if your natural shot is a draw, it might be better to find an option that allows you to play to your strength."

—Ben Crenshaw

Play to your strengths. That is always the best option.

Whatever your strengths are, play to them. Boost them. Build on them. Strengths are an asset. You need plenty of them to be a good golfer.

If you hit the hell out of that 5-wood, use it. Drive with it, putt with it. Hell, brush your teeth with it.

Practice is the time to work on "weaknesses." If your long irons are a worrisome thing for you, leave them to gather dust in your bag. Better yet, leave them home. What's to debate?

You know what your strengths are. And you know how strong your strengths can be when you are feeling the power. The more you rely on and call upon your strengths, the stronger they become. Use them!

Resolved: I play to my strengths.

March 14

"Quick fixes are not the route to lasting golf swings. What you need to do is work on solid fundamentals."

—David Leadbetter

Maintain a steadfast commitment. No quick fixes.

Put in your time. No quick fixes.

Pay your dues. No quick fixes.

No skipping steps. No quick fixes.

The author John Lancaster Spalding writes, "It is weakness to be resolved as to the end, and to remain irresolute as to the means." You may be looking for a quick fix if you are resolved to the end but not the means. Be resolved to the means. Let the end take care of itself. No quick fixes.

You must go through the alphabet to get to Z. There is no other way, as painful as it is to comprehend.

Even the young and truly gifted must go through the same steps as everyone else. They think that their gift allows them to skip steps, thinking it is unnecessary for them. All that means is they will have to learn them at a later date. Nobody skips steps and shoots low scores for long.

Look at Jack Nicklaus. You'd think if anybody could have skipped steps, it would have been he. When he was a boy his teacher held his hair to keep his head still during his swing. Young Jack cried out in pain every time he moved his head. In fact, Jack Nicklaus learned the steps better than anybody else; that's why he became Jack Nicklaus.

Learn the lessons you need to learn. No quick fixes.

Resolved: No quick fixes.

March 15

"It is better to throw a theoretically poorer pitch wholeheartedly than to throw the so-called right pitch with a feeling of doubt. You've got to feel sure you're doing the right thing, sure that you want to throw the pitch that you're going to throw."

—Sandy Koufax

Few men have ever thrown a baseball harder than former Los Angeles Dodger pitcher Sandy Koufax. Or better. He could really bring it. Hitting against Koufax, said one batter, was "like trying to eat soup with a fork."

A few things about Koufax are worth noting for golfers:

For one, he knew the theories on how to pitch. He was not just standing on the mound trying to knock over the catcher.

These theories, however important in their way, were not vital to his success as a pitcher. Of far more importance was his ability to register a "K" when Doubt stepped up to the plate.

This was a conscious act on his part. He knew he could not always control what happened to his pitches; sometimes a batter like Willie Mays hit them out of the park. But he always felt positive about what he could control—his state of mind.

This has tremendous relevance to golfers who spend time worrying about whether they have chosen the "right" club or whether they are swinging the "right" way. Step up, hit the ball with confidence. There is no wrong way to hit a golf ball if you hit it with the confidence that what you are doing is right. Theory means nothing; the only thing that matters is your steely inner resolve.

Resolved: I step up and hit with confidence.

March 16

"Hit fairways, hit greens, sink putts."

—Ernie Els

What are the elements of good golf? Hit fairways, hit greens, sink putts.

Ernie Els found himself in a tight spot in the South African PGA, a tournament he desperately wanted to win because he wanted to establish himself as a player of stature, at least in his native country. He had the lead at the end of the third round. But after bogeying three straight holes on the back nine on the final day, the lead was gone and he was leaking oil like the *Exxon Valdez*.

What was going wrong? For one, Ernie realized that he was trying too hard. Trying too hard to impress his countrymen, trying too hard to score birdies. He was trying too hard to be perfect, and this was causing him to take foolish chances.

As a remedy, he returned to what for him are "the basics":

Hit fairways.

Hit greens.

Sink putts.

Focusing on these three essentials allowed him to relax, to quit trying so hard. He no longer felt the need to take so many chances. Everything would be all right if he hit the fairways and greens, and made his putts. And he was right. He won the tournament.

Resolved: I hit fairways, hit greens, sink putts.

March 17

"As you read greens, remember: First sight is best sight."

—Charlie Epps, teaching pro

This is ancient golf counsel, the wisdom of our tribal elders. Trust your first read, they say. They are right.

Reading greens can be tricky, no doubt. But trying to follow the techniques for reading greens as put forth by some contemporary golf pros is like trying to understand calculus. And all it does is sow doubt.

Did I do it right? The way they said to do it in the magazine? I must have left something out. Something's not right.

Yeah, something's not right. *You missed the putt.*

We fall into lazy habits of mind when we give more credence to a system than what we know to be true with our own eyes. Even those who adhere to a system still miss putts, still misread greens.

Give yourself credit. You know a lot. You have seen a few greens in your lifetime. More important than any system in putting is confidence. Confidence comes with success. Success lies in trusting the reads you make, and knowing that your first sight is your best sight.

Resolved: I trust my first read.

March 18

"When I joined the Tour I studied the best players to see what they did that I didn't do. I came to the conclusion that the successful players had the Three Cs: Confidence, Composure, Concentration."

—Bob Toski

Instill the three Cs in your game. Make C the most important letter in your golfing alphabet:

Confidence: Cultivate a positive mental attitude the way a gardener cultivates a poppy. Know that you can do the thing that you are about to do, the thing that you have set your mind to do.

Composure. Be the eye of the hurricane. Maintain calm in the face of events. Maintain calm in every situation. Even out the ups and downs with a consistent mental approach. Let the ball bounce as it will. Control what you can control. Stay within yourself throughout all.

Concentration. Focus on a single thing and do it. Let go of distractions, details. Stick with what you know and do well. Play the course; let the other players take care of their own games. Maintain a steadfastness of purpose. Be clear about your target and take aim on it like a sharpshooter.

Resolved: I instill the three Cs into my game.

March 19

"I'm usually like a yo-yo out there. I play good and then I play bad and then I play good."

—Juli Inkster

Juli Inkster was the top-ranked women's collegiate golfer in the nation in the early 1980s. When she decided to join the LPGA Tour it was a foregone conclusion that she would qualify in a snap.

Oops. So much for foregone conclusions.

In the second round of the Qualifying School Tournament, she lost a contact lens. Her vision went blurry and so did her score. She missed the cut and failed to qualify for the Tour.

The defeat just crushed Juli. Everything had always come easy for her. She was young, gifted, athletic. She took up golf at the relatively late age of 15. By the time she graduated from San Jose State she had won three U.S. Women's Amateur titles and been named College All-American all four years.

The failure at Q-School hit her like a brick. But she had enough maturity to realize that in golf, the yo-yo swings down but always comes back up again. She returned to Q-School and got her LPGA card. She finished fifth in the first tournament she entered. Shortly thereafter, she won the first of many championships in her sparkling career.

The yo-yo always goes down, but you do not have to go with it. A bad attitude will only prolong the down times and make them seem worse than they are.

Stay positive, upbeat, and get ready to ride the yo-yo when it swings back up again.

Resolved: I stay positive during the down times.

March 20

"In our springtime every day has its hidden growth in the mind, as it has in the earth where the little folded blades are getting ready to pierce the ground."

—George Eliot

It is the first day of spring. Time for a golf housecleaning.

Time to sweep away all those negative thoughts. Time to get rid of those negative images and "you can't" voices. Time to fling open the doors and windows of what is possible and let the fresh air in.

We have all taken lessons from a pro or gotten a tip that we have tried hard to incorporate into our game. But why keep struggling with an idea that is not working? Sweep it out the door.

We have all heard those "shoulds" that are supposed to help us but instead just make us feel insecure or inadequate. Beat those shoulds like a dirty rug.

The benefits of cleaning out your personal Golf House are immediate. You may know instantly which ideas of yours are old ideas, tired ideas, dead ideas. They need to go. The same goes for those old ways that no longer work, or never worked in the first place. Who needs them? Junk 'em.

Spring is a time for new beginnings, a time to clear out the dust bunnies and cobwebs of your golf game. Step outside, see the new buds sprout. You have a whole bunch of great golf ahead of you.

Resolved: I let go of old thoughts that no longer work.

March 21

"There is unquestionably a world of grief ahead for the man [or woman] who continually goes all out after every shot."

—Bobby Jones

The temptation to go all out is at its strongest on the tee. Man, how we all love to crack that ball far out of sight down the fairway!

The only way to get rid of a temptation, said Oscar Wilde, is to give in to it. So the best thing to do in this case is to go all out. Only after you've purged your system of this impulse will you be able to adopt a more levelheaded approach.

On second thought, one never fully gets over the impulse. But most would agree that going all out on the tee will net you only lost balls and a strained back.

Look at how the PGA determines the best drivers on tour. It is a function of length and accuracy *over time*. This last is crucial. It is not enough to hit a long ball over a tournament or even a few tournaments. The best drivers have to do it over a sustained period of time playing on different courses in varying conditions.

This has meaning even for those who struggle to eclipse the 200-yard barrier. One drive will not make or break you. So relax. Hit the ball the best way you can, and it will all even out in the end.

Those who have the "boom or bust" mentality tend to do more of the latter than the former.

Strive for consistency in your tee game. It may be more boring than indulging your temptations, but it will serve you better over the long haul.

Resolved: I think "consistency" on the tee and relax.

March 22

Do you find yourself lapsing into predictable patterns when you golf, and are these patterns less than desirable?

Think about the last time things went awry on a golf course. Was it similar to the time before that, or the time before *that*? Is there a pattern you can distinguish?

The circumstances of each episode may be different. You may have been playing on different courses, or different holes on the same course. Your clubs may have been different.

But what was your response to what happened? Did you get mad? Mad at your partners? Did one bad shot lead to another? Did you hang your head in disappointment, sulk?

Think about this: Do you have a comfortable way of playing and acting on a golf course that works for you? Did you fall out of this routine somehow, and did *this* lead to things getting out of control the way they did?

It could have been a small series of events, not just a blowup. Maybe you just didn't handle yourself as well as you have at other times. Are there underlying patterns in the way you act that characterize these down periods?

Once you learn to recognize these patterns, you can break out of them. You can catch yourself as they are occurring or possibly stop them from occurring at all.

Resolved: I recognize the patterns I lapse into when I play golf.

March 23

"You need a purpose in mind when you practice."

—David Leadbetter

Don't practice with a dolphin; practice with a purpose.

In David Leadbetter's view, there is way too much free-lancing among golfers at the practice range. Says Leadbetter: "Responsible businesspeople, men and women who would never dream of entering a meeting unprepared, either don't practice at all or practice with no real purpose in mind. They simply go out to the range and beat balls. That's not practice, just exercise."

Want to put purpose into your practice? Try one of these techniques:

Leave the driver in the bag, or do not take it out at all. In relation to how many times you use a driver during a round, the typical golfer gives it way too much attention in practice.

Work on your putting first, then move over to the range— opposite the normal pattern. This way, the last ball you hit in practice will be with a full swing, preparing you for the full swing you take on the opening tee.

Practice all irons one day, or all woods. This allows you to focus on one type of club and improve its use.

Work the ball. Hit soft high approaches, as if over a hazard guarding a green. Keep the ball low, running it up to an imaginary green.

Work on your weaknesses. Work the ball from left to right if you are a natural fader. The opposite if you hit the draw.

Build on your strengths. Always feel good about what you do in practice. Hit the shots that give you confidence.

Resolved: I practice with specific intent.

March 24

"The last warm-up shot you should play should be with your driver."

—Tom Watson

This is how most of us practice: We go to the range and beat some balls. Then, if there's time before our round starts, we wander over to the practice green and hit some putts. It's like we're all reading from the same book, *How to Practice*, and we can't vary from a single word of its teachings.

Tom Watson apparently did not read this book, for he recommends a different way of practicing. "Most weekend golfers will go to the range, then to the putting green, then to the first tee," he says. "They warm up on the tee, cool down on the putting green, and have to warm up again to tee off." For Watson, this is a backward approach.

Go to the putting green first. Going there first will make you spend more time practicing your putting, which is only good. It will also shift the emphasis in your mind to the short game, which is, after all, the way a person really scores in golf.

After an appropriate time on the green, go to the range. Warm up gradually, taking half-swings at first. Use the high irons, then as you get warm work into a full swing with the woods. The last club in your hand before you take the tee is the driver. The last swing on the range is a full swing like your tee shot. "Then you are physically and mentally prepared for that crucial opening drive," says Tom.

Resolved: I practice my putting first, then move over to the driving range.

March 25

"I've never been to heaven, and thinking back on my life, I probably won't get a chance to go. I guess the Masters is as close as I'm going to get."

—Fuzzy Zoeller

Go to heaven. Go to the Masters.

March 25, 1934. Horton Smith wins the first Masters ever played, inaugurating the best golf tournament in this or any other solar system.

Ever been there? It is thrilling enough on television. Imagine what it would feel like to walk along those storied fairways, like walking through the colonnade at St. Peter's for a person of the church.

Amen Corner. Holes 11, 12, and 13. The golf world's most sacred triptych.

Rae's Creek. Azaleas, magnolias, wind whistling through the Georgia pines. You have to go.

Ben Crenshaw breaking down in tears on 18 after winning his second Masters.

Jack Nicklaus hugging his son after his sixth.

Larry Mize exulting in joy after his miracle chip.

Every year it seems we are moved and inspired by events at Augusta National. It is in the nature of the place.

If you build it, he will come. Well, they built it. Now it is time for you to go.

Resolved: I make a pilgrimage to the Masters.

March 26

"It takes care of you in more ways than one. It is a great leveler. The ball doesn't know who you are, the ball doesn't care who you are."

—Gary Morton

The ball doesn't care about Gary Morton, and it doesn't know who he is. It feels the same way about you.

The ball is indifferent. This may be the cruelest of all golfing facts. Your hopes, your dreams, the fact that you are a decent person, that you pay your bills on time, that you love your family, that you take your dog out for walks, that you tip 15 percent, that you respect the flag and love Mom and apple pie—*the ball just doesn't give a damn*. That's just the way it is and nothing you can do will ever change that.

Nevertheless, while the ball may not care about you, golf ball manufacturers certainly do.

Did you know that dimpled golf balls travel farther than smooth ones? Golf ball manufacturers do. They have done exhaustive studies on the subject of golf ball dimples.

This is a truly inspiring thought. While you go about your day, working at the office, running errands with the kids, visiting the unemployment office or whatever, brainy high-paid golf engineers are spending their time trying to figure out how to make your game better—and you don't have to lift a finger! Now, if that doesn't put a bounce in your step today, nothing will.

Resolved: I observe a moment of silence in honor of golf technology.

March 27

"Golf is in its essence a simple game. Where the average man goes wrong is in making the game difficult for himself."

—P. G. Wodehouse

The average man and woman can never go wrong reading P. G. Wodehouse, one of the best and funniest writers about golf who ever lived.

Even the great ones can learn from the Oldest Member and other characters in the vast Wodehouse treasury. Nancy Lopez quoted this passage of his in her book:

" 'Observe the non-player,' he writes in his quintessentially British way, 'the man who walks round with you for the fresh air. He will hole out with a single carefree flick of his umbrella the 20-foot putt over which you ponder and hesitate for a full minute before sending it off the line. Put a driver into his hands and he pastes the ball into the next county without a thought. It is only when he takes the game in earnest that he becomes self-conscious and anxious, and tops his shots even as you and I. A man who could retain through his golfing career the almost scornful confidence of the non-player would be unbeatable.' "

Funny guy, great points.

Earnest good intentions can lead to self-conconsciousness and anxiety. Keep it simple and fun. Simplicity builds confidence. Maintain the scornful confidence of the nonplayer and you will be unbeatable.

Resolved: I maintain the scornful confidence of the non-player (and read Wodehouse).

March 28

*"Self reverence, self knowledge, self control. These three alone
lead to sovereign power."*

—Alfred, Lord Tennyson

It is only natural to watch the pros on TV and try to imitate
them. But how useful is it really?

Bobby Jones's putter was named Calamity Jane. Bobby
named it that because it had suffered through so many calami-
ties, most of them coming at the hands of its tempestuous
owner.

Though he treated Calamity poorly, Jones was very
attached to it and each time he broke it he patched it back
together again, rejoining the two broken pieces of the shaft
with black tape or bands.

Bobby Jones was hugely popular in his time, golf's answer
to Babe Ruth or Jack Dempsey in the "Golden Age of Sport"
of the 1920s. What was for him a functional necessity—tap-
ing Calamity together—became for the golfing public a matter of style. Golfers around the country taped black bands
around their putters, thinking that some of Jones's magic on
the greens would rub off on them.

One thought: Style sinks few putts.

Another thought: What works for someone else, even a pro,
will probably not work for you. Golf techniques cannot simply be acquired and pasted on like black bands. It is like trans-
planting an incompatible organ. It is a foreign presence to the
host, and the body rejects it. The better way to go is to find
solutions that are organic to your golf game and make sense
for you. It is ultimately the only thing that works.

Resolved: I find solutions that are organic to my game.

March 29

"Addressing the ball in the proper position is the most important fundamental because it determines the kind of swing you will make. Unless you are trying to fade or draw the ball, it is important that you set up squarely to your target line."

—Peter Thomson

Set up squarely to your target line. It seems the most rudimentary form of advice. But like so many things in golf, it is more complicated than that.

The reason you get confused about your target line is that your target is so far away. Far targets are harder to *see*, much less hit. It is like chasing a long-term goal. The goal seems so far away, so remote, you lose faith that you'll ever reach it.

Never lose faith. Give yourself short-term goals on the path to achieving your big long-term goals. Aim for what is closer at hand.

The same principle exists in the physical act of setting yourself up to hit a golf ball at a target that may be hundreds of yards away. Pick out a leaf or a twig a few feet in front of you. Use it as your guideline in setting yourself up to hit the target. Put the ball on a track that passes over the leaf and watch it shoot like a laser beam toward the flag.

Replace the far with the near. Bring the future abstract into the present immediate. Make a long-term goal merely the culmination of a series of highly realizable short-term goals. Do this, and you will hit your target every time.

Resolved: I set up squarely to my target line.

March 30

"All things come round to him who will but wait."

—Henry Wadsworth Longfellow

The game is in the waiting.

How much of a three-hour round is actually spent striking the ball? Two minutes? Add in the setup, the waggling, the practice swings—what then? Fifteen minutes, twenty? The rest is walking, and waiting.

Other things being equal, a person who knows how to wait will be the one who wins the match. How you wait depends on who you are. Hogan was silent as a monk. Chi Chi Rodriguez is a chatterer. Fred Couples nonchalantly leans on his club.

Waiting time in a golf match is not dead time. A lull to one person is an opportunity for another. When you step up to hit are your thoughts strangely dispersed? Do you find yourself having to force them back to the task at hand? Are they leaping ahead to the next shot, or even the end of the round? You may need to rethink your approach to waiting.

You may be concentrating too much and need to loosen up. You may not be concentrating enough and need to intensify. Wait time is preparation time. Whether you are walking to your ball in the fairway, striding up to the green, or sitting on a bench watching your partners tee off, you must be readying yourself on some level to hit. At some point you must gather your energies together, harness them to a single intent, and like a tiger eyeing a lone gazelle that has wandered away from the herd, prepare to strike.

Resolved: I turn my wait time into productive time.

March 31

"Too many golfers underestimate the advantage of 'feel' in a golf swing."

—Jim Bellington, teaching pro

We think about it to the point of obsession. We try to control it and direct its path and progress. We flail at it. We curse it. We flatter it like a lover when it does what we wish.

It is amazing how much of our playing lives revolve around that little dimpled white ball and how little time we actually spend holding one.

Here's a thing to do, even as you are reading this book: Develop feel. Roll a golf ball around in your hands.

Jim Bellington thinks this is a good idea. He believes in a more tactile approach to golf. He thinks it will help your entire game, but especially the short game, to develop a better sense of the object you are striking.

Before you warm up, pick it up and roll it around in your hands. Before you play, on the tee, do the same thing. Feel the weight of it. Toss it in the air and catch it.

Do you have one yet? Go get it. Pull it out of your bag. Roll it back and forth between your hands. It might be a thing to do whenever you pick up this book. Pick up the book, pick up a ball. Having a feel for the ball will help you when you finally perch it up on a tee and start hitting it in earnest.

Resolved: I roll a ball around in my hands while I read *The Golfer's Book of Daily Inspiration*.

April 1

"Why always 'Not yet'? Do flowers in spring say 'Not yet'?"
—Norman Douglas

No fooling, no pranks. This is no joke. Today, you begin. Whatever you have been putting off or delaying for another day, begin it today.

"Another day" has arrived. Today is that day. No more not yets.

Whatever you have been thinking about, or mulling over, or trying to decide on, cease your contemplations. Begin it today.

Delay is a form of holding back. Quit holding back. Begin the thing you know you must do, the thing that despite being put off for so long always keeps coming back, that never goes away.

You know best of all what that thing is—in golf and in the rest of your life. Begin it today.

Are you somebody who has always wanted to play golf but can never find the time?

Today you get off the fence. Today you begin.

Or you may be a young person whose dream is to become the greatest golfer who ever lived.

Good for you. Today your quest begins.

Once you begin you will discover all you need to know, if you need to know anything more at all. Knowledge comes in the doing. Begin today.

Resolved: I begin.

April 2

"I'd rather be lucky than good."

—Branch Rickey

Luck is an important element of golf, as it is in all things. But golfers, being a superstitious bunch, do not like to talk about it much. They fear they may jinx themselves.

This is probably wise. One cannot force luck, on a golf course or anywhere else. Luck is a thing that happens, seemingly independent of a person's character or talents.

E. B. White's line about being young in New York City, "Any young person who comes to New York must be willing to be lucky," applies to golf as well. You must be willing to be lucky.

You cannot force golf, any more than you can force luck. Every golf game must leave room in it for serendipity.

Work, yes. Practice, yes. Refine technique, yes. Prepare, yes. Play always with sturdy resolve. But golf does not succumb merely to the harsh dictates of the will. There is more.

There is luck. The crazy bounce. The "How-in-the-hell did-that-happen?" shot. One can wish for luck to come, but in these cases it almost never does. All that you can do is open yourself up, allow it to happen, be willing to be lucky.

Then, when the ball bounces crazily out of the tall grass onto the green, take advantage of it. That is an important element of golf too. One person's luck is another person's missed opportunity. When a ball bounces your way, jump on it with both feet.

Resolved: I let myself be lucky.

April 3

"Arrange whatever pieces come your way."

—Virginia Woolf

Success in golf—in life, for that matter—depends on how you arrange the pieces.

If the ball lands in a ditch, play it from the ditch. Do not cavil about the existence of the ditch or your misfortune in landing there. Just play it.

If the ball lands on a roof, play it from the roof. Gary Hallberg did that one year at Indian Wells in the Bob Hope Desert Classic. The ball bounced up onto the clubhouse roof from a cart path. Hallberg was permitted a free drop, but he only had a clear shot at the green from the roof. He shot it from there, using a wedge, and made par.

Play the cards that are dealt you. Arrange the pieces you have. Make the best out of whatever situation you find yourself in.

Another example: Some years ago at the U.S. Women's Open, Donna Caponi and Peggy Wilson were tied for first going into the final hole. A thunderstorm broke out, chasing everybody off the course. Rain poured for fifteen minutes. After the storm passed Caponi returned to the 18th tee to finish her round. She made a birdie on the hole and won the tournament.

If you rage against whatever your circumstances happen to be, you cede your power to them. You are saying, in effect, "My situation controls me." Take control of the situation in which you find yourself, and find a way to make it work to your benefit.

Resolved: If my ball lands on a roof, I play it from there.

April 4

"You have to get yourself together, plan your shot, and trust your swing."

—Ken Venturi, on the three elements of a good golf shot

I get myself together. Before I step up I compose myself. I make sure I am ready. I step away if I need to. I take a deep breath, take another moment for myself. I focus on the task at hand. I am the one who is in charge here.

I plan my shot. I study the lay of the land. Observe distances, obstructions, my lie, the relation to the pin. I see the shot before I hit it. See the ball fly in my mind's eye to an area that I have designated. I pick my club. I know it is the right one because I have confidence in it.

I trust my swing. I step up. My focus sharpens. The other issues are decided; I am at ease. I take a practice swing— loose, free-flowing. Take it back slow, bring it down easy. I've done it a thousand times. Easiest thing in the world. Trust myself, trust my swing. I see the ball and I hit it.

Resolved: I get myself together, I plan my shot, I trust my swing.

April 5

"That's the worst thing you can do. Step up to a golf shot without a clear idea in your head."

—Scott Hoch

Scott Hoch knows what can happen to fuzzy thinkers on a golf course. Fuzzy thinking cost him a Masters.

It is 1989. The first hole of a sudden-death playoff with Nick Faldo. Hoch is 2½ feet away from donning the green jacket.

He steps up. Then he steps back for another look.

He steps up again. But his second look has only planted second thoughts. He yips the putt. Sends it five feet past the hole. Thousands of gallery onlookers and millions of TV watchers gasp.

After the tournament Hoch went back to check his reading of the green. His read was right, he just blew the putt—and a claim to Masters immortality. Faldo finished him off the next hole.

Listen to Scott Hoch. *He* knows. Step up to a putt with a clear idea. Doubts are inevitable in golf. But if you must doubt yourself, do so *after* the shot, not before. A head full of doubts produces doubtful shots.

Clarity leads to confidence. Step up with a clear idea. Then knock it into the hole.

Resolved: I step up to a shot with a clear idea.

April 6

"Whenever you are sincerely pleased, you are nourished."

—Ralph Waldo Emerson

Sometimes you can get motivated for an activity by thinking how good you will feel once it's over. Swimming, running, and pumping weights are particularly well suited for this technique.

Golf, however, is not. It is more like sex. It is an act to be relished while in the act. At its most fulfilling, it is nourishing as cheesecake and sincerely pleasing. When it is over, and it is good, you will want to do it again.

If 18 holes seems like forever and you find yourself always looking ahead to the conclusion of your round, you may, in fact, want to treat your golf like your sex life and give it a boost. Such as:

Get a new partner or partners to supplement your current ones. Variety is the spice of life.

Play around. Your home course may be getting stale. A new exotic environment may do wonders.

Be willing to experiment. You may be stuck in a rut without realizing it. If you're a morning person, try doing it at a different time of the day, for a change.

Give yourself plenty of time. Rushing it can cause performance anxiety.

Try an aphrodisiac. In golfing terms, this may be a Big Bertha driver or a new extra-long putter.

Make it "special." Wear something nice. You may be taking golf for granted. The surest way to lose a lover is to take her for granted.

⚔

Resolved: I never take golf for granted.

April 7

Use your powers. Give the ball a thump.

Today is the anniversary of one of the biggest thumps in the history of golf. April 7, 1935. The Thump Heard 'Round the World.

Gene Sarazen stood poised to hit his second shot on the 15th hole of the final round of the second-ever Masters. Sarazen was a short, stocky ball-striker with forearms like Popeye. He used a 15-ounce driver. Henry Longhurst described the sound when Sarazen's club met the ball as "a tremendous elementary thump." He really laid into it, swinging so hard he sometimes lost his balance. The journalist O. B. Keeler, Bobby Jones's muse, said that Sarazen gave "the impression of straining at the leash" when he swung. His playing style reflected his swing: He always attacked, always went for the flag.

Sarazen was 265 yards from the 4½-inch cup. He chose a fairway wood, a 4-wood. He stepped up, gave the ball an elementary thump, and watched it fly into history. The ball went into the hole. Sarazen's 2 on the par 5 tied him for the lead with a shaken Craig Wood, who lost their 18-hole playoff by five strokes.

Sarazen's immortal double eagle proves it. Give the ball a thump, and extraordinary things will happen.

Resolved: I give the ball a thump.

April 8

"Let me tell you how to improve your lie. Improve your clubs."

—Fuzzy Zoeller

How are your sticks?

How long have you had those clubs, anyhow? Getting a little long in the tooth, aren't they? You do know that wooden shafts are no longer in vogue, don't you?

All right, maybe your clubs aren't *that* old. But maybe it's time for a new set anyway.

It's like an automobile. At some point you are simply going to have to get a new set of wheels to obtain the performance you seek. You'll get a positive charge out of a new set of sticks, too. Doesn't matter what kind you buy. The simple fact that you treated yourself to new ones—that you thought enough of your golf game to spend the money—will radiate throughout your being and inspire your play, at least for a time.

Getting yourself new sticks is a way of placing value on your golf game and, by extension, yourself.

Improve your clubs. Improve your game.

Value yourself. Value your game.

Resolved: I buy myself a new set of clubs.

April 9

"The putter must be sought for with care and not hastily, for she is to be the friend, be it hoped, of many years."

—John Low

John Low wrote these words in a 1903 essay on golf. The message was as true then as it is now: Choose your putter with care.

Putters *are* commercial products. But you will never develop the touch you need to excel on the greens if you view your putter as a mere thing to be bought and sold, like a tube of toothpaste. A hammer is a tool. A putter is not. It is more on the order of a magic wand. Nobody knows why it works— or how. But it turns scullery maids into princesses.

Good golfers name their putters. This is not an affectation. Their putters have an identity, why not a name? Putters are as individual as people. The good ones are irreplaceable.

Like people, putters have finite lifetimes. A putter has a certain number of putts in it—times when it will make the ball go in. When it has used up its allotted putts, it is a worthless thing fit for the dustbin of history.

The only question to ask in choosing a putter, and the question that no one can answer, is: How many putts (made shots) does it have in it? That is why it matters little if you have an old putter or a shiny new one, whether you buy it at a pro shop or a toy shop. The essential mystery of every putter is how many putts it has in it.

Keep looking. That four-leaf clover is out there for you. You'll find it.

Resolved: I find me a putter with lots and lots of putts in it.

April 10

"Address the ball any way you want. Hold the putter how you want. Stand on your head if it feels comfortable. However you get the ball to roll into the cup, that's the right way to putt."
—Steve Smyth Jr., golf writer

Is there a right way and a wrong way to putt?

Yes, there is. When the ball rolls into the cup—that's right. Everything else is irrelevant. As Fuzzy Zoeller has said, "If it takes using a broomstick, use *that*."

No doubt if one of the Tour's leading money winners started sinking putts with a broom, golfers around the world would begin using them. Somebody would make millions on the book and video series, *The Broomstick Guide to Better Golf*.

If you are making your putts, that is all you need to know. The rest is simply *noise*.

Let's go further. Let's get rid of all the "rights" and "wrongs" of golf technique. Does it work? Are you having success? Those are the only questions you need to ask.

Thoughts of right and wrong—should and should not—only create confusion and doubt. Absolute standards are for discussion in religion and ethics, not golf. Golf is about what works.

Do what works for you, in putting and everywhere else on the course.

Resolved: I do what works.

April 11

"All the past can help you."

—Robert Henri

Learn from the past. Recapture its glory in your game. Remember your past successes and repeat them.

Greg Norman won the 1995 World Series of Golf with a 66-foot chip from off the green, beating Nick Price and Billy Mayfair in a playoff. Before he took the shot, Norman had a case of déjà vu.

"Believe it or not," he told reporters afterward, "I said, 'Let's do a Doral.'"

Five years earlier, Norman had won the Doral Invitational with a chip on 18. Both the shot and the circumstances were similar to what he faced in Akron at the World Series. This memory put him in a confident, positive frame of mind. He hit a 7-iron, and the ball went in the hole.

There is only one Greg Norman. But all of us have our personal Dorals.

The past contains moments of glory for every golfer. Keep those records in an "Active File" in your mind and refer to them as needed.

Make the past a harbinger of great things to come. Let it work for you in the same way it works for Norman. You have played before; you have had success. Burn those images of success in your mind. When you come to a shot that looks similar to one in which you had past success, use that image to achieve current success.

Knocked it in before? Knock it in again!

⌧

Resolved: I call on my past successes on the golf course.

April 12

"Meditation is a contented but perfectly conscious dwelling of the mind on something likely to elevate our life."

—Ernest Dimnet

Take a moment for yourself. Meditate before you play.

Clear your mind of work. Clear your mind of what troubles it. Clear your mind of distractions. Find a quiet place to be alone and compose yourself.

Meditation slows you down. Slowing down is good for your game. "If I meditate for even just a half hour," says one person who meditates, "it's easier for me to set up my priorities. It's as if while I'm meditating, an inventory is taking place." Take a mental inventory. Prepare yourself for the game to come.

Golf itself is a form of meditation. But you put yourself into a better state to absorb its unhurried meditative pleasures if you take a moment for yourself ahead of time.

A moment of preround meditation may serve your game better than a half hour of hitting balls. Think positive thoughts; drive away the bad.

Playing golf is as much mental as physical. Spend time on your mental game. Take a moment for yourself even as you are playing.

Use this book to help you in your meditations. Read the daily message and think about what it says. Perhaps it will stimulate unrelated thoughts of your own.

The important thing is to give yourself a moment to speak to itself. The benefits to your golf will be enormous.

Resolved: I take a moment to compose myself before I play.

April 13

Golfers have a charming way of putting themselves down. "What's your handicap?" they are asked (the typical question of the nongolfer).

"My putting, my driving, my chipping, my irons, etc.," they respond playfully.

That's an old joke, but it does reflect the skeptical frame of mind of many who play the game. And, to a certain extent, this is an admirable quality. No one likes a person who takes themselves too earnestly.

Let's put it in another context. Suppose you were looking at new houses and you complimented the builder on the one you had just seen. "Thank you," he said, adding with a sly smile: "But I wonder if the roof will hold."

Would you want to buy the house?

Or say you were looking at cars and you asked about a shiny red convertible on the lot. "It's okay," said the salesman. "But the clutch needs work and the brakes are almost shot." That probably wouldn't fill you with a lot of confidence either.

Negative talk *does* matter. You listen to it when you hear it from other people. Then why do you put your golf game down? Talking down about yourself affects the way others see you. It erodes self-confidence.

Say positive things about your game. You can do that without pumping yourself up to the extreme. From positive words will flow positive thoughts and deeds.

Resolved: I say positive things about my golf game.

April 14

"In this world, if everybody followed the rules, the world would be a better place, people would be better."

—Roberto de Vicenzo

April 14, 1968, is one of the most infamous days in golf. That is when Roberto de Vicenzo was deprived of a Masters title because of a scorekeeping error.

Every golfer knows the story of how Roberto's playing partner, Tommy Aaron, who was keeping his scorecard, had mistakenly written down a 4 instead of the correct 3 on one of Roberto's final-round holes. De Vicenzo signed the inaccurate scorecard, adding one more stroke to his total. According to the rules, this meant that Bob Goalby, who actually recorded as many strokes as de Vicenzo during the tournament, was the winner. Roberto was awarded second place.

But there's a happy ending to this story that never gets told. This apparently unlucky break turned out to be the greatest thing that ever happened to the native-born Argentinian. Roberto received far more attention than he would have if he had won the title. He earned hundreds of thousands of dollars in endorsements—money he would not have seen otherwise—and widespread public sympathy, including more than a million letters and telegrams of support.

The moral of the story: Follow the rules. The short-term loss you experience may be eclipsed by a hidden long-term benefit.

Resolved: I follow the rules.

April 15

"Golf has made more liars out of people than the income tax."

—Will Rogers

Is it cheating if everybody does it?

Well, yes.

But what if it is a commonly accepted practice as old as the game itself?

Sorry. But yes, technically it is still cheating. Whether you fudge on your handicap or toe a ball with your shoe to get a better lie or mark down 6 when it was really 8, *you are not supposed to do it.*

But look on the bright side. At least there is no IRS in golf. Nobody is going to attach your bank account if you whiff on your tee shot and happen not to count it as a stroke.

Then again, you may be one of those rare souls who play on the strict up and up. More power to you. Take power from your virtue.

However you approach the game, this is not a day for beating yourself up. You have done enough for your country. You have received enough punishment for one day. Now go out and have a good game of golf.

Resolved: I imagine the ball is the IRS and pound the hell out of it.

April 16

"Play with a controlled mad."

—Sam Snead

Swing under control. Play with a controlled mad.

Get hot, but not too hot. Play with a controlled mad.

If you are throwing clubs, stomping around, and cursing the heavens, your anger has gotten the best of you. You have lost it. More precisely, your game is lost.

Anger can be a motivational force if directed. It is like a mountain river. Within its banks a river is a powerful, onrushing, nearly irresistible force. But once it spills over its banks, its unfocused energies become dispersed, robbed of their potency. It is the same with your anger. Keep it focused. Send it racing down a channel that serves your ends.

On the last day of the Masters several years ago, spectators cheered when Ian Woosnam hit a ball into Rae's Creek at 13. Woosnam, a Welshman, was locked in a tight battle with Tom Watson, the crowd favorite.

The gallery reaction angered Woosnam, but he realized it was something he could not control. He ignored the jeers. If he had let the crowd get under his skin it would have wrecked his chances. He made his anger an ally and stayed on track. He came back to birdie 15. The tournament came down to 18. Woosnam, Watson, and Jose-Maria Olazabal were all tied. The latter two made 5s and Woosnam made 4, and he became the 55th Masters champion.

Use your anger. Make it your ally. Make it work for you. Play with a controlled mad.

Resolved: I play with a controlled mad.

April 17

"The presence of the young lightens the world and changes it from an oppressive, definitive, solidified one to a fluid, potentially marvelous, malleable, variable, as-yet-to-be-created world."

—Anaïs Nin

What can we learn from playing with and watching players who are younger than us? Let us count the ways:

Confidence, confidence, confidence. A young player at the height of his or her powers exudes the stuff.

The ability to act decisively. The tendency to overanalyze that so afflicts and impairs older golfers is far less prevalent among the young.

Optimism. A young person's frame of reference is the future, not the past. They are always looking ahead.

Length off the tee. The years tend to shorten the backswing. What a joy it is to see a golf swing with full range of motion, swinging long and free.

Their attitude on the greens. They are surprised when a putt does *not* go in; they expect every one to drop. This is the attitude of every good putter.

They are positive, upbeat, energetic. They've got their health and their youth. What more could a person want?

It is inspiring to play with younger players. They may remind you of a person you used to know—say, 10, 20, or 30 years ago. Namely yourself. Not only that, a young person has one more valuable thing going for him: He may not have heard all your jokes.

Resolved: I play with a younger partner.

April 18

"Within I do not find wrinkles and used heart, but unspent youth."

—Ralph Waldo Emerson, at age 61

What can we learn from playing with men and women who are older than we? Let us count the ways:

They are very forgiving. Always let an older person tend your card. You will be amazed at how many 8s become 6s.

They know lots of jokes, some of them even funny.

They are compassionate. They know how heartbreaking golf can be, for they have suffered so many heartaches themselves over the years.

Some play "winter rules" all year round. Kick the ball into a better place. Hell, it's only a game.

They are very complimentary. They encourage and support. They enjoy seeing young people take up the torch.

They are, in contrast to the miserly stereotype, generous. They will likely buy you lunch or drinks after.

Older golfers are emissaries from another time. They know lots of history—not only about the game, but about the times that came before the times in which we live.

Golf is a lifetime endeavor. If playing with an older golfer is a vision of the future, one can be content with what lies ahead of us. These are people who have been living and loving this game for years and years. Look at how well they do! It is a model to which we can aspire.

Resolved: I play with an older partner.

April 19

"If I wrote one, it would consist of two sentences. Take the club straight back. Then swing it straight through."
—Peter Thomson, asked why he had never written a golf book

Take it straight back. Swing it straight through. Simple as that.

Now, your first reaction might be "Hey, golf's more complicated than that. At least *my* game is."

But that's not the point. The point is that Peter Thomson won five British Opens (three of them in a row, from 1954 to 1956) by keeping things simple. By simplifying his game. By reducing golf into small, manageable elements that he could easily control.

Take it straight back. Swing it straight through. Two sentences equal five British Opens.

When you go out on the course today, there will be so much to think about. You may be battling a case of the nerves. You may be playing with someone new and you're not sure what he or she is like. Maybe it's someone from work and you want to impress him. Maybe you've never played this course before. You're wondering how you'll do. You've heard it's hilly and the wind comes up, and you hate playing in the wind.

All these things and more go through a person's mind before he or she plays golf. So it's vital to keep it simple. You can concentrate better when you have fewer things on your mind.

Straight back. Swing through. Peter Thomson didn't have to write a book. He said it all in two sentences.

Resolved: I take the club straight back and swing straight through.

April 20

"Nothing is so exhausting as indecision, and nothing is so futile."
—Bertrand Russell

Be decisive on the golf course. Make a decision, make it fast, and stick with it.

It is ironic and often painfully comic how indecisive businesspeople can be on a golf course. They snap off decisions right and left in the office. They take charge, they take full responsibility, they move ahead.

But put these same decision-makers onto a golf course and they turn into Hamlets in spikes. Should I or shouldn't I? Do I or don't I? Am I right—or wrong? How's a person to know?

Bring that powerful, decision-making side of you onto the golf course. Make no excuses. Be decisive. Act. Forge ahead.

Stick with your first impulse in golf. It will always serve you better than all the others that follow. Play the 8-iron. Or if you choose, play the 9. Either is preferable to a waffling indecisiveness that can ruin your game and your confidence.

A decisive player will always beat an indecisive one. The decisive player plays more crisply. He gets into a good rhythm, settles on his choices, and takes his cuts. The indecisive player, in contrast, plays haltingly, overcome by the numerous potential choices that exist with every golf shot.

A decisive player quickly leaves the past behind. He does not look back in regret. What's the good in that? He looks ahead, always ahead, and trusts himself to respond to whatever situation arises.

Resolved: I play decisively.

April 21

"Put things into their places, and they will put you in your place."

—Arab proverb

Ever watch Nick Faldo putt? There is practically a one-beat pause from the time the blade of his putter makes contact with the ball to when he looks to watch the ball's progress. It's almost inhuman. The thing that golfers most want to do in the world, as quickly as they can do it, is watch their putt after they stroke it.

This is maybe not such a good idea, though. As Miller Barber says, "One of the most destructive faults in putting is looking up or moving the head." Giving in to the urge to look spoils the results we want to see. Everybody knows this, and yet everybody looks anyway. It is human nature to want to see how you did as soon as you can.

This is one of the problems with negative instructions. Telling someone "Don't move your head" triggers a subconscious response to do exactly that. All you can think of is not moving your head or not looking at the ball, and you lose track of what you want to do.

Here's a better way to think of it. Stroke, then look. Almost two beats, like Nick Faldo.

You would not put your socks on after your shoes, would you? You would not watch television before you flipped it on, would you? It is the same with putting. All you are doing when you stroke, then look, is following the natural order of things. First do one thing, then go on to the next. Everything in its place.

Resolved: Stroke, then look.

April 22

"Ninety percent of the balls that fall short of the hole don't go in."

—Yogi Berra

"Never up, never in" is one of the oldest saws in golf. Here is U.S. Women's Open champion Meg Mallon giving it a modern spin:

"Think about the times you've three-putted. The problem is normally in the distance you hit your first putt. When you leave the ball well short of the hole or hit it way too hard, you put too much pressure on the next putt."

We all know it. The ball has got to reach the hole to have a shot at going in. But how often do we still leave it short?

Make this pact with yourself. In today's round (or the next one you play), no putts short. Everything to the hole. NO exceptions. Even if you are 100 feet away, make sure it gets there.

You can talk all you want about putting stroke, judging distances, reading the greens. This is not about that.

This is a matter of willpower. If you have the will to get the ball to the hole, you will find a way to get it in.

Resolved: I leave nothing short.

April 23

"Method or technique is less than 5 percent of putting."

—Bob Charles

Method is 5 percent of putting. The rest is confidence. Here is a practice putting method that will give you confidence:

Walter Travis was one of the most accurate putters in the game in the early part of this century. Tommy Armour and other fine golfers admired and copied his practice techniques.

To practice long putts he stood 25 feet away. His object was to come within three feet of the cup. If he did that he was happy. Though Travis was such a virtuoso on the greens, many of his long-rollers of course fell in.

Travis spent most of his practice time on short putts from two to six feet. The Old Man—so called because he first took up the game in his middle 30s—started at two feet, placing balls at the north, south, west, and east points around the hole. Then he'd putt them in. Missing, however, carried a penalty. If he missed one he had to start all over. He moved on only after he made four in a row.

Then he moved out to three, four, five, and six feet, repeating the procedure at each distance. Tommy Armour has noted that each person must work out his putting in his own way. But, he adds, the Travis method is "a much better way of learning and practicing putting than putting a half-dozen balls alongside each other, then tapping them to the hole," as so many people do.

Resolved: I give the Old Man's method of practice a try.

April 24

*"Fitness can help your game. Fitness seems to inspire confidence.
All things being constant, a fit golfer should be the better
one, especially if you exercise your golf muscles as well as
your heart."*

—Leonard Schwarz, physician

Being fit will improve your game (not to mention your sex life
and other nongolfing activities). Here are a few simple exercises that you can do in the course of your everyday life that
will build fitness. Why not start today?

Walk every chance you get. Take a fast, half-hour walk during lunch. Using hand weights while you walk will double the
calories burned. Forget elevators (unless your office is, say,
on the 67th floor). A philosopher once said that every stair
you climb adds a minute to your life. Go up the stairs two at
a time if you feel inspired.

Squeeze a rubber ball or a grip device. This will build the
strength in your hands, wrists, and forearms that is essential
to good golf. You can do your squeezes while watching TV,
chatting on the phone, or reading one of those boring office
reports.

Stretch. It's vital to stretch before playing, but it's something
you can do at your desk or even while in line at the movies.
Do toe raises (working the calves) or maybe even squats
(thighs), using the wall to support your back.

The nice thing about golf is that one does not have to be
a gym rat to play it and play it well. But being physically fit
still helps. Other things being equal, it will give you an edge
over other players.

Resolved: I take the stairs today.

April 25

"Humiliations are the essence of the game."

—Alistair Cooke

Now, there's a happy thought for you! Don't you just feel like going out and playing some golf now?

Motivational tomes such as this one tend to avoid such concepts as "humiliation." In golf, however, this would be like living along the Mississippi River and denying the possibility of floods. It happens. There is no hiding from it. All you can do is be ready for it when it comes.

The question for the day, though, is: Do we think too much about calamity as golfers, and therefore hasten its arrival?

The only possible answer is: Yes. We start thinking about the Train Wreck Hole looming ahead on 14 and top our approach on 11. That sours our mood, and we begin to play poorly. When we finally reach 14 we are down on ourselves and our game. We are no match for this hole, we think. Look at how badly we are playing. Then we shoot a 47 on the hole and confirm our worst expectations.

Is there a way out of this trap?

We have already accepted that humiliations do occur—that bad things can happen to good people on a golf course. First, you must accept that you *can* control these events. They are not happening to you; you are making them happen.

Second, know that you have experienced this before. This, too, shall pass. You will get through it, just as you've gotten through similar experiences in the past. Your job is to make that happen sooner rather than later.

Resolved: I keep events under control by keeping a positive frame of mind.

April 26

"Nothing is ever going to go perfect in this life. You have to expect a little detour now and then."

—Greg Norman

On his way to golfing fame and fortune, Greg Norman has developed a rather unusual visualization technique for those times when he is headed down a street the wrong way and needs to get straightened out again.

You want to try it? Okay, here is what Greg does:

He likes to sit down in a quiet place and, as he confessed to Roy Firestone, imagine himself on the toilet. He is not actually sitting on a toilet, mind you, just imagining it.

Then, in a nod to his Australian heritage, he "pulls the chain." (Americans may prefer to visualize a handle.)

"I flush away all the bad," said Greg. "I pull the chain and it's gone." Good-bye to all those negative thoughts, sayonara to all those bad vibes. And he stands and feels *much* better.

Flush those troubles down the drain. There is your positive visualization technique for the day. Hey, if it works for Greg Norman, who's to knock it?

Resolved: I flush my problems away.

April 27

Are you a golfer for whom it hurts to think? Take heart. There are lots of others with similarly painful thoughts.

After squandering a big lead and losing the Canadian Open, Mac O'Grady came up with a novel approach to venting his golfing frustrations: He wrote a letter. "Dear Mrs. Golf, I hate you," he wrote at three in the morning, unable to sleep. "Why do you continue to mutilate me with these merciless acts?"

Such is the cry of a man in pain. We all know how he felt. Maybe you feel that way now.

But what about his technique? Do you think writing a letter to the Golfing Gods will help your case? It's like when a kid writes Santa Claus, only with more swear words.

No? You don't think so? Well, what about these other techniques for venting one's displeasure with the Golfing Gods:

Breaking your club.

Throwing your club.

Burning your clubs.

Screaming maniacally at the top of your lungs.

Climbing a tree on the 18th fairway and refusing to come down.

Renouncing all family and friends, taking a vow of celibacy, and wandering the face of the earth for the rest of your life.

Better still, why not just have a drink and forget the whole thing?

Resolved: I have a drink and forget about it.

April 28

"If you can't quit looking at the trouble, very often it is better to aim at the trouble instead of trying to avoid it."

—Steve Caulkins, teaching pro

Leo Diegel was a talented, if highly erratic, golfer who played in the 1920s. If Prozac had been available then, he would have been a prime candidate for it. Nothing was too slight for worry. All signs augured doom. Still, he won two major titles and might have won more had he not been plagued by a chronic case of the yips.

The Riviera Country Club in Los Angeles used to have horse stables in the out-of-bounds area off the first fairway. Leo came to play a tournament there, and naturally began to obsess about the stables. Stables, stables, stables. He dreamed stables at night, he saw stables in his eggs at breakfast. And on his practice round he did what he most feared, hooking his drive into the stables.

This is one of the natural laws of golf, much like Newton's Laws of Gravity. By seeking to avoid trouble, we find it. So, Leo decided, why not just be done with it and hit it there?

Come tournament time, Leo stepped up to the tee and did exactly that. He hit it into the stables. It cost him a penalty stroke, but it was well worth it. In a peculiar but very real way it helped him relax and forget about the stables altogether. He hit his next drive down the fairway and played the hole flawlessly the rest of the tournament. Would this ever work for you?

Resolved: I try a change in tactics. I aim for a trouble spot.

April 29

"Given that even the best players land in hazards all the time, you better make friends with hazards. Enjoy them."

—Bob Rotella, teaching pro

Some years ago the broadcaster Curt Gowdy sought to inject a new term into our sporting vocabulary. When two football teams tie at the end of regulation, they play "sudden-death overtime." The team that scores first, wins.

But Gowdy thought this phrase overly morbid and began using, on the air, "sudden-victory overtime" in place of it. The term never caught on, and in fact Gowdy caught a lot of flak for using and advocating the term.

Nevertheless, Gowdy's point makes some sense when it comes to bunker play. "Hazard" is a negative term with negative connotations. The only things that can happen to a person who lands in one are bad.

But is this strictly true? Sometimes it is nicer to be in a smooth, well-raked bunker than the rough. A hazard can be a boon to the golfer who plays it well. Everyone, in time, lands in one, as Rotella suggests. When your time comes, if you get up and out you may pick up strokes on the person who struggles when he encounters one.

How about saying "challenge" or "opportunity" in place of "hazard"?

Nah, the word is fine. But there is nothing stopping us from improving our attitude when we find ourselves in a bunker.

Resolved: I come to appreciate the challenge of sand play.

April 30

*"The practice of self-denial is good; it may be learnt. More
difficult than self-denial is enjoyment, rejoicing in that which
ought to delight us."*

—Mark Rutherford

We have talked a lot in these pages about setting goals as a method of improving your play.

Set limited goals and work to achieve them. Even if you just simply want to play more, make that your goal. Once you achieve your goal you will find yourself already on the way to accomplishing still greater goals down the road.

But let's never forget: We're in this for fun. The greatest goal—and we've missed everything if we've missed this one—is to enjoy ourselves.

When you achieve a goal, reward yourself. You deserve it, right? You have worked hard. Satisfaction comes not just in the striving but in the feeling of having done what you set out to do, as in the happy, exhausted face of a marathoner crossing the finish line.

You need to pause and give yourself credit for the job you've done. If you don't, who will? And if you don't, how can you expect others to?

Treat yourself to a movie, a night on the town, a massage, a weekend getaway—or more golf. You deserve it!

Resolved: I treat myself to a nice dinner for all my hard work this month.

May 1

"He will through life be master of himself and a happy man who from day to day can have said: 'I have lived!'"

—Horace

Be a happy person. Make golf a part of your day today and every day. Here are a few suggestions on how to do that:

Read this book.

Talk golf with a friend (should be no trouble for most golfers).

Practice putting on the carpet of your office or home (subject to approval by spouses and bosses).

Chip balls into a backyard net.

Watch golf on TV.

Roll a ball around in your hands to promote "feel." (If your golfing lags, you may discover heretofore unknown skills as a juggler.)

Swing a club (preferably in an open, unobstructed space) or just grip it, again for crucial reasons of feel.

Play an imaginary hole or round.

Play a round of the real thing.

You will become a better golfer—and a more satisfied one at that—if you can do one golfing thing a day, even if you cannot make it out to the course and even if it is only for five minutes. Five minutes can grow into 10, and 10 into 20. But even five minutes is worthwhile.

Resolved: I spend at least five minutes on golf today.

May 2

"To me every hour of the light and dark is a miracle. Every cubic inch of space is a miracle."

—Walt Whitman

Here is a mental exercise for you: all positive thoughts, all day long.

While you're at work, all positive thoughts. When you're out at the golf course today, all positive thoughts. Before the round, after the round. Before each shot, after each shot.

If a negative thought occurs take it out and examine it, as if you were a car mechanic who found a defective part in the engine he was working on. What caused this to happen? How long has it been like that? Where did it come from? Then toss the part away and replace it with a new one.

All positive thoughts all day will make you aware of how ingrained negative thoughts are in your mental processes. Thinking positive thoughts requires discipline. We have grown accustomed to our negative patterns of thought. We accept them as part of ourselves. We have thought our negative thoughts for so long, we are only dimly aware of how they hinder our performance.

Positive thoughts give a jolt to the system, like charging a battery that has gone dead. How much easier it is to criticize a painting than paint one, criticize a book than write one, criticize a speech than deliver one. Similarly, how much easier it is to criticize a golf swing than to do it.

The critical faculties have their place. But they work so hard normally, let's give them a rest. Have a nice day!

Resolved: All positive thoughts, all day long.

May 3

*"In the life of a young man or woman the most essential thing
for happiness is the gift of friendship."*

—Sir William Osler

One can make a friend in the time it takes to play a round of golf. A stranger on 1 is a confidante by 18. The serendipitous ways in which friendships are formed on a golf course is one of the game's chief pleasures.

Here is another way to make a friend in golf: Join a club. Not a country club, but a golf club. These clubs consist of as few as 10 people and are sanctioned by local chapters of the USGA. They are men and women, frequently single, who like to combine golf with socializing. They organize outings to golf courses and receive the added benefit of group rates. These clubs advertise their outings in the recreational listings of the newspaper or may be contacted through the USGA.

Your reason for joining a club may be to meet people. What better people to meet than golfers? You can play a little golf while you're making friends.

Joining a club can also be a great motivational tool. You may be more eager to learn the game and improve your skills knowing that after your round is over you are going to have to come back and report the news to the others in your group.

Resolved: I join a golf club.

May 4

"The more I practice, the luckier I get."

—Gary Player

Learn to play good golf. Practice.

Turn a liability into a strength. Practice.

Get lucky. Practice.

Good things happen to those who practice. Make good things happen. Practice.

Be ready when opportunity knocks. Practice.

Practice before you play. Practice after you play. Be the first on the practice range in the morning. Be the last to go home at night.

Develop your strengths. Practice.

Practice is another name for work. Work builds character. Be a person of strong character. Practice.

Practice better, play better. The better you play, the more you enjoy. Therefore, practice increases enjoyment.

Practice your fundamentals. Good habits produce good golf. Practice is the best habit.

Dull, uninspired practice reflects a dull, uninspired mind. Be imaginative. Assert your impulse to play and make practice fun. Practice left-handed shots; practice trick shots.

Practice in the summer, winter, fall, and spring. Practice, practice, practice.

Resolved: I practice.

May 5

"When I am idle and shiftless, my affairs become confused. When I work, I get results: not great results, but enough to encourage me."

—E. W. Howe

Today, I go out and hit some good shots. I may not achieve great results, but those really aren't the results I'm looking for. I just want to hit some good shots.

I don't much feel like keeping score today. That is not my purpose in playing. I want to have some fun, and hit some good shots.

Hitting some good shots is a very worthy goal. I know that a round that is slipping and sliding can develop traction when a player hits a few good shots in a row. You get some momentum and pretty soon everybody else is breathing your exhaust.

But I'm not out to conquer the world today. I just want to hit some good shots. I don't even care if they're back-to-back. That may indeed be too much to ask. If I get a good shot on 3, a good shot on 7, and maybe a few on the back nine, I'll be happy with that. I'll take my good shots where I can get them.

Am I selling myself too short? I don't think so. I kind of like my attitude. Every great round of golf includes lots of good shots. I'll start with some good shots and leave greatness to the history books.

The rest of the world can just go hang. I am clear about *my* goals. I get good results today and walk away encouraged.

Resolved: I hit some good shots.

May 6

"As long as one keeps searching, the answers come."

—Joan Baez

Keep searching. The answers will come.

Frustrated by your putting? Keep searching. You will get it right.

You love the feeling of the long ball, but the driver is so hard to control. Keep searching. You will figure it out.

Your long irons are a problem. How does *anyone* play them? Keep working—and searching. The answers will come.

The joy of golf—and, to be sure, the challenge and frustration—is in the searching. To be a golfer is to be a searcher.

John Updike knows. He, too, is a searcher. "Even from the start," he writes, "I could now and then hit a shot that felt and looked thrillingly right. Yet as the hours and the summers on the golf course mounted in number, I seemed as far as ever from discovering how to hit such shots all the time. Or even half the time."

Half the time? You are lucky indeed if you can make the right discovery as much as that.

When we play golf we discover about the game itself—how to play this shot or this club in ever-changing circumstances and conditions. But we also discover much about ourselves. The fact that we do it at all—that we spend those hours and summers—tells us *something* about ourselves, though even such an astute observer of the human condition as John Updike may be hard-pressed to say what.

Keep searching. In golf and in life. The answers will come.

Resolved: I keep searching.

May 7

"We all know golf is a pretty sensitive, delicate game and it doesn't take much not to hit it as well or putt as well. The funny thing is if you make a few putts, all of a sudden the ball-striking becomes easier."

—Mike Donald, U.S. Open runner-up

Make your game easier. Make a few putts.

We tend to divide golf into pieces: the game, approaches, chipping, bunker play, putting, etc. But it is all one game, and the surest way to realize this is to make a few putts.

Get your whole game going; make a few putts. This will trigger an enthusiastic response that will carry over to all aspects of your game. You will drive better after you make a few putts. You will hit your irons better. You will even have more energy.

When you are grinding away, golf does seem all about distinctions and differences. But when you are in the flow of your game these distinctions evaporate like the dew. One shot leads to the next, which leads to the next, and all have a common goal: ball in the cup.

How do you get in the flow? Make a few putts. Walk onto the green with an attitude of "This is where it starts. This is where I get it going." And you *will*. Even if you are strugggling, you can resurrect your game by making a few putts.

Sometimes just one putt will do it. Sink a tough one and watch how you have to battle your enthusiasm to keep it under control as you walk on to the next tee. That great drive you hit really started on the last green.

Watch your game surge. Make a few putts.

Resolved: I make a few putts.

May 8

"Change a losing game."

—Bud Collins

Bud Collins made this comment during a televised tennis match. One player was whipsawing the other around the court. The match seemed a foregone conclusion unless the losing player changed tactics. Bud advised him to charge the net, alter the pace of his second serves, *anything* to throw his opponent off stride. But he never did, and he got creamed.

The contest in golf is against the golf course, not other players, but the advice remains solid: Change a losing game. Change a game that is not working.

Easily said, not so easily done. Because people get defensive about their golf.

"This is the way I did it in the past," you say. "This is the way I have always done it. Are you saying I was wrong to do it that way?"

No. And we're not talking about you anyway. We are talking about your golf game. There is a difference.

Sometimes the past is all we have to hang on to, and we defend it out of all proportion to its current value to us. Is it working for us today? That is the question we need to ask ourselves. It is like getting rid of the old clothes in your closet. Why keep them hanging around if you don't wear them anymore?

Changing a losing game requires a mental adjustment more than a physical one. It is a matter of opening your mind to new ways of thinking, new ways of doing things, new possibilities that were not conceived of before.

Resolved: I change a losing game.

May 9

"Always have the situation under control even if losing. Never betray an inward sense of defeat."

—Arthur Ashe

The degree to which you exert control over a golf course is the degree to which you are successful.

This is what makes the game so damnably difficult, of course. Control is illusory, fleeting at best. Serendipity comes into play, sheer dumb luck, the bounce of the ball.

But go look in the mirror. That is what (or whom) you can control. And that is a lot.

You can control your expectations, desires, emotions, thoughts, confidence. You can control how you handle pressure, how you cope with a bad break, whether you let the weather get to you—the whole program inside your head.

Step up to the tee with the attitude "I'm in control." Then let nothing that occurs alter this attitude. Even in a disintegrating situation, as Arthur Ashe suggests, you can remain in control. That is when control becomes paramount. Staying under control will stop the situation from deteriorating further and help you pull yourself together again.

Resolved: I control myself, I control my golf game.

May 10

"Never be a hero when you don't have to be. Play for the scorecard, not your ego."

—Jack Nicklaus

Declare today an "Ego-Free Golf Day."

An Ego-Free Golf Day is kind of like a nuclear-free zone, when a city says that nuclear materials cannot be transported through its jurisdiction. Today we refuse to transport our egos to the golf course.

If we feel like laying up, we lay up. We don't think twice about it.

If everybody else takes their driver out of their bag, but you feel more comfortable with a fairway wood off the tee, you play the wood.

If someone scores a three and you take a five on the hole, you congratulate him for his good play and move on. You know you'll get it back later on.

If you are in the rough with an obstructed view of the green and your partner says, "Go for it," but you feel more like playing it safe, you pitch it nice and easy into the fairway to set up your next shot. Then you hit *that* shot stiff to the pin.

If you miss a makable putt or chili-dip a ball beyond the green, you do not rage like a mad despot. You let it go, and recover on your next shot.

The ways in which Ego can interfere with—and ruin—a golf game are as many and diverse as there are egos. The biggest ego stroke of all is to put a good number on the board at the end. Everything else is meaningless.

Resolved: I declare today an Ego-Free Golf Day.

May 11

"Failure sometimes enlarges the spirit. You have to fall back upon humanity and God."

—Charles Horton Cooley

Sometimes the best thing you can do with failure is let go of it.

People—golfers in particular—tend to hash and rehash their failures, as if by going over them again and again we can answer the unanswerable questions of "Why? Why did it happen to me?" You can make yourself crazy with questions like that.

Reliving a failure again and again is a form of self-torture. We repeat the act in our mind and pull blame over ourselves like a blanket. We have to accept the failure, quit torturing ourselves about it, turn off the light, and go to sleep.

The past is past. It cannot be undone. Even if you could reach back in time and change it to fit your ends, what would be the point? Your failures can teach you a better lesson than your successes ever will. If you wish to remake the past, you have probably missed the lessons it teaches.

Golfers are famous self-analyzers. We can take an octagon and analyze it nine different ways (or more). But a little self-analysis goes a long way. It's like clearing your desk of papers after you've finished a project. With your desk freed of clutter you are ready to tackle something new. By clearing your mind of past failures (which were probably exaggerated anyway), you open your mind to the success that is surely coming.

Resolved: I accept my failures and move on.

May 12

"I would like to be the perfect mom, the perfect wife, and the perfect golfer. But I've found that it's almost impossible."

—Nancy Lopez

It's Mother's Day. Treat yourself to a round of golf.

You love the game. Only, you don't get to play as much as you used to now that you have kids.

Hey, it is *your* day today. Go out and knock it around.

Golf takes time. It is hard to get five minutes for yourself in a day, let alone five hours. But today is different. Today you take the time. You tee it up.

You may be a working mom. Actually all moms are working moms, whether they stay at home or are employed outside the home. All the more reason to chuck it all for a while and cut loose on the links.

But you may be one of those working moms who feel guilty about leaving their kids during the day and want to spend every moment of free time with them.

Well, that's fine. But today, worry only about your long irons—nothing else. Your kids will survive.

You *are* the perfect mom. Look at those kids. Could they be any more splendid?

And you are the perfect wife. Look at that lucky stiff of a husband. What could be better than to be married to you?

So it's your golf game that needs pampering. Go ahead, treat yourself. Maybe it will turn into a delicious regular habit.

Resolved: It's Mother's Day. I treat myself to golf.

May 13

"To aim at the best and to remain essentially ourselves is one and the same thing."

—Janet Erskine Stuart

Goal for the day: all two-putt greens.

That is 36 strokes on the greens, the regulation number. Ever done it before? Ever consciously strived to do it? It's not impossible, but first you must try.

Be relaxed about it. The purpose is not to put a bunch of extra pressure on you. The purpose is to set a high target—and see if you can make it. Aim for the best. Achieve yourself. That is the underlying goal for the day.

Be conservative. Be daring. Do whatever it takes to hole it in two. You may need to be both daring and conservative on the same green.

On long putts, shoot to get within a three-foot circle around the hole. Then knock it in. If you slip, you slip. No big deal. See it as a game within a game. You can make it up when you bang home a 25-footer on 13.

Does that seem overly confident? Is too much confidence possible in putting? You can stroke it firm and run it past the hole. But that is probably due more to misjudging the distance than being aggressive. At least you are going for the hole! The ball has no chance to go in unless you get it there.

Set a high standard for yourself and toughen up your game. Your attitude will improve. You will fight not to give away strokes. You will walk onto every green with the confidence it takes to be a good putter.

Resolved: All two-putt greens today.

May 14

"A good swing begins with a good grip."

—Tom Watson

And what does a good grip begin with? Lightness of touch.

"Don't put a death grip on the club," adds Chi Chi Rodriguez. "You have to be able to feel what you are doing."

Feel what you are doing. Be light about it. Bobby Jones, ever the gentleman, likened it to a polite handshake. "The grip should be no firmer than it would be while shaking hands with a lady," he said.

Some question the practicality of such advice. A pro or expert player with strong hands and forearms is better equipped to take a club "lightly" and see good results. An ordinary player may have to take a firmer grip.

Still, the key word—the key thought—is lightness. "Like you would hold a bird" in Sam Snead's famous maxim. "You mustn't hurt it."

Walk lightly. Grip lightly. These are good golf maxims to live your life by.

Resolved: I hold the club as if shaking hands with a lady.

May 15

"Every dedicated golfer I know wants to improve."

—Chuck Cook, teaching pro

Want to be a better player? Play with better players.

A young boy or girl who wants to improve will play with kids a few years older (and presumably better). It is the same principle. Improve your play by improving the company you keep.

This is not a knock against your regular gang. They are great guys (and gals). They're comfortable with you. You're comfortable with them. It's a comfortable situation.

That's the point. To improve, you have to get out of your comfort zone. Challenge yourself; see how you measure up against a higher standard of play.

If only for a day, hook up with the head pro or one of the top players at your club. (You can always go back to your regular group.) Don't see it as a competition. That's discouraging. See it as a chance to watch and play and learn.

You'll learn the most by playing a round with these players, not just watching them on the range. Without imitating their swing or specific techniques, "go to school" on them. Watch how they handle themselves, how they respond to certain situations, their strategy on the course. Observe them critically. What are their strengths? Their weaknesses? What would it take for you to play in their league?

You may be intimidated at first. Then again, you may say to yourself, "I can do that." And you can. Before improvement comes the desire to improve, and you have made a major step.

Resolved: I play with some top players.

May 16

"A journey of a thousand miles must begin with a single step."

—Lao-tzu

So you are thinking about taking up golf, are you? Good for you. You have the right attitude. Certainly you have the right book.

And yet, what's that you say? You're still not sure. You're worried that you will look stupid or clumsy or both. You're worried that you may hit someone with your ball. You're worried that you won't be very good. You're worried about all sorts of things.

The simple solution to your worries, whatever they may be, is this: Start.

You will always have doubts and worries, even after you have played for years. It is in the nature of the game.

What you need to do is start. Once you start you will see. You will find the answers to your questions. Then you will form new questions. That is in the nature of the game too.

It's a great game. Entertaining, invigorating, challenging, a game that is played outdoors and among friends, rich in history, full of laughs and surprises, as pleasing and rewarding a sporting pursuit as yet devised by humankind.

You will love this game. You really will. If you give it an authentic go, it will absorb you like nothing else.

But.

To experience the wonders of the game, you must . . . *start*.

Make it today. Start today, and check back here tomorrow for a postround appraisal.

Resolved: I do it. I start to learn.

May 17

Hurrah! You did it. You looked fear in the face. You played golf.

You took yesterday's message to heart and played a round of golf, your first ever. How'd it go?

That bad, eh?

Today, spend a little time talking to other golfers. Venture down to the coffee shop at the course. Don't be shy. Golfers love to talk about golf. Some of them can talk about nothing else. They will talk your head off.

Sidle up to that golfer at the counter—yeah, that one there, the one in the greasy John Deere cap who's smoking the unfiltered Camels—and ask *him*. Ask him if he has ever experienced, or if he knows anyone who has experienced, a round worse than yours.

See what he says.

If he is like every other golfer on the face of the planet, he will tell you tales that will make you sick to your stomach, tales that will make your skin crawl. You think your round was bad? Wait till you hear what happened to *him*.

But does he give up? Does he give in to despair? Granted, he smokes a pack of cigarettes a day and drinks three shots of whiskey before noon. But he does give up? No!

There is truly only one thing to do. You must do the thing you absolutely cannot. You must play again.

Resolved: I go out again today.

May 18

Now, that's more like it!

You played for the first time the other day. Then, despite initial discouragement, you played again. Give yourself a pat on the back.

And how'd it go this time? Better, right?

(Pause.)

Well, wasn't it?

You say you conked one of your foursome on the head with your tee shot? Your brakes went out on your cart and you crashed into a ditch? You lost three balls on the opening hole alone? You shot 150 after the first eight holes and stopped counting after that? You say a 98-year-old woman in the group behind you disparaged you for slow play? And when you made a snide remark in reply, her bodybuilder grandson chased you into the out-of-bounds area brandishing a 4-iron perilously close to your head? And you hid in the bushes until they played through?

Oh well, those things happen. But you're making progress. That's what's important. It's a great game, isn't it? Didn't we tell you? Now keep it up!

Resolved: I play again first chance I get.

May 19

"He had a simple, childlike talent for meeting life. 'I am terribly afraid,' he said, 'but the other fellow is afraid too.'"

—Sherwood Anderson, on Ulysses S. Grant

The last few days we have been having some fun talking about what it is like to play golf for the first time and the kinds of things that people go through when they do.

This may not sit well with some. It is like discussing airplane crashes with a person about to take a flight. Some people are genuinely uneasy—scared, nervous, apprehensive—about taking up a club and striking a ball.

One friend says, "The first time I played golf I was petrified. You know why? I didn't know how to stick the tee in the ground. How do *they* do it? I wasn't sure. When I did it I had to push and push before the little pointy end went in. And then the ball kept falling off. It was like the ball was doing it intentionally. Every time I'd step back it'd fall off. It was a race to see whether I could step back and hit the shot before the ball fell off. Finally, I figured it out."

That's right: You figure it out. One way or the other, you figure it out.

Keep it in perspective. That's a good message for everybody, novice and seasoned golfer alike. Every golfer has had those kinds of fears, and many still do. There is always performance anxiety, a fear of how you will do every time you approach the first tee, driver in hand. But never let it get the best of you. Meet the game as you would meet life, and keep playing.

Resolved: I put my fears behind me and play.

May 20

"There are two things to aim at in life: first, to get what you want; and after that, to enjoy it."

—Logan Pearsall Smith

Set goals for yourself. Establish short-term goals on the road to your long-term ones. Give yourself rewards, incentives along the way. Be sure to enjoy what you are doing as you pursue these goals.

We have talked about all these motivational techniques in this book. Here's another: Set a deadline.

Journalists, businesspeople, students, homemakers—everybody functions under deadlines of one type or another. Deadlines get you going. They spur you into action, light a match under what may now be deposited in the seat of a chair.

Your golf deadline could be a tournament coming up in a few months, or a business-related golf outing. It could be a high school reunion of your old golf team. You could be planning a golf vacation in Palm Springs and want to get your game in shape before you go. Almost anything can work.

Now, some people may bristle at the thought of a deadline. They have so many social and professional commitments in the rest of their lives, the last thing they want to do is add deadline pressure to their golf.

That's okay. Completely understandable.

On the other hand, a deadline may be what you need to get into gear. When you reach the target date, you can use it as a signpost to show you how far you have traveled on the road to golfing self-improvement.

Resolved: I set a target date to chart my golfing progress.

May 21

"You're here only for a short visit, so never forget to stop and smell the flowers."

—Walter Hagen

It is the most banal of utterances: Stop and smell the flowers.

Walter Hagen, a man who appreciated the finer things in life, including roses and rosewater, uttered it in a golfing context and it has become part of his—and the game's—legacy.

Stop and smell the flowers.

Simple, banal, true.

The phrase resonates on two levels: Flowers really *do* smell great, especially right now when they are in their full and gorgeous springtime bloom.

The second level is metaphorical. There is more to golf than hitting balls. There is more to life than making money. Take note of the good things in life before it is too late.

Again, simple, banal, and powerfully true. That is one of golf's best features—how much the natural world is part of it. Never forget to frolic a little while you're out there.

Resolved: I stop and smell the flowers.

May 22

"He that riseth late must trot all day."

—Ben Franklin

If old Ben had been a golfer he might have said it this way: "He that getteth to the course late must play catch-up."

We have all heard the story (or stories like it) of the golfer who, hurrying to make his tee time, rushes up without stretching or warming up, uncoils a mighty swing, and promptly throws his back out. Whether a piece of urban folklore or not, the tale has a good cautionary ring to it, teaching us:

One should rush only at one's peril.

Stretching is wise before playing.

Getting to the course early can only help.

Unless you are a Walter Hagen (and you most certainly are not, seeing that he has been dead for decades) and your tardiness is a tactic calculated to psych out the opposition, getting to the course ahead of time is always the best strategy.

The benefits are obvious. You can hit some balls. You can stretch. You can jive a little with the guy behind the counter at the pro shop. You can think about the golf to come. If you are running late, chances are your mind will still be back at where you came from—home, office, wherever—rather than on the game at hand. And your play on the opening holes will likely reflect this preoccupation.

Give yourself the time. You deserve it.

Resolved: I get to the course in plenty of time.

May 23

"A person's mind once stretched by a new idea, never regains its original dimension."

—Oliver Wendell Holmes

Today's mission: Make all the makable putts.

Makable, in golf, is a relative term. One person's makable is another person's impossible. Nor is makable simply a matter of real estate. A five-foot downhill putt with a break can be much trickier than a straightforward 10-footer.

But today, we're ignoring all talk of relativity. We're in the mood for an absolute. We're making all the makable putts.

"You can't say that," you say. "You cannot simply declare, 'I will make all my makable putts!'"

Why not? They're makable, right? Everybody has a makability range. Whether it is 3 feet, 8 feet, or 15 feet, or 30 feet, we all have a range in which we feel we have a legitimate shot at making a putt.

First you make the makable putts. Once you make the makable ones, your range will naturally grow outward. Once you stretch your mind with a new idea, things can never quite be the same again. Make all your makable putts, and you have stretched your putting world into a new shape.

Do what you can do. Find what your range is. Establish your limits and the realm of what you know. Then exploit it to the maximum. Once you do that, your limits will expand.

Resolved: I make all my makable putts.

May 24

"My problem was something I'm sure most amateurs can relate to. I was walking into the sand with a negative attitude. In truth, I was happy just to get the ball on the green a lot of the time."

—Andrew Magee, touring pro

Magee was talking about his fear of the sand—a not unfamiliar feeling for many of us.

"Sandies" is a game to play to build confidence in the sand. It is a betting game. Play it with your foursome. Whoever gets a ball out of the sand and into the cup in two strokes garners a "sandie." The one with the most sandies at round's end wins the bet.

If you are not the gambling type—or if you don't feel confident enough yet in your sand game to risk money on it—that's fine too. Play Sandies by yourself. When you go into a greenside bunker, get it up and down in two.

"But I don't have the technique," you protest. "I don't have the skills."

Rubbish. Technique, though important, is a distant second to a positive frame of mind in achieving success in golf. Let's get out of a pattern of thinking where we dwell on what we lack. Let's avoid negatives in describing our game altogether.

Create a habit of mind. Adopt a can-do attitude. Up and down in two.

Resolved: Up and down in two.

May 25

*"You've got to go in believing in yourself. I don't mean thinking
you'll just give it a good try, but believing that you've got it
already done. The actual climb becomes only a follow-up on
that visualization."*

—Lynn Hill

Lynn Hill is one of the world's best rock climbers. In the parlance of the mountains, she climbs free—without a rope. She climbs 3,000-foot granite walls in Yosemite Valley without a rope to catch her if she falls. *Nobody* catches her if she falls.

Here are more thoughts from Lynn on how she does what she does: "You must stay relaxed but concentrated, so you can hold a positive image in your mind and avoid negative self-talk. Negative thoughts interrupt the positive flow. If you allow that, you arrive at a handhold with no idea of what to do next. Your momentum stops, and you fall as a direct result of that thought."

Hold a positive image in your mind. Stay relaxed but concentrated. Avoid negative self-talk. Keep that forward momentum going.

These are all powerful concepts that every golfer can relate to and put into practice. Another important concept of hers translated to golf: When you stand at the tee, imagine the hole as already completed. Work back in your mind from the hole and see the strokes that you took and how you did it. The actual playing of the hole merely becomes a follow-up on that positive visualization.

Resolved: I visualize a hole as being already completed before I play it.

May 26

"Never tell people how to do things. Tell them what to do and they will surprise you with their ingenuity."

—George S. Patton

The *what* of golf is getting the ball in the hole. The *how* of it is up to you.

A round of golf is a kind of performance, but no one knows the script until the curtain goes up. It is an improvisation. Who knows what will happen for the next few hours? Not even the actors can say for sure.

Wrap your putter around a tree? To heck with it. Putt with an iron.

Ball caught in the branches of another tree? Climb up and hit it from there.

Once you enter into a spirit of improvisation, the obstacles you face will seem far less forbidding. You will possess the confidence to play your way out of every situation.

Your driver's acting up today? Well, then, hit a wood off the tee.

Your ball keeps visiting the rough? Fine. We'll hack away and make it work.

Golf is endlessly varied. No two shots are ever the same. The best golfers learn to think and act on the spot.

But first, you must give yourself up to this idea. When you play golf you must be willing to throw out all your carefully considered plans in a moment. Let go of the what; revel in the how. You will surprise yourself with your ingenuity when you do.

Resolved: I open myself up to a spirit of golf improvisation.

May 27

*"I couldn't tell you what exactly I like about golf, just when you
think you've got it mastered, it lets you know that you haven't.
I'm just crazy enough to do it."*

—Clint Eastwood

Today is a milestone day in golf history. The first-ever Aerial
Golf Championships occurred on May 27, 1928, at Old Westbury Golf Club, New York.

From its humble beginnings at Old Westbury, "The Aeri-
als," as they came to be known, grew to become one of the
most prestigious stops on the PGA Tour. It was the fifth leg (or
"fifth wheel") of the Grand Slam, along with the Masters, the
British and U.S. Opens, and the PGA.

Actually, no, none of that is true. The Aerial Golf Championships were just a loony stunt by some golfers who were
crazy enough to do it.

Teams consisted of two members apiece and an airplane.
Two teams competed. One person rode in the airplane (not,
however, as pilot) and dropped a golf ball down onto a green.
The object was to get the ball as close to the hole as he could,
for his teammate on the ground had to putt it in.

What was the point? Who knows? They were just some
guys having a gas, which *is* the point after all. You can just
imagine them sitting around their local 19th-hole establishment throwing back shooters of Cuervo Gold and one of them
says, "Hey, I got this idea . . ."

In celebration of the anniversary of Aerial Golf, do something crazy today. The effect may be exhilarating.

Resolved: I do something slightly daffy on the golf course.

May 28

"When I got back into boxing people would say, 'George, your jab is slow.' I'd totally resist that. But when someone said 'George, I'm going to show you how to make your jab quicker,' that's what I would take."

—George Foreman

Life begins at 40. Just ask George Foreman.

George may not know from golf, but he does have a handle on motivational psychology. And everybody can learn from him, whether you are middle-aged or not.

When George announced he was returning to the ring after years of retirement he became a subject of ridicule. He was fat as a walrus. He was the worst sort of fool—an old fool. He was going to disgrace his sport (an impossibility, that) and himself and possibly endanger his health when he stepped into the ring again.

The carping ceased when, at age 45, George reclaimed by knockout the heavyweight title that he had lost 20 years earlier.

The message of Foreman, large of body and heart, is clear: Liabilities are liabilities only if you think of them that way. George never did, and look at what he achieved. He saw his so-called weaknesses merely as areas in need of improvement, opportunities for greater advancement along the road to achieving his dreams.

In the physiognomy of golf, being 40 is like being a baby. It is only the beginning. There is so much more ahead of you. Take a cue from George. Your supposed liabilities are only liabilities if you think of them that way.

$$\boxtimes$$

Resolved: When thoughts of middle age weigh me down, I remember George Foreman.

May 29

The first-ever back-to-back holes in one by a woman occurred on May 29, 1977. The lucky golfer was named Sue Press. She got her aces on holes 13 and 14 at the Chatswood Golf Course in Sydney, Australia.

Now, put yourself in Sue's shoes. You have just hit a hole in one on 13. You're ecstatic. It is the first ever in your career.

Now you are standing on 14, another par 3. You're still jazzed from the previous hole but you're trying to hold it down a little bit. You are suddenly feeling real loose and you want to make a good swing on this hole too.

This is where we can take a cue from Sue Press. Some people might think, "Well, I just got a hole in one. That's it for me, there's no way I'll get another." They count themselves out. Fortune has already smiled on them and there is no way it will smile their way again, they figure.

It is true that if you go around wishing for back-to-back holes in one in golf you are liable to be *very* disappointed. But there is every reason to believe that good things—no, *wonderful* things—can happen to you again . . . and again . . . and again.

Leave yourself open to the possibility of magic. When you step up, like Sue Press, to the next par 3 after a hole in one, give yourself the chance to experience amazing good fortune. Who knows what will happen?

Resolved: I open myself to the possibility of amazing good fortune.

May 30

"In choosing a set of wedges that is right for your game, don't underestimate the value of visual preference. It's a lot easier to have confidence in clubs you like to look at."

—Paul Azinger

This is a wonderful, even radical thought, one that flies in the face of the grindingly utilitarian teaching we receive from the pooh-bahs of golf.

There are aesthetic considerations to the game, and these considerations deserve respect. How we look and dress. How the courses look—the beauty of our surroundings. These aesthetic concerns extend even to our clubs, notably those glistening wedges.

It is not just the composition of the shaft or the degree of loft in the clubface that matters. The way the club looks matters too.

Nor are these aesthetic concerns superficial. Visual preference affects how we feel, how we play. It works for Zinger. He plays better with clubs that look good to him.

Still, the motive in buying clubs stays the same whether your concerns are aesthetic, utilitarian, or purely economic. Buy the ones that give you confidence. You can hit with a stick if you have confidence in it.

Resolved: I buy a set of glistening new wedges.

May 31

"How can a guy think and hit at the same time?"

—Yogi Berra

Yogi made this remark about hitting a baseball, not a golf ball, but its comic wisdom applies equally well.

Here is another thing Yogi said: "I never like to play golf in the morning and play a ballgame at night. I don't like to think twice in the same day."

Another way to say this would be: To cerebrate repeatedly prior to, or in the process of, a stipulated action—such as the act of striking a multidimpled round object—may not produce, indeed may even inhibit, the attainment of one's desired ends.

Keep it simple. Leave the thinking to Einstein, and hit the cover off the ball. Yogi always did.

Resolved: I keep it simple.

June 1

"Vitality shows not only in the ability to persist but the ability to start over."

—F. Scott Fitzgerald

It is the first day of the sixth month. The official beginning of summer draws near.

At the start of the year we resolved to make this the greatest year of our golfing lives. How are you doing on that quest?

You may have set more specific playing goals, such as topping your best score ever or bringing your scores down six or eight strokes on a consistent basis. You wrote your goals down on paper, perhaps even posted them in your office or home as a reminder to yourself to stay vigilant.

Are you making the progress you hoped?

It may be the case that you started out the year with grand hopes and, well, things have slowed down since then. You got busy with other things. They distracted you from your golf, and you fell off the wagon.

There is still plenty of time left if this is the case. Typically a person who falls short of goals fills himself—or herself—with recriminations. Forget recriminations. **Forget** your supposed shortcomings. You are fine just the way you are.

Just start over.

The ability to start over is a sign of vitality. It shows heart, courage, strength. It is a gesture of faith in yourself and a game that eventually always rewards the faith you show in it.

Give yourself—and golf—a second chance. Start over.

☒

Resolved: I renew my vow to make this year the best year of my golfing life.

June 2

"There is no greater panacea for every kind of folly than common sense."

—Baltasar Gracian

Use common sense. Improve your golf game.

Asked how to correct a problem of always hitting left, Ben Hogan said, "Hit right."

Englishman Ted Ray was a burly power hitter in the early years of the century. Approached by a young boy on how he could hit his drives farther, Ray replied, "Hit 'em a sight harder, mate."

Then there is teaching pro Hank Haney's advice to those golfers struggling with a closed stance. "If your setup is closed," he recommends, "open it."

We tend to look for answers in golf as if they were rare East Indian spices that we need to journey around the world to find. But the answers may be plain as vanilla and found in your kitchen cupboard. Is there a plain vanilla remedy to your situation?

Exploit the obvious. Use common sense. Improve your golf game.

Resolved: I apply common sense to my efforts to improve.

June 3

"The pleasures of this game are among the happiest of life's delights."

—Colman McCarthy

You cannot improve unless you play. Speaking more positively, you improve when you play.

It is the first fundamental, the fundamental upon which all other fundamentals rest. *Nothing* begins until you play.

Not the fun.

Not the exercise.

Not the good times.

Not the beery camaraderie on the 19th hole.

Not the satisfying sensation of a well-thumped 3-wood.

Not the pleasure of slipping on that leather glove, or the familiar reassuring sound of spikes clattering on pavement.

Not the rising surge of enthusiasm you feel as you walk down a rolling green fairway as wide as a river.

Not the joy of a birdie.

Not the chance for an ace.

Not the pure unalloyed joy of a ball that rolls and rolls and rolls and disappears into the bottom of the hole.

None of that—*none of that*—is possible until you play. So what's stopping you?

Resolved: Nothing stops me. Today I play.

June 4

"If you can convince yourself the ball is going in the hole, you'll get it there more often whatever kind of stroke you use."

—Gay Brewer, Masters champion

Today I am sinking a long putt. I am going beyond "going for it." I am making it.

Putting is all confidence. I have it today.

Sure, long putts are tricky. What's the right pace? The right line? The condition of the green? If you hit it too firm you will shoot it past. But you don't want to leave it short. You want to give yourself a shot at making it. All these factors come into play.

One way to play a long putt is to think of it as two strokes. The first long one sets up the second short one. You're shooting to get it within a three-foot radius of the cup. That's your objective.

That is a reasonable approach to take, and maybe some days that is what I will do. But not today.

Today I am knocking a long one in. I promise to consider all the variables. But the biggest variable in my golf game—me—is not varying from his goal today.

I am determined to do it. I am going to wow everybody who sees it. I am going to read it, stroke it, and watch it roll and roll and roll and roll and roll into the cup.

Resolved: I hole a long one today.

June 5

"Make up your mind what you are going to do. Then go ahead and do it."

—Bobby Locke, on the secret to good putting

Three-foot putts are the hardest. The reason: You are *supposed* to make them. It's almost, but not quite, gimme range. You miss one of those, it is humiliating.

But that's a negative attitude. You're thinking miss, you're thinking about the consequences of failure. You're beating yourself before you start. You let doubt weasel its way into your psyche. The putter twitches and the ball slides past.

We all know that scenario. Let's envision another one:

Every ball from three feet or less in the hole. You step up, you make your practice stroke, you punch it in. Just like that. Like ringing a bell. You pick the ball from the hole, and smiling, step away.

Every hole is like that, *every one*. You make up your mind, you do it. You feel so good about your putting, you decline offers to pick up. Your stroke feels so good, you want to experience it every chance you can.

What happens, it becomes infectious. Short turns to long. Because your short putts are going in, you start finding the range on the long ones too. You nail an 8-footer and a 10-footer. You sink one from another zip code. It is not luck. You're feeling it. You *know*. You know that ball is headed for the bottom of the cup.

The latter scenario is just as possible as the first. Start with the short ones. Make them all. Then build on that confidence for the longer distances.

Resolved: I hole my short ones.

June 6

*"I have never been a heavy practicer from the standpoint of just
  beating balls."*

—Jack Nicklaus

If Jack Nicklaus wasn't a heavy practicer, why do we need
to be?

Practice for Nicklaus was "hitting balls in preparation for
playing and finding out how your swing was working." More
of a laboratory-like testing process than a rote repetition of
stroke. Nicklaus never went out with "the idea to beat 500
balls" and think that he had accomplished anything by the
sheer fact of having done it.

Nor did he practice a set amount of time. He might take
half an hour or half a day. When he was satisfied with the
results he was getting, however long or short it took, he
stopped.

Though it may seem a waste of money, it may actually be
good for your golf game to walk away from a bucket of balls
with balls still in it, if you are happy with your stroke.

Nicklaus said he never practiced putting when he was
young because it aggravated his back problems. More important than repetitions was feel. More important than mechanics was attitude.

The sole purpose of practice is to help us play better. There
is no inherent virtue in it. The results of practice are to be
found only on the golf course itself. Hours on the driving
range or practice green count for nothing. Only results count.

What is the point of practice? It is time to take a break from
it if you are asking yourself that question.

Resolved: I lay off practicing for a while.

June 7

A golfer is large too. He or she contains multitudes.

Flipping through this book, the careful reader will find contradictions in the advice being so liberally bestowed.

One day talks of the virtues of practice. Another speaks of the mundane nature of practice and recommends skipping it. One day says to see a pro if you need to. Another says avoid experts like the plague. One says be wary of tips. Another says keep your mind open to them because you never know when you might stumble onto a pearl.

One response is (if a response is needed): A year is a long time. Over the course of a year a person experiences many moods and changes. Accept these changes as you would the changing of the seasons, and celebrate them.

Another response is: Contradictions? Every golfer is filled with them. Something works one day, but strangely not at all the next. You may go along in a certain pattern for a while. Then you make a change and you think to yourself, "How could I have ever done it that way? What was I thinking?"

This is in the natural way of things. Golf is a process, not an end. Every golfer is in a constant state of experimentation. Testing this, testing that. Even if a thing is working well, he or she will want to jimmy with it to make it work better. By all means, plunge ahead. Reverse yourself and all that you formerly held true if such a reversal will help you play better golf. A foolish consistency is the hobgoblin of bad golfers.

Resolved: I gladly reverse myself if it helps me play better golf.

June 8

"All of us, from time to time, need a plunge into freedom and novelty, after which routine and discipline will seem delightful by contrast."

—André Maurois

For many of us (the enlightened of the world), that plunge into freedom and novelty is golf. But when we plunge, do we really plunge?

What about that pager on your belt? Or that cell phone—ever make work calls during your match? Do you try to get in a little golf, while still staying in touch with the office? When you play golf, do you leave your work behind? Really leave it behind?

"Increasingly," writes the *Wall Street Journal*, "stressed-out business people are finding that the only way to get away is to find a place with no phones, no fax machines, no modems—indeed, no gadgets whatsoever, that connect with offices, bosses, employees, and clients." The golf course is just such a place, if we allow it to be.

When you play golf, play golf. When you work, work. You will be better at both if you concentrate on each in its own time. Golf can constitute a real break—real relaxation—but not if you see it as an 18-hole office.

If it is simply impossible to cut yourself off from the lines of communication at work for that length of time, at least curtail it. Call on the ninth hole and no other time. Then forget about it. Work will still be there when you get back.

Resolved: When I play golf, I play golf.

June 9

"I told myself: 'Take the club back slower, set my hands at the top, and swing down smoothly to accelerate through the ball.'"

—Hale Irwin

Hale Irwin won his third U.S. Open by making a midround adjustment to his swing. He was in an 18-hole playoff with Mike Donald, but he was hitting his irons poorly and he was struggling.

"My swing had got too short, " he said, "and I was wishing at the ball instead of swinging through it."

Wishing at the ball, instead of swinging through it. Most golfers will recognize this predicament. What the Baxter Springs, Kansas, native did to fix his problem was go back to basics.

Take the club back slower. Set your hands at the top. Swing down smoothly and accelerate through the ball.

"You have to understand yourself and your tendencies in different situations," explained Irwin. "The game's not nearly as complicated as these modern support systems make it seem. If you understand the delivery of the club to the ball, you can play."

Irwin's self-diagnosis worked. Standing at 16 at Medinah, the toughest hole on the course, he sat 207 yards out with an uphill lie and the wind blowing in his face. He hooked a 2-iron around some trees and rolled it up six feet from the cup. Irwin, a drop-dead putter who learned on greens of sand, sank the birdie putt and once more became Open champion.

Resolved: I take the club back slowly, I set my hands at the top, and I swing down smoothly through the ball.

June 10

"A great round of golf is a lot like a terrible round. You drift into a zone, and it's hard to break out of it."

—Al Geiberger

Today we make a breakthrough. Today we drift into a zone and play a great round of golf.

Today was the day in 1977 that Al Geiberger made *his* breakthrough, one of the more amazing feats in the history of golf. He shot a 59.

Now, going out and eclipsing the 60 mark may be a little out of our league. But we can make our own sort of breakthroughs today.

Shoot 79 if you have been trying to break 80, or 89 if your goal has been 90. Heck, put a 129 on the board if you have been trying to get under 130. Whatever your personal goal, make a breakthrough today.

What's that, you say? You say that any fool knows that you cannot simply go out and have a breakthrough day in golf.

This is certainly true, but let's go back to Geiberger's once-in-a-lifetime round to see how he did it. With three holes to go he—and his ecstatic gallery—realized what was at stake. He would make a 59 if he played the last holes under par. When he realized how close he was, he did not pull back. He kept pushing. He saw what he could achieve and he did it.

You cannot arbitrarily decide to make a breakthrough. But you must show courage if you get close. Do not pull back in sight of your goal. Keep pushing. Never waver, never falter. It's right *there*. Right at your fingertips. You can almost reach out and touch it. . . .

Resolved: I make a breakthrough today.

June 11

"What you have to do is believe what you see, trust it, and putt it on the line."

—Ken Venturi

Believe what you see (your read).

Trust it (it is the *right* read).

Putt it on the line (make the ball follow that imaginary path to the hole).

These are the essentials of putting. But we sometimes forget them under pressure.

The degree that we feel pressure is the degree that we internalize outside events or circumstances. We make our circumstances worse than they are by worrying, overthinking, overanalyzing.

The players who perform the best under pressure are the ones who do not internalize the external. Their reactions, their judgment, their thinking, their emotions are unclouded by circumstance (or, more exactly, by their *perception* of their circumstance). While others falter, they ascend.

The way they are able to do this is by doing the same things they always do, things they have done thousands of times before.

Let it be that way for you too. When you step up to a putt today that you really need, treat it as you always do.

Believe it. Trust it. Hit it on the line.

Resolved: I make a putt that I really need.

June 12

"Competitive golf is played mainly on a five-and-a-half-inch course: the space between your ears."

—Bobby Jones

Beth Daniel's game was in ruins. Once one of the most promising ball-strikers on the women's tour, she had lost all confidence in herself and her putting.

"I felt like I was going to have to quit," she recalled. "I just didn't believe in myself anymore." She had won Rookie of the Year and Player of the Year honors in successive years in the early 1980s. She had won over a dozen tournaments with one of the sweetest swings around. But her putting had collapsed and taken the rest of her game down with it. She had not won a tournament in more than four years.

One of her problems on the greens was pace. She rushed her stroke, indeed her entire putting routine.

That was the first thing: slowing herself down. Settling into a rhythm that was comfortable for her.

Still, it wasn't enough. She was still missing putts. Then her brother Tony suggested this simple technique:

Look at the hole, not the ball, when on the practice green. It worked almost immediately. She made a respectable showing at that year's U.S. Open and then went on a title-winning run that drew comparisons to the young Nancy Lopez. And Daniel still looks only at the hole, not the ball, on short putts.

Daniel's talent was never in question. That was always there. All she needed was a trigger to turn her game around in her head. Once she found it, her putting and everything else fell into place.

Resolved: I look at the hole, not the ball, when I putt.

June 13

Those who want to know the United States of America learn about Lincoln. Those who want to know golf learn about Hogan.

Ben Hogan was the greatest self-made golfer ever. He was a pretty good player in the 1930s and early 1940s. But Hogan was not satisfied with pretty good. He retooled his swing and after World War II became the most dominant player in the game.

On February 2, 1949, a Greyhound bus smashed head-on into his car. He suffered multiple fractures and underwent emergency surgery that saved his life. A year and a half later he competed in the U.S. Open with bandages on his legs. He beat Lloyd Mangrum and George Fazio in an 18-hole playoff to win what would be the second of four National Open Championships in his career.

June 13, 1953, was the day of his fourth Open title. Hogan beat runner-up Sam Snead by six strokes. That year he also won the British Open and set a scoring record to claim his second Masters.

Hogan practiced as hard as a person can practice. No one was better prepared for a tournament. He believed in both— practice, preparation–with the avidity of a religious disciple.

Practice, preparation, determination, perseverance. These are good lessons to take away from *The Life of Hogan*. Here is another: striving for excellence. How often do we settle for pretty good in our own lives?

Resolved: I remember Ben Hogan the next time I settle for "pretty good."

June 14

"Life is short, health vital, and dollars incapable of transfer to the next world. Therefore, there is much to be said for a reasonable enjoyment of life in this."

—Lord Birkenhead

Lord B. penned these words after World War I. He was making the case for why businessmen and -women ought to occasionally cease from the business of making money and play golf.

He makes some good points, namely:

Life is short. A conventional truism but one that still packs a punch. When you die you are dead a long time. You might as well have a spot of fun while you have the chance.

Dollars are incapable of transfer to the next world. This, too, is a fact. While some wealthy individuals may have tried to do it, none, so far, has succeeded. (The IRS won't allow it.) We spend a great deal of our abbreviated lives accumulating capital. Capital is good. The more the better. But what is the point of piling high the capital if we do not take a moment every now and then to enjoy it?

There is much to be said for a reasonable enjoyment of life. Heck, there is much to be said for an *unreasonable* enjoyment of life. Birkenhead was British, though, and therefore all the enjoyment he permitted himself was of the reasonable kind.

To sum up:

Time is running out. You can't take it with you. Therefore, make hay while the sun shines. Enjoy yourself. Kick up your heels. What's the point of playing golf if you're not? What's the point of anything?

Resolved: I have a little fun today on the golf course.

June 15

"When you are deeply absorbed in what you are doing, time gives itself to you like a warm and willing lover."

—Brendan Francis

One of the unique qualities of golf is the absence of a clock. Our time on the course is not regulated by hours and minutes but by the number of holes we play.

At its best this feeling of timelessness provides a wonderful feeling of contentment—that we have escaped, if only for an afternoon, the tyranny of the clock. It is like we are playing hooky from school. We take temporary leave from our daily responsibilities and go on a mini-vacation in a green world.

Ordinarily we are like Harold Lloyd hanging from the hands of a clock. Time runs our lives, entangles and traps us. It defines our lives—our existence spanning a finite number of years and no more.

But while out on the golf course, all of that falls away. When the sun is shining and the sky is a light clear blue and your partners are good and the putts are dropping, those of us who play this game engage in a glorious grand gorgeous illusion. For us, time stops.

You will soon enough return to the world of responsibility. Today, or the next time you go out, give yourself up to the timelessness of a round of golf and the sense of freedom that goes with it.

Resolved: I let the time pass on a golf course and pay no mind.

June 16

Think back to a Masters of about a decade ago:

Jack Nicklaus shoots a 65 on the final day, roaring down the back nine in 30 heartstopping strokes to win his sixth and last Masters. He is 46, the oldest player ever to don the Green Jacket.

Accompanying him on his epic quest is his son, Jack Nicklaus Jr. Jackie caddied for his dad, and with the championship in hand, the two men embrace on the 18th green. It is a wonderful, deeply moving tableau: father and son sharing their family triumph.

Golf is a great way to get to know people. Those people may even include members of your own family. Golf bridges the generations. Families play together. Fathers and sons, mothers and daughters—while they may not have many other things in common, they have golf.

You talk. You hit. You talk some more. You hit some more. That's golf, and that's a good way to spend an afternoon with your dad.

You're lucky to have him. Make a gesture, show him your love. Let him show you what has delighted him about the game over the years, and you show what pleasures you have found. What you discover—about him, about you, about each other—may last a lifetime.

Resolved: I play a round of golf with my dad.

June 17

"Almost any game with any ball is a good game."

—Robert Lynd

There is the game of golf. Then there are zillions of games within the game—single shot or other games (betting optional) that may relieve the tedium of a long day's journey across 18 holes. Some suggestions:

- Closest to the Hole. A golf classic. Play it anytime, on almost any type of shot. On a par 3, play it on the first shot.
- One Club Golf. Pick one club—driver, putter, iron, whatever. Then stick with it for the entire hole (or round).
- First on the Green.
- Longest Drive. Accuracy matters here too. If your ball goes off the fairway, you lose.
- Fewest Putts. Keep track of the total number of putts for the round. The person with the fewest putts wins.
- Closest to the Line. Whoever hits their tee ball closest to the center of the fairway (draw an imaginary line).
- Sandies. Getting the ball out of a bunker and into the hole in two shots earns you a "sandie." The most sandies by round's end wins.

Playing a game of this sort, while fun in itself, can jump-start a round that has begun to sputter and backfire. Instead of being always concerned about your overall score, you focus harder on the shot in front of you, and it gets your engine going again.

Resolved: I play Closest to the Hole.

June 18

"It isn't so much a man's eminence of elementary faculties that pulls him through. It is the steam pressure to the square inch behind that moves the machine."

—William James

Arnold Palmer was as good as dead on this day in 1960. Beginning the final round of the U.S. Open at Cherry Hills, he was seven strokes back of the lead. Fourteen golfers were ahead of him. Put a fork in him. He was done.

But nobody informed Arnold of this fact. Think of John Daly at the tee. Palmer in his prime had that kind of magnetism—and raw power. "When he hits the ball," a fellow pro remarked, "the earth shakes."

The first hole at Cherry Hills was 346 yards tee to green. Arnold hit the ball. When the earth stopped shaking the ball was on the green. Thus began "the most explosive stretch of subpar golf any golfer has ever produced" in championship golf, said Herbert Warren Wind.

Arnold shot a 30 on the front nine. By the next hole he had made up the seven strokes, climbed over all 14 of those bodies, and captured a piece of the lead. By the 12th hole, the lead was his alone. He shot a 65 on the day to win his first and only U.S. Open.

Falling behind? Make the earth shake.

Need to come back? Make the earth shake.

People counting you out? Make the earth shake.

Approaching the first tee? Make the earth shake.

Resolved: I make the earth shake.

June 19

"Today, there is so much money at stake in golf tournaments that it overpowers all other considerations. It is the rare player now who seems to enjoy his sport and to regard it as something more than a means to an end."

—Herbert Warren Wind

Wind was speaking about the pros, but there is some relevance for amateurs too. Not in terms of money, but in terms of keeping score.

Sometimes we get so caught up in scoring that we forget everything else. It overpowers all other considerations. We get so absorbed with reaching a desired end that we ignore the process of how we are getting there.

Results versus process. It's an age-old conflict. Means versus ends. Results *do* matter. Your score does matter. But at what price? Can you get good results and still enjoy the game?

You most certainly can. In fact, pleasure and fulfillment—results and process—go hand in hand. Enjoy the game. Play to win. You can do both.

You enjoy yourself the most when you play the best. You play the best when you are enjoying yourself.

But do you need to keep track of your score *every* time you play? Results, in golf, are best measured over time. Progress is a gradual accumulation; you do not need a daily accounting. Today, when you go out, forget the scorecard. Just play.

Concentrate on your strokes and swing and leave the numerical assessments for another time.

Resolved: I leave the scorecard behind today.

June 20

"Club selection is crucial in chipping. You must choose the proper club for the distance. You have to get the distance right if the ball is to have a chance of going in."

—Tom Watson

On this day, June 20, 1982, Tom Watson got the distance right, very right. He holed a chip off the 17th green at Pebble Beach and won the U.S. Open.

It was a spectacular shot. One author described it as "the greatest golf shot ever made." Those who saw it rated his chance of making it at 1 in 10,000—and they may have been too optimistic. The ball lay in the deep rough off a green that was, in Dan Jenkins's words, "slicker than tile."

Watson pulled a sand wedge from his bag. At the time he was tied for the lead with Jack Nicklaus, who was pacing the carpet in the clubhouse. "Just get it close," Watson's caddie told him. "I'm going to chip it in," Watson replied. His confidence was born of success and hard work. Watson said later that he had practiced similar shots thousands of times over the years.

Watson has advised amateurs to go for the hole on a chip off the green because there is always the possibility you will make it. On this magical day, he took his own advice. He went for the hole and sunk a birdie 2 that made his day and ruined Nicklaus's. It gave Watson a U.S. Open to add to his Masters and British Open titles.

Confidence. Hard work. Getting the right club in your hands. Going for the hole. In honor of Watson's great accomplishment, *you* do it too.

Resolved: I hole a chip off the green.

June 21

"Now it is summer and as usual, life fills me with transport and I forget to work. This year I have struggled for a long time, but the beauty of the world has conquered me."

—Leo Tolstoy

Now is the start of the best season, the warm season.

Summers are made for golf. For forgetting about work, for playing, for giving yourself up to the unconquerable beauty of this world and this game.

The days are longer. You can start earlier, end later. It is warm, luxuriantly radiantly breathtakingly warm. You are loose as soon as you walk on the tee, ready to bite into that golf course as if it were a peach.

Mornings are blue, afternoons are blue. Marshmallow clouds drift by. The breeze is as benign as a smile.

In what other activity are we outside for three, four, five hours at a time? Some days you wish it was longer.

Everybody is out, including all the animals. Chipmunks, squirrels, robins, Canada geese, bluebirds, a family of mallards on the pond. In the early evening the sun recedes and shadows stretch across the landscape. Deer come down from the hills.

A day of golf in the summer is as relaxing as a massage. You find shade under a pine, wipe your face with a hand towel. Your partner hits and you walk along together, pulling your bags, saying nothing.

At round's end you stop in at a clubhouse as pleasant as a tropical cabana. You order up, thinking how good today was and how much better tomorrow will be.

Resolved: I celebrate the first day of summer. I play golf.

June 22

Rediscover your personal fountain of youth. Immerse yourself in golf, at least for a while.

One way to immerse yourself in golf is to go on a playing vacation. Play and play and play. Take a lesson, practice a little. Go to bed, get up. Play and play and play some more. Full immersion in the game of golf can produce amazing dividends in a relatively short period of time.

Another immersion method (suitable mainly, it is true, for youngsters) is a golf camp.

There are day camps and overnight camps. These camps usually last a week. The overnight camps are the way to go, because the kids really get to eat, sleep, and drink golf.

Campers receive instruction from teaching pros and even real-life playing pros. They play obstacle course games, in which they must chip over wooden barriers or through car tires, and target practice games. They form relay teams and compete against other teams. They get to experience what they normally do not get a chance to in this solitary game, the joy of being on a team.

Mostly, of course, they play. They play in the morning, they play in the afternoon. They play and play and play and their game improves.

There, we've got it all worked out: your summer immersion plans. Kid goes to golf camp, while you take a golf vacation and rediscover your personal fountain of youth.

Resolved: I sign my kid up for a golf vacation this summer.

June 23

"Even if you're on the right track, you'll get run over if you just sit there."

—Will Rogers

Don't just sit there—enter a tournament!

The summer and early fall are traditional times for tournaments. All sorts of tournaments are held, at virtually every golf course, in a variety of formats for all levels of players.

What, you say you're not the competitive type? Come on. Everybody competes on some level in their professional lives and in other ways. Competition does not equate with cutthroat. Tournaments are a great way to meet people and make social contacts.

Tournaments are frequently team events consisting of pairs or foursomes. A popular game for tournaments is Best Ball. You team up with another player. You play your own ball, but only the better score on each hole counts for your team. The team with the best score overall wins.

Competition is the best way to judge your skills against those of your peers. Most important, it will improve your game. You will learn how to cope with pressure. Competition is the whetstone that will sharpen every implement in your bag, as well as your mental approach to the game.

Besides all that, it's fun. Give it a shot!

Resolved: I enter a tournament.

June 24

"Never let what you cannot do stop you from what you can do."
—John Wooden

John Wooden coached the UCLA Bruins to ten NCAA basketball titles. He is widely regarded as one of the greatest coaches and motivators of all time, in any sport.

Wooden had an interesting philosophy. He never scouted opposing teams. He let other teams worry about the Bruins, and did not prepare them differently for one opponent than any other. His feeling was that opposing teams took themselves out of their own game by being overly concerned by what the Bruins were going to do. They hurt themselves by changing their methods and approach just because they were facing UCLA.

Conversely, Wooden wanted his Bruins to concentrate on their own strengths, what they wanted to accomplish as a team. Everything would work out fine as long as they did that.

Another characteristic of Wooden was that he was a great bench coach. He responded to each game as it presented itself. He and his teams could adapt and overcome whatever adversity they met.

Some principles of the Wooden Way as applied to golf:

Focus on what you do best as a player and what you need to do to succeed.

Focus on what you want to accomplish, what your goals are.

Let the other competitors take care of themselves.

Expect adversity, and be ready to adapt to it when it comes.

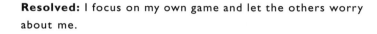

Resolved: I focus on my own game and let the others worry about me.

June 25

"Let me win. But if I cannot win, let me be brave in the attempt."

—Special Olympics motto

When Art Pease was a baby his parents tied him to a crib and beat him. Before authorities intervened he had suffered permanent brain damage.

As a young boy he was saved from a life of being moved from institution to institution by an Oregon High School coach and his wife, who adopted him. In an environment of love and nurturing, his athletic talents were recognized. He began to run as a teenager. He really loved it, and he was good at it.

He entered a local five-mile race. It was combined with a marathon. The long-distance runners ran alongside the five-milers in the early part of their race. Art missed the turnoff and kept running with the marathoners. At the 17-mile mark he began to realize what he had done. But he kept running. He had never run this far before in his life. He finished the marathon in just over four hours. He now competes in the Special Olympics Marathon and other competitive road races.

What can we learn from young Art?

One: Leave yourself open to possibility. You may surprise yourself at what you can achieve.

Two: You think you got problems?

Resolved: I am brave in the attempt.

June 26

"I like to expect the unexpected."

—Greg Norman

A friend from North Carolina writes, "I remember playing one summer in Jacksonville. That is northeastern Florida. It is more like southern Georgia there than what most people think of as Florida. The water table is so high you can dig a hole in the ground and the hole will fill with water.

"I was working for the railroad at the time. A group of us went out on a Saturday. It was stinkin' hot. You hardly wanted to move, it was so damp and hot. If we'd had any sense at all we'd have been inside in an air-conditioned rib house downing a pitcher of Sangria.

"I was hitting the ball all over the place. That's my usual style. The only safe place to stand when I hit is in the middle of the fairway. I hit the ball way left into this swampy area. It was kinda cool in there, I must admit. There were some trees and brush, and it was protected from the sun. I'm in there thrashing around, looking for my ball, and I step on something. No kidding. I look down and for a split second I see it: I am stepping on an alligator's tail.

"Now, I have been golfing a while. I think it's a good policy to expect the unusual. That way you're always prepared. Nothing gets to you. But I'm telling you, a lot of this philosophical stuff goes straight out the window when you try using an alligator's tail as a footstool. Actually I couldn't tell you who got out of there faster, me or the gator. I never did find my ball."

Resolved: I expect the unexpected, including alligators.

June 27

"If you must play, decide upon three things at the start: the rules of the game, the stakes, and the quitting time."

—Chinese proverb

Here is a way to inject instant motivation into your golf game: Put a little money on it. Nothing gets the blood beating faster than incentive of the economic kind.

For some people, playing golf is little more than an excuse to gamble. Nothing wrong with that. Golf and gambling go together like salsa and chips.

Gambling will teach you better than any book or teacher how to play under pressure. The famous Lee Trevino line comes to mind: "You don't know what pressure is until you play for five bucks with two bucks in your pocket."

Good line. Not good advice, though. Better to heed Sam Snead on this one: His rule was to always play for something, but never for more than what you have in your wallet.

Another good piece of advice comes from Dave Marr, this on the subject of whom to play *against*: "Never bet with anyone you meet on the first tee who has a deep suntan, a 1-iron in his bag, and squinty eyes."

A Nassau is the most common golf game. It is commonly played four ways. Five dollars for whoever wins the front nine, $10 for the back nine, and $5 for the match. Dollar amounts are negotiable.

Those who gamble can just be thankful that of all the technological innovations that have come to the game, at least they haven't put ATMs on the golf course. Not yet, anyhow.

Resolved: I play a $5 Nassau next time out.

June 28

"I go back to the word 'desire.' I became a good player because of desire."

—Bob Toski

Nothing stops desire.

A pretty good player will beat a great player if the pretty good player has desire and the other does not.

A person with limited skills will beat a naturally gifted player if the limited player has desire and the other relies on his talent alone to carry him. Desire moves mountains. Desire expands the range of what a person can achieve.

Check the standings at the end of a tournament. Check the name at the top of the list. That is the person who wanted it the most. Be that person. Play with desire.

Golfers are not born, they are made. Desire makes them: desire to practice, desire to improve, desire to win. A person who starts with all the advantages, who receives the best teaching, uses the best equipment, plays the finest courses—this person will achieve nothing in the game if he lacks desire. He or she will surely squander his material advantages because he lacks the emotional wherewithal to convert them into the currency of excellence.

A player with heart has nothing to fear against a player of this ilk. A player with heart has nothing to fear at all. The world stretches out before him, ripe for the taking, like Columbus setting out across the Atlantic.

Resolved: I play with desire.

June 29

"Be content with your lot."

—Aesop

There is much to be said for nine holes and only nine holes. It is shorter. It takes less time. It takes less out of you. And yet there is a completeness to it, a wholeness. The circuit you travel brings you back to the clubhouse just as when you play the full 18.

Nine holes provides a measure of one's play. There is a score worth noting, a score that means something. Doubling the score for nine provides an approximation of how one would have fared over a full round. Though a nine-hole score is a worthy number in its own right.

Some disparage nine holes as somehow less. It is not real golf, not a true test.

Actually, playing nine holes is like that old glass of water thing. Is the glass half empty, or half full?

The answer is easy. Nine holes is a half-full glass that can be wholly satisfying. The discoveries you make on 18 holes you can make over nine as well. You may find that you put less pressure on yourself when playing nine. You may not be as score-oriented and you may enjoy yourself more. These are all noteworthy things.

It all depends on what you make of it. Certainly, nine holes are nine better than none at all. Today, squeeze in half a round if you cannot afford the time for a full one. However you add it up, it's still golf.

Resolved: I get in at least nine today.

June 30

"I like it because it's a walk in the park. There's an honor system, and that's really valuable. It's character building. I know it's made me a better human being."

—Actor Craig T. Nelson, on why he likes golf

What do you like about golf? "Coach" says it makes him a better person. How about you?

A happy golfer is one who knows what he wants from the game. He never asked golf for low scores, so he doesn't feel cheated when he doesn't shoot them. He gets from golf what he wants, and his game is more enjoyable and productive because of it.

One man plays strictly for business reasons. He plays only when he entertains clients, and he shoots in the 100s because his attention is on them, not his game. This is just fine with him. He's clear about what he wants from the game. He's a happy man.

Get from golf what you want to get from it. Play golf for your reasons, not someone else's. This is the way to find happiness in the game.

We've touched on this topic before in these pages and we will touch on it again. It's a good thing to review, much as you would periodically assess your performance goals over time. Happiness in golf is a very worthy goal unto itself.

Resolved: I spend my golf time the way I like.

July 1

"We are always the same age inside."

—Gertrude Stein

At the age of 65, Arnold Palmer traveled to St. Andrews, Scotland, to play his final British Open. Reporters asked him what his goal was.

"There's only one," said Arnold.

Arnold came to win.

Now, everyone knew Arnold had an ice cube's chance in hell of winning the tournament. He had not won a title of any kind in years. His presence in St. Andrews was largely ceremonial. His last British Open Championship came during the Kennedy administration. Was he being disingenuous, then? Putting the press on?

No. Arnold was in earnest. He meant it.

Crazy? Hmm. Maybe a little. Self-deluded? Possibly that too. But despite the passage of years, despite his aging body, despite the fact that his skills had eroded, Arnold's heart was unchanged. The spirit-core that had guided him back when he was winning all those championships was as youthful as ever.

Do you have doubts about yourself? Do you have trouble believing in yourself when your limitations are so painfully obvious to yourself and therefore everyone else?

The answer is simple. Though it may seem strange at first.

The answer lies in the kid you used to be The part of you that never ages. Tap in to it. Respond to it. Listen to it. You have what you need to play the very best golf you are capable of . . . right now.

Resolved: I open my heart to the part of me that never ages.

July 2

*"There are those who are so scrupulously afraid of doing wrong
that they seldom venture to do anything."*

—Vauvenargues

It is one of the axioms of golf that championships are lost, not
won. A corollary axiom is that the best golfers are the ones
who make the fewest mistakes. This is true enough. But every
golf champion will tell you that an attitude of sitting back and
waiting for others to make mistakes will not get you very far
in golf.

You have to go out and make things happen. In life as in
golf, you must fire at the flag.

Think of Greg Norman, Jack Nicklaus, Arnold Palmer, John
Daly. What do we admire about them as golfers? One jointly
held attribute of theirs is this: They take chances. They risk
it all. They dare greatly. They fire at the flag.

Join them. Join Norman, Nicklaus, Palmer, Daly. Fire at the
flag.

Waiting for others to stumble before you can move ahead
breeds timidity. You become a spectator even as you are playing. You privately hope that fortune will be unkind to others
and smile upon you. While you adopt an attitude of passivity, the fearless in the field charge right past you. They risk
mistakes, but they also risk greatness. The curse of the timid
is second place.

Be aggressive. Make things happen. Fire at the flag!

Resolved: I fire at the flag.

July 3

"Keep it smooth and slow. Think smoo-oo-ooth."

> —PGA champion Larry Nelson, on the golf swing

A quick reminder: When you go out today, take your swing back sloo-oo-oow and smoo-oo-ooth.

Sam Snead was paired in a pro-am with a guy with a machete-chop swing. Snead found out he was a musician and advised him to swing in waltz time. The tip worked. The guy slowed his swing down and found the right tempo.

Flip to the classical station on your drive over to the club. Maybe they will be playing a waltz by Strauss.

Another musical tip, this one from Tom Watson but with the same purpose: Slow the swing down into a nice easy rhythm.

Remember "Edelweiss" from *The Sound of Music*? Watson suggests humming the three-note structure of the song—"E-del-weiss, E-del-weiss"—to relax you and instill a feeling for the rhythm of the swing.

One caveat: Just don't start yodeling and singing "The hills are alive with the sound of music . . ." around the club. People may talk.

Resolved: I take it back slow.

July 4

"Bold is freedom, the breaking thing. Freedom lies in being bold."
—Robert Frost

Today is Independence Day, and today I declare my independence from:

Timidity. I play bold when I play golf. That is the only way to play.

Fear. Why be afraid of a simple golf shot and its consequences? It's just golf. Stand up strong and confident and give it a ride.

Negativity. Negativity can come from many places in golf. It can come from outside sources and from inside my skull. I declare my independence from all forms of negativity.

The blame game. Blaming others or external factors for the things that happen contrary to my wishes. I accept responsibility for what I do on a golf course, for I know that is the path to greater power and control.

Jealousy. How come he's so good? Why can't I play like that? I reject such thoughts and use the example of a better player as an inspiration—and a challenge—to me.

Self-pity. Self-pity can lead to feelings of frustration and hopelessness.

Today, break away from your own form of golf tryanny—the thoughts that hold you down—and play boldly and confidently, the way Thomas Paine would have played if he had been a golfer. Then go home and have a barbecue with the family.

Resolved: I play boldly and confidently.

July 5

"He seems a man of cheerful yesterdays and confident tomorrows."

—William Wordsworth

Project confidence and you will play with confidence.

Observe a player who is doing well. She is relaxed, smiling, the very picture of confident self-esteem. Positive vibes emanate from her like perfume. You can tell she is on her game by the way she looks (her facial features) and the way she carries herself (her body language).

Contrast this picture to a golfer who is struggling. He is grim-faced, tight-lipped. His posture slumps after every shot. He looks haggard and tense. It is as if he is on an 18-hole forced march. He looks like a beaten player, and he is.

Logically, one would conclude that the first player is happy and confident because she is stinging the ball and scoring, while the second is miserable because he is not. Reverse the roles—the first player struggling, the second on top of his game—and you would see corresponding changes in each's behavior, right?

Not necessarily.

Be a person of cheerful yesterdays and confident tomorrows. Project a positive outlook and you will more likely have a positive outcome.

Attitude is all. Project the golfer you want to be and then *be* that golfer. Model a certain image and live up to it. Appear relaxed and confident in ordinary play and you have a better shot at being relaxed and confident when things get tight.

Resolved: I project confidence. I play with confidence.

July 6

"Dum Spiro Spero."

—Golf towels in shops near the Old Course at St. Andrews
bear this Latin inscription, which means:
"While I breathe, I hope."

You arrive on the tee in a foul mood. You three-putted the last green and you're ticked.

You take a deep breath. You know you have to leave that hole behind and concentrate on this one.

You hit a banana ball. It starts down the middle, then bends right into the trees. You slam your driver into your bag and walk off.

Your ball is in a bad spot. Bad lie, low-hanging branches, the whole works. Nothing to do but chip it back onto the fairway into a better place.

Your third is your worst shot yet. You hit a 7-iron fat. Your ball squirts up like a one-winged bird learning to fly and plops down, exhausted, into a sand trap.

But you dig it out, and chip up. You watch helplessly as the ball rolls back down the hill and stops at your feet. You try it again and somehow manage to crest the plateau of the green.

You lie 10 feet away. You have to give yourself credit. Others may have gotten discouraged. You didn't. You hung in there. You worked hard on every shot, and now you can salvage some measure of dignity with a good putt.

You run it five feet past the hole. It takes two more strokes to get it in. "Oh, well," you say to yourself as you scoop your ball up. "Get 'em next time."

Resolved: While I breathe, I hope.

July 7

"Let's play two."

—Ernie Banks

It is summer and the days are long—so long that you can consider playing 36 holes today—a sort of golfing doubleheader. Mister Cub would approve.

Going around twice used to be far more common than it is today. They frequently decided major tournaments by playing 36 holes on the final day.

But times have changed. Golf courses today are like Grand Central Station with fairways—people coming and going, rushing hither and yon. There is barely enough time to squeeze in 18 holes, let alone 36. Only kids on summer vacation have time to do it now.

Maybe in your case it has to wait until vacation, when the demands are fewer and there is more time in the day. Still, make a point of it. Play 36 holes.

Do it as a lark. Do it for the experience. Devote the whole day to golf and see how it feels. Sunup (or thereabouts) to sundown (roughly speaking). Eighteen in the morning, a leisurely lunch, another 18 in the fading light and lengthening shadows of late day. You will be tired. But it will be an honest tired, a tired that you can look back on with pride, a tired that will, curiously enough, be one of the most energizing days of golf you have ever experienced.

Resolved: I play 36 holes the first opportunity I get.

July 8

"I don't like to talk about putting. There's a tendency when you do to focus on one element of your stroke and then start to overdo it."

—Paul Azinger

Be quiet as a monk when it comes to putting. Let your putter do the talking. For in putting, silence is golden.

Putting is a mystery, and like all mysteries one must approach it with a kind of reverential awe. A humble quietude is part of this.

A person who talks about his putting is not worth listening to, for if his putting was worth a damn he wouldn't be talking about it. On the other hand, when a person says nothing about his putting, keep your hand on your wallet. He may be locked into something good.

Like Paul Azinger, Chi Chi Rodriguez knows what can happen to a motormouth putter. A magazine hired him to write an article about his technique. "Then I started trying to figure out what I did, and I suddenly didn't know what I did," he said. Chi Chi talks plenty, but only when it suits him.

Ever been in a situation where you've talked about a thing and ruined it because of that? Putting can be like that. Then again, you may be the type of person who likes to talk, and if you can talk about your putting without overanalyzing and overdoing it and throwing your stroke off, more power to you.

Resolved: I let my putter do the talking.

July 9

In 1956 an Iowa club pro named Jack Fleck beat Ben Hogan in a playoff for the U.S. Open in what many still refer to as "the greatest upset in golf history."

On the sixth hole of their playoff at the Olympic Club in San Francisco, Hogan had a short birdie putt while Fleck's ball lay 25 feet from the hole. Fleck was nervous, in a rush. He was nervous about being the focus of such attention, nervous about playing in a playoff for the greatest championship in golf, and nervous about doing it against the best golfer of his time.

"I'll be out of your way in a minute," Fleck said as he hurriedly sized up his putt.

"Take your time," said the stoical Hogan. "We have nowhere to go."

The comment seemed to settle Fleck down. He slowed down and sunk his long putt (Hogan missed his). He went on to make birdies on 8, 9, and 10 en route to a three-shot win.

Purposeful play is not slow play. Take the time if you need the time. Let the others wait; you have waited for them. Hold every moment sacred on the greens. As the great man said, there is nowhere else to go. Stand over it, sight it, sink the putt.

Resolved: I take the time I need before I putt.

July 10

"When I'm in the trap, I play the shot that will get me out."

—Grier Jones

When you're in a trap, play the shot that gets you out. Grier Jones, an excellent bunker player, was referring to sand traps. But the advice extends far beyond that.

When you're in the trees, play the shot that will get you out of the trees.

When you're in the rough, play the shot that will get you out of the rough.

Let's extend the advice still further: When you're in trouble, play the shot that will get you out of trouble. When you're down, play the shot that will bring you up.

When you're struggling, play the makable shot. There is a tendency among many of us to take the hard way out. We ignore the simplest option, because it seems so obvious, so elementary. We tend to place more value on the complicated and difficult, though it may not serve our ends as well as the plain and simple solution staring us in the face.

Simplicity is best. Play the shot that gets you out. With this commonsense wisdom in mind, everything becomes clear: your choice of club, your plan of attack, even your mental approach. You stay within your capabilities, maintain control, and keep your game under command.

Resolved: I play the shot that gets me out.

July 11

"One friend, one person who is truly understanding, who takes the trouble to listen to us as we consider our problem, can change our whole outlook on the world."

—Elton Mayo

When you take a lesson from a pro, are you the student or the teacher?

This is not as crazy a question as it seems. Ask any pro. They have all dealt with people who come to them seeking advice and yet already know what is wrong with their swing and what needs to be done to fix it.

This may be due in part to the fact that many golfers are successful in business and are more accustomed to telling, rather than listening:

"Here, this is what is wrong. Let me tell you."

Going to a pro constitutes a kind of role reversal—from boss/authority figure/person with the answers to student/listener/asker of questions. It is a tough switch to make sometimes.

Suffice to say that all you need to do is show a pro your swing and he or she will be able to recognize what's wrong with it without explanation, however helpful, from you. The best thing you can do during a lesson is cast yourself in the role of willing and eager listener.

Also, if you truly knew what was wrong with your swing, wouldn't you just fix it yourself? A pro can give you directions on how to change your golfing outlook. But first we need to listen to what he or she says.

✕

Resolved: I go to a pro with an open mind.

July 12

"Never hurry and don't worry."

—Walter Hagen

Walter Hagen never hurried when he played golf, and he almost always arrived late. Both were the acts of a calculating mind.

Hagen did everything slow on the day of a tournament. He ate slow, dressed slow, brushed his teeth slow—all to slow down his golf. You'd think a man moving at such a turtle's pace would give himself plenty of leeway to make it to his match on time. But Walter, who put the one in one-upmanship, never put much stake in punctuality, at least not if it went against his interests to do so.

And yet when he did make his entrance—a half hour past his scheduled tee time, probably in a limousine, possibly accompanied by a damsel or two, impeccably altered in the fashion of the '20s (him and the ladies), his opponent no doubt seething volcano-like—he was unfailingly courteous and apologetic, ever the dignified gentleman distressed at inconveniencing so many good people.

The contrite Mr. Hagen would then politely go about the business of dismantling his opponent, who was frequently discombobulated by all the commotion caused by Walter's arrival. Match play was very big back then, and Walter was the Bruce Lee of match play.

So what can we learn from Mr. H?

1. Never hurry.
2. Never worry.
3. Be late when it suits you.

Resolved: I never hurry and I never worry.

July 13

"Most slicers know that the best way to cure their affliction is to develop a hook."

—John Elliott

This advice falls under what might be described as "The Commonsense Guide to Teaching Golf."

Hitting it right too much? Well, then, *hit it left*.

Slicing the ball? Okay. Hit a draw.

Slicing gets a bad name because it signifies a lack of control. This is really what the issue is. Not that the ball goes right, but that the ball goes right all the time. It is chronic. Out of control.

What does a chronic slicer need to do, then? Get control. If all he thinks he has to do is "stop slicing," he is kidding himself. His slice is merely a manifestation of the larger issue of control.

How do you turn it around? Change your point of view. See the slice not as a liability but as a tool, one that you have taught yourself to use very well. Now, it is time to learn to use some new tools, such as the draw or the slice's better-behaved cousin, the fade. Go out to the range. Work the ball from left to right. Then right to left. See what you are doing; try to get control of the process.

You are the master of your golf shots. Make them slaves to your will. The ball is not slicing of its own accord; you are hitting it that way. And you can—you *can*—hit it other ways if you choose.

Resolved: I see my slice as a tool and get control of it.

July 14

"Close up his eyes and draw the curtain close; and let us all to meditation."

—William Shakespeare

A fascinating moment occurred at the centennial National Open at Shinnecock. It occurred on the final hole of the final day. From about 225 yards out, Corey Pavin, the eventual winner, struck a beautiful curving 4-wood shot that flew down the fairway and over a bunker and bounced onto the green a few feet from the pin.

The TV cameras caught the shot perfectly, and it is destined to be replayed for many years to come. But the replays never show what Pavin did after he hit the shot of his life.

He ran down the fairway to see where the ball landed. He was like a little boy, he was so happy. He threw his arms up in victory and let the cheers of the gallery swell over him. They knew, as did he, what the shot meant.

Then—and this is what the replays never show—Pavin stopped his exulting. He squatted down and closed his eyes. This was a very gripping thing to see. Amid the roars of the crowd, he sought inner counsel. He closed his eyes for a moment of prayer or meditation, or simply to compose himself.

This is a very good thing to do even if you have not just hit a title-winning shot in the National Open. Whether you are exulting in triumph or battling anger, take a moment to compose yourself whenever you need to during a round. Seek inner counsel. It will calm and strengthen you for your next shot.

Resolved: I take a moment to compose myself during a round.

July 15

"I was very patient. I knew this guy was going to be a fighter."
—Tiger Woods, after besting an opponent in match play

Be a fighter on the golf course. Be the type of golfer who, if you were playing Tiger Woods, he would have to be very, very patient to beat.

A fighter on the golf course never beats himself. Others may beat him through their outstanding play. But he does not beat himself. He does not give up on himself. He never quits.

He is like Smokin' Joe Frazier. He keeps coming and coming and coming until he wears you down and drops you to the canvas. Be a golfer the way Joe Frazier was a boxer.

A fighter on the golf course is relentless. He finds a way to win. Even on a bad day, he keeps fighting.

Victory is a maze with a thousand doors and one opening. A fighter on the golf course keeps knocking on doors until he finds the right one. It is dark. He winds through tunnels. Lesser spirits quit because of the lack of light and seeming hopelessness. Let your heart like a miner's headlamp lead you through the darkness into the sunlight.

A fighter on a golf course keeps going because he knows that in this game especially, anything can happen.

A fighter on a golf course will not win every time. But he knows that he did everything he could in order to win. And this provides him with satisfaction at the end of a battle.

Resolved: I am a fighter on the golf course.

July 16

"The woods are full of long drivers."

—Old Scottish saying

Short off the tee? Doesn't matter. You can still beat the pants off those long drivers.

Use Paul Runyan as your inspirational model. On this day in 1938, he simply crushed a much longer hitter to win the PGA Championship.

His victim was Sam Snead, one of the sweetest swingers ever. Runyan's swing was sweet too; the ball just didn't travel as far when he hit it. Snead's drives went 50 yards or more farther than Runyan's, who needed three shots on a long par 5 to cover the same distance that Sam covered in two. But Little Poison (Paul was also small in stature) whipped him 8 and 7, which means he was eight strokes ahead with seven holes to play, clinching the match play title after only the 11th hole.

How did he do it? The same way you can:

Refusing to be intimidated.

Playing your own game.

Concentrating on your strengths.

Picking up strokes around the greens.

Sinking those putts.

Nothing unnerves a big swinger faster than to see the putts of another player start falling in.

Resolved: I beat a long-driving player with my short game.

July 17

"I felt like every hole was 700 yards and I had the longest putts in the world."

—Annika Sorenstam

Ever had that feeling? Some of us have it all the time. But the thing to remember is that if you have that feeling, you can come back from it.

Annika Sorenstam experienced that feeling, big-time, in the 1995 U.S. Women's Open. With four holes left to play, she had a three-stroke lead. The tournament seemed hers. She was playing superbly. She seemed locked in that "zone" that athletes in all sports talk about when they can do no wrong.

Then, on 15, she sneaked a peak at the leader board. Only 24, a native of Stockholm with no LPGA wins to her credit, Annika saw her name at the top of the board. The reality of what she was doing hit her. She freaked.

She lost her concentration. She thought beyond the moment she was in. Just like that, she was out of the zone.

On 15 she found a bunker and bogeyed. On 16 she three-putted for another bogey. But she managed par on the next two holes, and when runner-up Meg Mallon's putt for birdie on 18 went wide, Annika was champion.

What happened to Annika can happen to anyone. You can have it. You can lose it. But if you hang tough, you can get it back.

Resolved: I hang tough.

July 18

I loaf and invite my soul to play a round of golf with me. Then I call in sick.

Life is short. Too short for work, school, responsibility . . . *all the time.*

Today I am taking the day off from all that. Today I am playing golf.

"Hello? Mr. Painintherear (cough, cough, sputter)—I don't know what happened—all of a sudden—last night (hack, spit) . . . I know I sound terrible. I feel even worse. It's like any minute—uh, excuse me—gotta go. I'm going to ralphhh . . ."

Later, sucker!

You say I'm abandoning my duties? I say the world will survive one day without me. And if it all does come to a stop today, well then, I am glad I will be spending the Last Day of Planet Earth on the golf course, where I belong. I just hope I can get in a full 18 before it all ends.

Tomorrow, I promise, I will return to my responsibilities as a dues-paying, taxpaying, blues-gathering, burden-shouldering citizen of the world.

But today, oh today, the skies are blue, the fairways are green, and I'm playing golf!

Resolved: I take the day off and play golf.

July 19

"The hours we waste in work and similar unconsequence.
Friends, I beg you do not shirk your daily task of indolence."
—Don Marquis

Hmm. That was kind of fun. Yesterday, I mean. Calling in sick and spending the day at the golf course instead.

I mean, it was *really* fun. Spring has sprung and all that. Flowers blooming all over the place, it was like a damn arboretum out there. The air crisp and sharp.

I don't usually get a chance to play midweek, either. And in the morning. Nobody was there. It's like they rolled out the red carpet for me. I practically walked on. Got into this group with these three old guys, retirees. They were a kick.

And I hit the hell out of the ball. Really. The old guys were oohing and aahing like I was John Daly or something. It was great.

I kept halfway expecting my department supervisor, Mr. Painintherear, to pop out from behind a bush and bust me. But he never did. It was completely cool, all day.

I go back today, of course. Two days in a row, that's pushing it. I got work to do. Jack needs my help on this project we're working on. Then there's the aptly named Mr. Painintherear. He's gonna be suspicious. Besides, it's just not right. Work is work and play is play and that's all there is to it.

"Hello, Mr. Painintherear (cough, sputter, hack). Oh yeah, it's terrible. I'm going to (hack, hack) a doctor today. It may (cough) be (cough, sputter, spew) pneu—(cough, cough, cough)—monia . . ."

Yes!

Resolved: I play the string out for all it's worth. I play golf again.

July 20

"Afoot and lighthearted, I take to the open road.
Healthy, free, the world before me."

—Walt Whitman

Oh, well. What's done is done. No sense crying over spilt milk.

I guess two days in a row *was* pushing it. But how was I supposed to know Mr. Painintherear would be entertaining a client that day at the very same golf course where I happened to be?

Jobs come and go. I'll find a better one. I suppose. Someday.

I *know* I'll find a better boss than that ole Painintherear, that's for certain. I can still hear his snide voice saying, "Driving the ball pretty well for a man on his deathbed, Mr. Shirker. . . . I see you're a man of swift recoveries, Shirker, on the course and off. . . ."

Please. A man calls in sick to play golf—okay, so *fire* me. But don't insult my integrity. That's not right.

Now what?

Well, first, I call the unemployment office. I bet they're a lot more understanding about guys who'd rather play golf than work. I bet they see lots of guys like me.

Listen, I'll bounce back. It's like in golf. You get into trouble, you hack away until you get out of it. I'll be all right.

Hey, that's what life is all about. A little rain must fall and all that. Sometimes it turns into a monsoon and floods the house. What do you do?

Tell you what I do. I'm healthy, I'm young, I'm free. What the hell? I'm playing golf.

Resolved: I let tomorrow take care of itself. Today I play golf.

July 21

To take trouble is to strengthen the character. That's true for men and women. Take the trouble today. Go out and buy some new golfing duds.

Many women (and some men) do this: When they are feeling blue they'll go shopping. It is a form of therapy. They browse through the gleaming racks of merchandise and they buy something nice for themselves. And they feel better for having done it.

Feeling a little blue? Feeling down on your golfing luck? Go out and spend some money.

This principle applies very well to golf too. Many a golfer has reported, upon purchasing a new driver, more length off the tee when he first put his purchase into action. And if, over time, the novelty of the club wears off and your drives return to their previous distance, so what? You felt real good about yourself for a time. What's wrong with that?

New clothes can have the same effect. The way you look is not an irrelevancy in golf. If it is, why do all the very best players look so put together? How you look is a reflection of how you play, the confidence you feel.

Go buy yourself a new pair of pants or a slick new golf shirt. Those Foot-Joys are looking a little ragged; a new pair wouldn't hurt. Hell, revamp the entire wardrobe! Take the trouble. You deserve it. The next time you go out to play, you'll be stylin'.

Resolved: I buy some new golf duds.

July 22

"It is of the essence that a game of golf can't be quickly and over done with, but must dominate the day."

—John Updike

Critics of golf use time as a cudgel against it. Too slow, they say, takes too long to play.

But those who love the game know better. This is at the heart of why we play. Because it takes so long.

We experience a form of temporary amnesia when we play golf, forgetting those concerns we left behind on the first hole and will return to after the last. The sheer number of hours we spend on the course contributes to our forgetfulness. Like a sailing voyage around the Cape, it takes a while—a long while—before we come back home again.

Another thing about golf (and this is what contributes to the challenge of it): It requires our attention while it demands our time.

Advertisers make 15-second TV commercials because they feel that the attention span of the audience demands it. People will flip the channel if the message lasts longer than that.

Now look at golf. Look at how fully we must focus ourselves, and for how long. Three, four, five hours or more.

One way to play better golf is to find a way to increase your attention span, the length of time you can concentrate on a given task. Stretch your attention span like taffy and elongate it. Meditation may help in this regard.

In the meantime, enjoy the voyage. Hitch your vessel to the sun and track it across a brilliant unclouded sky.

Resolved: I relish the sheer length of time I spend on the course.

July 23

"Give us grace and strength to forbear and to persevere."

—Robert Louis Stevenson

It was a marvelous moment for watchers of TV and of the human spirit: the 72nd hole of the 124th British Open. Italy's Constantino Rocca needs to sink a 65-foot birdie putt to tie America's John Daly, who is in the lead cooling his heels in the clubhouse at hoary old St. Andrews.

Rocca putts. Improbably the ball goes in, creating a tie and forcing a playoff. Rocca falls to the ground in a prayer of joy. Daly is stunned. His face gets real hard, like a hit man who has just gotten his assignment to go kill somebody.

The playoff that followed was anticlimactic. Apparently Daly had enough drama for the day. He went par-birdie on the first two playoff holes to Rocca's bogey-par. Then he made a four to Rocca's seven on the Road Hole, and all that was left for Daly was a victorious stroll across Swilcam Burn Bridge at the foot of the glorious Royal and Ancient.

How did Daly do it? How did this recovering alcoholic bounce back from the disappointment of seeing Rocca's putt roll in? "I don't know what happened," he said, in explaining how he played so well in the playoff. "I got real *strong*."

This sort of strength, however inexplicable, is available to us all. It is not superhuman. Is there a golfer who wears his flaws more openly than Daly? Any of us can reach down and get that strength if we need it.

Maybe we have to live a little. Let us hope we don't have to go to the bottom and climb back up, as Daly has done, in order to find it. But it is there, *it is there*.

Resolved: I get real strong on the golf course, real strong.

July 24

"I always knew I was a good player. I just needed the opportunity to show it."

> —Woody Austin, after winning his first PGA Tournament,
> the 1995 Buick Open

You know you are a good player too. All you need is the opportunity to show it, just like Woody Austin.

Woody Austin is a former bank teller whose game came together only after he committed himself to it full-time. He is no different than anyone else. Your dreams are not so far-fetched if you commit yourself to them. If Woody can do it, you can do it.

Sometimes opportunity knocks. Other times you are going to have to kick the door down to find it. Here are some ideas on how to create opportunity for yourself:

Make the time. That's hard to do sometimes; there are plenty of distractions. But you must commit the time in order to succeed.

Play, play, play. The only way you are going to do the thing you so ardently want to do is to do it.

Practice. What's that old saw about genius being 1 percent inspiration and 99 percent perspiration? Well, it's true.

Hang in there. The actor who achieves "overnight stardom" probably played off-off-off-Broadway for years while supporting himself as a waiter.

Set your sights high. Accept short-term concessions only as a means of achieving your long-term goals. Keep your eye fixed firmly on the prize.

Resolved: I give myself the opportunity to play at a high level.

July 25

"Just because you're nervous doesn't mean you can't hit great shots."

—Paul Azinger

You're sweating bullets. The adrenaline is pumping. And why not? It's a tough putt.

Your heart is pounding. It's like a bass drum inside your chest. It's pounding so loud, it is a wonder that no one else can hear it.

This is what Paul Azinger does when he gets in those situations: he breathes in four counts slowly and breathes out four counts slowly.

Always four counts. The breathing in and out helps him, and so does the simple counting: "One–two–three–four."

You reach the green. You check out the line. You make your practice stroke.

Everybody gets nervous when they face a tough putt. *Everybody.* But you can still be nervous and make tough putts.

You step up. Your eyes narrow on the hole. You calmly drain it. "One–two–three–four."

Resolved: I breathe deep, calm my nerves. Then I sink a tough putt.

July 26

"The game of golf is not how many good shots you hit, it's how few bad shots you hit."

—Jack Nicklaus

Bobby Jones, Nicklaus's boyhood idol, said that over the course of a normal round he hit only a half-dozen shots that truly pleased him. The rest, while not "mistakes" or "bad shots" by conventional standards, were less than ideal according to Jones.

Nicklaus possessed a similar perfectionist beat. If the shot did not go as he envisioned it prior to striking the ball, he found reason for discontent.

Besides their perfectionist natures and supreme accomplishments in the game, what Nicklaus and Jones shared was this:

They made their mistakes stop at one. A mistake was always a singular event with them, not plural. If they hit what was for them a bad ball, they followed it up with—ah, the wonder of their talent!—a good ball.

Of course, they might make another mistake down the road. But again, the bad ball was left an orphan. They instantly put it behind them—for that is what you must do—and they followed it with a winner.

That must be your attitude too. It is a sort of "The buck stops here" attitude. It is not enough to "limit our mistakes." We must stop them dead in their tracks.

One mistake is enough. That's it. No more. Boom! End of discussion.

Resolved: I leave every mistake an orphan.

July 27

"Give yourself the benefit of the doubt."

—Jack Burke Sr.

Jack Burke Sr. was an old-time golfer and golf teacher. He finished in a tie for second in the 1920 U.S. Open. He was one of a long line of Texans (Hogan, Nelson, Trevino, Penick, Crenshaw, Kite, etc.) who have had an influence on the way the game is played in this country. His son, Jack Burke Jr., won both the Masters and PGA in 1956.

Jack Senior told Jack Junior and all the golfers he taught to give themselves the benefit of the doubt. Golf is hard enough. We don't have to make it any harder by being so critical of ourselves.

This is sound advice for off the course too. Life is not exactly a bowl of cherries, and yet our toughest critics are often ourselves. Do we have to be so tough?

We set standards for ourselves—based on what? Based on what our friends or colleagues (or rivals) are doing? Based on what our parents think? Based on what we think a person our age should have accomplished?

Being comfortable in your own skin. That's a good standard to shoot for.

We treat ourselves to golf. We play because it is fun. Fun to be outside, fun to be with friends, fun to whack a little white ball around. Let's not beat ourselves up about it in the process.

Resolved: I cut myself some slack—on and off the course.

July 28

You can observe a lot by watching the women's Tour.

The LPGA Tour is the oft-ignored stepchild of pro golf, but there are many excellent reasons to watch the ladies play. Among them:

At the risk of appearing sexist, the ladies are nice to look at. It is far more pleasing to watch Annika Sorenstam than Craig Stadler any day.

More to the point, they are excellent golfers. And they are excellent in a way that average golfers can relate to, namely:

They really work the ball around the course. A Greg Norman or John Daly drives over everything. On the women's tour, while there are certainly big hitters like Laura Davies, sheer length does not surmount every obstacle. Bunkers come into play.

Watching the women reminds us that golf is not a game of brute strength. As Louise Nevelson said, "True strength is very delicate." Golfers come in all shapes and sizes. That is an inspiring thought for those who may not be "natural" athletes.

For women or men, the universals still apply. The short game is king. Finesse around the greens and with the putter is what makes great golfers, and the women have finesse in abundance.

Resolved: I watch the women pros with an open mind.

July 29

"People say, 'Play the course; don't play the man,' but I never believed that. Especially in match play, you have to keep one eye on your opponent."

—Sam Snead

Learn to play the man (or woman). Play match play.

The most common way of assessing golfing ability is stroke play. The fewest number of strokes wins the round or tournament. Match play is head-to-head golf. Total strokes do not count; beating your opponent is what matters.

Match play tournaments are played mainly on the club level now. The professional tours have largely abandoned it because of television. Television sees it as a rating killer, despite the phenomenal success of the Ryder Cup. Match play has a long and glorious history in golf. The PGA was once a match play event.

Match play is a wonderful alternative. It gets those competitive juices flowing like Niagara Falls.

Enter a club tournament, or play on your own in your group. The rules are simple. The player who takes the fewest strokes on a hole wins the hole. If there is a tie the hole is "halved."

It sometimes happens that the winner in match play would have lost in stroke play or by figuring fewest strokes over the round. But it also frequently occurs that a person shoots his best stroke total ever. Match play sharpens concentration and teaches stick-to-itiveness. You may lose a hole, but if you bear down you can make it up on the next one or later on down the road.

Resolved: I play some match play golf.

July 30

"The way I see it, if you want the rainbow, you gotta put up with the rain."

—Dolly Parton

Into every golfer's life a little rain must fall.

We are not talking metaphorical rain here. We are talking real rain—you know, the wet stuff.

First rule: Anything short of Hurricane Ollie, play through. A few drops never hurt anybody.

Second rule: All rules are immediately suspended if the storm brings lightning. Be very, very careful about lightning. It is nothing to play around with.

One out of five deaths caused by lightning in the United States occurs on a golf course. To paraphrase Lee Trevino, who was once hit by lightning, dogs that chase cars and golfers who play in lightning storms do not last long.

Another Trevino-ism: Pull the 1-iron out of your bag during a lightning storm. "Not even God," said Lee, "can hit a 1-iron." A better survival technique is to scrunch yourself into a ball close to the ground. Put your feet together, head down, and if you're lucky the lightning will pass over you and strike something else.

The last word belongs to Bob Hope: "Personally if I'm on a golf course and lightning starts, I get indoors fast. If God wants to play through, I let Him." Good advice, that.

Resolved: When God wants to play through, I let Him.

July 31

"Golf is most popular with a small sliver of the lunatic fringe."
—Peter Andrews

Have you done anything crazy (in a golf sense) lately?

On a July day in 1956, an American named Don Schuck was sitting around his Tokyo apartment with a few of his pals. A young Englishman had recently attempted to hit a golf ball from London to Oxford, and they were wondering if one of them couldn't try a similar stunt from Tokyo to Yokohama. "We'd get killed in traffic," said one.

Vetoing that idea, they decided on the next-best thing: hitting a golf ball up 12,395-foot Mt. Fuji.

Schuck was the one who actually performed the stunt. It took him 1,275 strokes—3 under par—to make it to the top of the mountain. Air Force Sergeant Lee Torliatt recorded the event for posterity with his camera. A Sherpa guide named Satori Amano accompanied them, steering them away from the out-of-bounds areas.

It took 10 hours to get to the top. Amazingly they only lost 27 golf balls. Schuck had the hardest time in a rocky section of the mountain where his drives ricocheted around like a pinball.

Schuck completed his golfing ascent by sinking a ball in a hole—the two-mile-wide crater at the top of Fuji. Then he hit one down the side of the mountain and watched it bounce and roll seemingly forever.

Schuck, Torliatt, and their Sherpa guide are esteemed members of golf's illustrious lunatic fringe. The group is always looking for new members. Care to join?

Resolved: I partake in the inspired lunacy of golf.

August 1

Keep trying. Never quit. Find a way. This is how you succeed in golf.

Here is the story of a man who found a way: Ken Venturi. Now a TV analyst, he was, in 1964, a 33-year-old San Franciscan trying to win the U.S. Open championship.

Talk about heat. They had it that year at the Congressional Country Club in Washington, D.C. One-hundred-degree temperatures, body-deflating humidity. Back then they played the final 36 holes of the Open on Saturday—18 in the morning, 18 in the afternoon.

Venturi shot a 66 in the morning to pull within two strokes of the lead. Between rounds his doctor told him to quit playing or risk losing his life. Venturi suffered from heat exhaustion, dehydration, and fatigue. "Do not go out again in that heat," his doctor said.

We mortals would be well advised to listen to our doctor's warnings and avoid playing in such conditions. Venturi did not, of course. He shot a heroic 70 with his doctor accompanying him every step of the way. When he reached the 72nd green he looked as if he had walked across the Sahara.

But he had done it. He had done what he had to do. He had found a way. He had won the Open.

The stakes may not be as great for you, but the requirements for success are the same. Keep trying. Never quit. Find a way.

Resolved: I find a way.

August 2

"Under the pressure of trial and responsibility we are often stronger than when there is no pressure."

—Mark Rutherford

Kids need to learn to play under pressure just as adults do. "Nickel Sinks" is a good game for teaching youngsters how to putt and play under stress.

It is a betting game. But the stakes are very mild. Every time a player sinks a one-putt, the other players in the group give him or her a nickel. Sometimes everybody wins on a hole; sometimes no one does. Nickels are given and taken back according to how one performs. It is highly possible for a person to play an entire 18 holes of Nickel Sinks and spend only a quarter.

It is remarkable what you can find out about people when they must perform under pressure. Some love it. Others simply cannot stand it. For them the fear of failure is too much. They worry about screwing up in some horrible way and so they refrain from playing at all.

This is the worst possible outcome for kids. It is always better for them to play than not to play. The rewards are so much greater.

Play Nickel Sinks. Kids as well as adults will profit from it. The monetary rewards are small, but the potential for learning to cope with pressure is vast.

Resolved: I play Nickel Sinks.

August 3

"One of the basic lessons of golf is take what you can get."

—Jim Litke

Be realistic. Take what you can get.

Accept the situation as it is. Take what you can get.

Accept weather conditions as they are. Take what you can get.

Seize opportunity. Take what you can get.

Be cautious or bold. Be stubborn or flexible. Shrewdly evaluate the circumstances. Take what you can get.

Aim high, if high is what you can get. Never sell yourself short. But take what you can get until you can get something better.

Accept the existence of a dynamically changing golf universe. Take what you can get.

Accept that things may not always go your way. Take what you can get.

Avoid absolutes. Take what you can get.

Play within the rules, but take what you can get.

Seize the moment. Take what you can get.

Adapt and overcome. Take what you can get.

Know your abilities. Know your strengths and weaknesses. Take what you can get.

Go against the odds. Fight conventional wisdom. Take what you can get.

When things begin to go your way on the golf course, take what you can get. And then some.

Resolved: I take what I can get.

August 4

Maybe you were good when you were younger. Then life intervened, and you let your golf drop.

Here is a goal for you: Play better than you did when you were young and didn't know any better. If you are 30, play better than when you were on the college team. If you are 50, earn a lower handicap than when you were 30. If you are 70, drive the ball farther than you did in your 20s and 30s.

What? That's impossible, you say? Not so. Paul Runyan, for one, could drive the ball farther at the age of 70 than he could when he was winning championships as a tour player.

It is well documented how Olympic swimmers have retired from competition in their early 20s, then returned to the pool in their 30s and 40s and beaten the times they turned in in their so-called athletic "primes." It is the same with many runners and track stars. Prime is what you make it.

We golfers are lucky because we play a game where you truly can get better with age. We can be what we used to be, and more.

Resolved: I play better than I did when I was younger and foolish.

August 5

Enjoy your game. And when you do something really fine, celebrate it.

When Hale Irwin sunk a 60-foot birdie putt to tie for the lead on the final hole of regulation in the 1990 U.S. Open, he took a spontaneous victory lap around the 18th green, slapping high fives with the spectators.

That's a good rule of thumb. Make a 60-foot birdie putt, take a victory lap.

Other golfers, upon winning tournaments, have plunged merrily into nearby water hazards, sometimes dragging their happy caddies with them.

Jump in a lake. Take a victory lap. Buy a round for your buddies. Hell, buy a round for the bar.

How you do it is up to you. Just be sure to do it. Golf is a tense, demanding sport that requires a chess master's concentration. It is good to release all that bottled-up emotion at the appropriate time and place—and maybe even at an inappropriate time and place. (You be the judge of that.)

A celebration taking place also assumes something else: that there is something worth celebrating.

Do something grand today. Then go out and celebrate.

Resolved: I sink a long birdie putt on 18, then I take a victory lap.

August 6

Never walk away from a hot streak.

Nobody knows for sure why a hot streak starts or ends. All we can know is this: If you walk away from one, you are spurning a gift from the gods.

Playing well? Keep playing. Play as much as you can. Play whenever you can. The way to keep a hot streak going is to play.

When you receive this gift do not respond with a puzzled look and ask, "Why me?" Open the package, smile broadly, and say thank you. Who more than you deserves such good fortune?

A hot streak will show you how good you really are. It is as if a curtain has been lifted and behind it is the player you know you are. Past and future concerns are swept aside. You are living and playing in the fully realized, electrically charged present.

A hot streak may last a few weeks, a few rounds, or a few hours. Use that time to springboard your game up to a higher level, the level where you truly belong.

Every day you walk on the course, the possibility exists that you will get on a hot streak.

Today is your day. Today you get it going. Today you play like you've never played before.

Resolved: When I get on a hot streak I run with it.

August 7

"First thought, best thought."

—Allen Ginsberg

Golf would become much less of a cerebral exercise if we followed our first thought and ignored our second, third, fourth, and fifth thoughts. In time these afterthoughts, stung by your repeated rejections, would sulk away like an unhappy suitor and leave us alone.

Observe these "firsts" the next time you play:

Follow your first read on the green and trust it.

Hit the club you pick first and trust it.

Do whatever pops into your mind first—play it safe, take a risk, whatever—and trust it.

Expect some tough slogging initially. Following first thoughts takes discipline and courage. Those second and third and fourth thoughts have had their way so long they will not like the way you are treating them. They will harass your first thought and call it crazy or stupid or worse. It could get pretty nasty for a while.

It is well worth the effort, though. Listen to your first thoughts. Let them lead you down a path of greater confidence and more inspired play.

Resolved: I follow my first thoughts.

August 8

"The most important thing on the golf course is executing that first shot. Then that shot is gone and your next shot is the most important shot."

—Greg Norman

Norman is talking shots. Let's talk pars.

A traditional motivational technique is to tell yourself: "One." Jog one lap. Do one repetition. Write one page. Once you do one of whatever you are doing, numbers two, three, four, etc. will come.

In golf, make one par. Start with one. Or, if you are an exceptional player, make one birdie. Once you get that first one under your belt, others will follow.

Your most important par is your first one. You can get a second only after you get the first. Get that first par and then go get another. And another. And another.

Resolved: I get that first par.

August 9

"Mighty things from small beginnings grow."

—John Dryden

Beginnings are everything. Make that first short putt.

Success breeds success. Make that first short putt.

Make that first short putt on the first hole today and it could provide the springboard for an entire afternoon of made putts.

This is what Ken Venturi thinks—and tries to do. "On short putts, grind hard on the first one of the day," he says. "The result will set your confidence level for the rest of the round."

Grind hard. Make that first short putt.

Set your confidence level for the rest of the round. Make that first short putt.

Make that first short putt and get your motor running.

Make that first short putt and make a whole bunch of putts after that, long and short.

Resolved: I work hard to make my first short putt.

August 10

"What matters is not the size of the dog in the fight, but the size of the fight in the dog."

—Bear Bryant

You are in the match of your life against the best player you have ever played.

Refuse to lose.

He is up a hole with two holes left to play. You are being tested as you have never been tested before.

Refuse to lose.

The 17th green. You are on in two. He has a sure four. If you miss he wins the match.

Refuse to lose.

You make the putt. Your birdie 3 sends it to 18, dead even.

Refuse to lose.

You hit. He hits. Your Titleist outrolls his in the cultivated grass.

His 9-iron approach is pretty as a picture. It spins back toward the pin as if it's controlled by a string. You need one just as pretty.

Refuse to lose.

You hit it on the nail. It stops inside his ball.

Shaken, he misses his birdie putt from eight feet away. Now it is your turn. You step up. All the marbles are riding on this one stroke.

Now let's talk about the size of the fight in *this* dog.

Resolved: I refuse to lose.

August 11

"I just came here to play golf and got lucky and won. Everybody knows I'm a Cinderella story."

—John Daly

One of the truly great days in the history of golf and sports. August 11, 1991. John Daly caps four days of astounding, improbable, awe-inspiring golf to win the PGA Championship at Crooked Stick Golf Club outside Indianapolis.

The man with the big stick wins at Crooked Stick, at 7,300 yards one of the longest layouts for a major tournament ever. What was Daly's secret?

"All four days, I didn't think, I just hit it," he said. His caddy's name was Squeaky, and Squeaky told him all he needed to know: "Squeaky said 'Kill,' and I killed it."

Age 25, Daly came out of nowhere. He was a Tour rookie with a big driver but not much else. It has become part of golfing lore that he was not even supposed to play in the tournament. Earlier in the week he was ninth on the list of alternates. By Wednesday eight had dropped out and he was first alternate. Daly got in the car and drove all night from Memphis, still not knowing if he was going to play. He reached Indianapolis at 2:30 Thursday morning. He made a call and found out that one more person had dropped out—Nick Price, to be with his wife for the birth of their first child—and that he was in. He had never seen Crooked Stick before.

Two swing thoughts for the day, in honor of John Daly's grand achievement:

Don't think, just hit.

Surprise people.

Resolved: I surprise people today.

August 12

"You must swing smoothly to play well. And you must be relaxed to swing smoothly."

—Bobby Jones

Concentration is vital to good golf. Focus on what you need to do and do it. But be careful. You can focus so much that you can get out of focus.

Physicians call it "focal dystonia." Your vision does not actually become blurry. What happens is that an intense form of concentration causes an abnormal or irregular action of the muscles. It happens to basketball players who tighten up on the free-throw line and miss the basket. It happens to billiards players and, of course, golfers.

There are physical limits to focus. Limits to how much you can concentrate on a given thing. And if you concentrate too hard it can harm your performance.

To avoid this, play easy. Let your mind freely wander at the appropriate times. Take your mind off golf for a moment. Share a laugh with your partners. Walk down the center of the fairway and drink in the beauty of the day.

You cannot stay in a highly focused state every minute of every hole. It wouldn't be desirable even if you could. You have to let go. You have to let the mental part of you out to play, along with the physical side. Otherwise it will bang against your interior walls and cause a frightful disturbance.

Allow yourself to relax when you are playing. Allow your mind to wander freely when the moment permits. This will sharpen your focus and intensify your concentration when you step up to hit.

Resolved: I find ways to relax even during periods of intense concentration.

August 13

"Be brave, be bold, and take your best shot."

   —Gay Brewer, advising amateurs on how to play in pro-ams

Peter Andrews asked some pros for their advice on how amateur golfers can hold up their end of the bargain in a pro-am. Here are their choicest tips:

Play the same as you always do. Trying to impress the pro will only create problems for yourself. Stick with the tried and true, at least during the tournament.

Go easy on yourself. If you walk up to the first tee talking about how many pars you are going to make that day, you are putting unnecessary pressure on yourself.

Play to your handicap. As Mason Rudolph says, "A 17 who tries to play like a good 17 can be a lot of help. But when he tries to play like a 12, he ends up hitting like a 22, and then he's no use to anybody."

Take enough stick. Amateurs tend to underclub themselves in pro-ams.

Relax. Nerves can make you tense up and throw your game off. Play at your usual tempo and speed.

Give your driver a two- or three-hole tryout. Chuck it if it isn't working. You will do fine with other clubs.

Finally, the best advice is worth keeping in mind not just for pro-ams but for every time you play:

Be brave. Be bold. Take your best shot. Forget about the pro. Forget what he is doing. Go out and do your best.

Resolved: I am brave, I am bold, I take my best shot.

August 14

"Nobody wants to win more than I do. But if I give it my best shot and fail, then life goes on. Golf, in the final analysis, is only a game."

—Jack Nicklaus

Over the years the greatest golfer in the history of the game developed an attitude he calls "positive fatalism," meaning:

You try as hard as you can. You give it your best shot. You do your best to win.

But:

Nobody wins everything. Everybody loses. If you lose it is not the end of the world. There will be other matches, other tournaments, other days.

You fight like hell to win. But you recognize the possibility of defeat. This is positive fatalism.

You may lose a tournament. But nothing and no one can defeat *you*. This is also positive fatalism.

Nicklaus said the attitude helped him stay cool as a tournament headed into its final holes. "You can enjoy and relish the experience [of competition] without getting traumatic about its consequences," he said, adding that this approach helped him focus better on the task at hand, too. Pressure can make you do funny things. By remembering that it's only a game, that there will be a tomorow, that life goes on, you can focus more sharply on what you need to do today to produce positive results.

Resolved: I develop an attitude of positive fatalism.

August 15

"If you can see a fairway out there for 300 yards and your caddie tells you to hit it down the middle, what else do you need to know?"

—Joey Sindelar

That is all anyone needs to know. Get it in the fairway.

Playing a tournament? Want to put pressure on the rest of the field? Get it in the fairway.

Want to take the pressure off yourself? And stay relaxed? Get it in the fairway.

Few things in golf are as disappointing as following a good putt with a less-than-stellar drive. You walk onto the tee flushed with success. You walk off crushed.

Concentrate on this simple thing after a good putt: Get it in the fairway.

Golf is a difficult game, but the road to success is clear. It's green, it's grassy, it's mowed.

You will get off the fairway. It's inevitable. When you get off, get back on. It's a good habit to develop. You never know when you will *need* to get a ball in the fairway. The more you cultivate the habit in your leisure, the more likely you are to do it under pressure.

Another way of saying "Get it in the fairway" is "Keep it in play." Keep yourself on the right track. Stay in the flow of your game. Getting the ball in the fairway, keeping it in play, is a form of staying on task, an external embodiment of your inner directedness.

Build on the things you accomplished the previous hole. Start this one right. Get it in the fairway.

Resolved: I get it in the fairway.

August 16

"Practice yourself for heaven's sake, in little things; and thence proceed to greater."

—Epictetus

Before he reached his 40th birthday, Nick Faldo estimated that he had hit 7 million balls in his life. That's a lot of balls.

This means that Nick has averaged 175,000 balls per year—that is, if you include his infant and toddler years, when even Nick would have been hard-pressed to hit a full 175,000 per year.

If we subtract those tender early years and assume that Nick, like most babies, did not spend the bulk of his time on a practice range, we arrive at an even more impressive average of 189,000 balls per year (rounded figure).

Hitting 189,000 balls over a year computes to 15,750 balls a week. His daily average is 2,250. Remember: This is every day, every week, every month of his life.

So Faldo whacks 2,250 balls a day—ignoring rainouts, travel days, vacations, injury, rest periods, and the like, which would, of course, boost his average higher. Now, for the sake of argument let's just assume that Nick is a light sleeper and logs only five hours a night. That means he hits an average of 118 balls per waking hour, or nearly two balls a minute for virtually every minute of his waking life.

One way of looking at it is that while you have been reading this page (est. time: five minutes) Nick has hit 10 balls. Better get busy. You've got a lot of catching up to do.

Resolved: I hit some balls today.

August 17

"The most important factor in playing a championship is to be fully prepared."

—Ben Hogan

How's this for preparation? When Ben Hogan was on the Tour in the 1950s, it was said that he charted out his round—shot by shot—in his motel room each night before he played.

That may be a bit much for most people. But Harv Penick has some solid suggestions for golfers preparing to play a big match. They are good even for golfers who are not competing in a tournament but who want to play their best on a given day. They include:

Stick to your normal routine. Eat the same as you always do the night before, at the same time. If you hit the sack normally at 10 P.M., hit it at 10. A sudden change of habits is what throws the body—and mind—off.

In the same vein, warm up as usual. Whatever you do normally to warm up, warm up that way.

No last-minute changes of grip or swing. What got you there must be pretty good, or at least work on some level. So stick with it.

Most important, "put the results of the big match out of your thoughts," says Harv. The worst thing to do is dream about what would happen if . . . Stick to business, the shot that is in front of you, and good luck!

Resolved: I stick to my normal routine on a big day.

August 18

"Your game counts for you and mine for me. In other words, look out for Number One."

—Gene Sarazen

Look out for Number One.

It is a powerful, raw, almost primal sentiment—and essential for winning golf tournaments.

You have to want it more than the other person. You have to want it so bad it goes beyond the realm of desire into need.

Bob Toski, the golf teacher and former touring pro, puts it this way: "When I play I am into myself. I am selfish, self-centered, mean. I want to beat somebody. I want to beat them all I can. Everybody who is a player of any renown is selfish."

Selfish, self-centered, mean. Another way to say it: Nice guys finish last.

Before and after the tournament be Clark Kent. During the tournament be Superman with an attitude. Be charming and gracious when accepting the winner's trophy.

If being selfish helps you shoot birdies, be selfish. Let your ego go on an 18-hole rampage.

Many of the game's greats have been accused at one time or another of being selfish: Nicklaus, Sarazen, Hogan, Greg Norman. Don't worry what others call you, as long as they call you "winner."

Selfishness does not mean expecting to win every time out and throwing a tantrum if you don't. But it does mean: Get yours. Get it because you deserve it. Respond when challenged. Always make your best effort. Demand nothing less of yourself.

Resolved: I look out for Number One.

August 19

"One can go a long way after one is tired."

—Proverb

Those who say golf requires little physical stamina have obviously never played 18 holes on a hot and humid afternoon in August.

On the 15th or 16th hole, toward the end of the third or fourth hour, on an afternoon pocked by long, restless periods of inactivity followed by bursts of adrenaline, the sun still up and blazing, walking, the shirt and pants damp with sweat, the clubs heavy as a bag of rocks and the strap digging into your shoulder, the arms and legs weary, the eyes nearly blurry from so much concentrated *seeing*—a body does get tired.

But there is a mental as well as a physical component to finishing up strong.

You feel tired. You're beat. You're ready to throw in the towel. Now watch what happens if you shoot a birdie or do something exceptional.

Where's that fatigue now? In all likelihood, it has vanished with the wind—swept away in the sudden wave of enthusiasm you feel from sinking that 35-foot putt or holing that chip off the green.

Remember this the next time you are struggling on the backside of a long, long day. You are one stroke away from energy, one stroke away from new life. All you need to do is tap into your latent energy, pop the cork. One stroke will do it. Keep firing away. You can still accomplish great things when you're tired.

Resolved: I keep firing away.

August 20

—"Ace" in *West Side Story*

It is the dead of August and it is hot, real hot. Fry-egg-on-the-sidewalk hot. Be like Ace. When the heat is on, play it cool.

Studies have shown that people do strange things in the heat. A Rice University study of 260 cities showed that when the temperature rose above 90 degrees, the violent-crime rate jumped 7 percent. Police are well aware of this phenomenon. People are outside more in the heat. They drink more alcohol during the day. It is a potent mix.

Even if you do not tend toward violent crime, you should recognize the effects of heat and adjust your play accordingly.

Play in the early morning if you can get up. Or late in the afternoon or twilight time. If you can't beat the heat, at least you can avoid it.

Take a cart. Even if you are dead set against the infernal mechanical contraptions, it may be wise in extremely high temperatures. You can bring along cool drinks.

Some people love the heat and flourish in it. Others do not. Figure how you fit in this scheme and adapt. Maybe nine holes or a light practice is all you care to do.

Realize that the heat can affect your mood, your energy, your level of play. The same as with your partners. Patience seems to be the first casualty in the heat. Take all of this into account, and give yourselves the benefit of the doubt.

Maintain an even keel. Hot, cold, windy, or whatever, play your game whatever the weather's like.

Resolved: I stay cool in the heat.

August 21

"Nothing great was ever achieved without enthusiasm."
—Ralph Waldo Emerson

Nick Price was going through one of those spells we all go through—when the game seems less a game and more an ordeal to be endured. Eighteen holes of agony.

Price, who has won a pair of major titles and a host of minor ones, missed the cut at two consecutive tournaments, the second of which was the Masters. This forced him into a reckoning. "I just need some time off, pure and simple," he explained. "I've got to try to stop the problem I've been having, which is not enjoying myself on the course."

This is a marvelous insight. It explains much about Price's greatness as a golfer and how he achieved it. His game was having problems. To solve them he did not need to work on his long game or his short game or his game in between. He did not need to *work* at all. What he needed most was to restore his enthusiasm for playing.

His solution? Take a little time off. Get that enthusiasm back.

Technique, without enthusiasm, is like a body without a beating heart. It's lifeless, dead. Enthusiasm is the wellspring, the source; everything good in golf flows from it. Enthusiasm, desire, the love of playing for its own sake—these are the hallmarks of a champion.

It is possible that you may also suffer from a lack of enthusiasm from time to time. Simply follow Nick Price's prescription when you do: Take some time off. There's no harm in it at all. The game will be waiting for you when you come back.

Resolved: I take some time off when I need it.

August 22

"I have an incredible feeling of respect for the touring pros. I'm a sports buff anyway, but golf is something special. You're alone out there. You get no help from a teammate passing the ball."

—Jack Lemmon

The PGA, LPGA, and Senior tours are like the circus. Sooner or later they will come to a town near you. When one of them does, go check it out. They all put on a good show.

Pop quiz: Say you want to go to a men's tournament. You want to really get close to the players and breathe their air, so to speak. What day should you attend?

Sundays are a zoo. Fergeddit. All those bodies competing for the same space—you get enough of that trying to get a seat on the commuter train to work. Saturdays are equally bad. It's a weekend. Everybody comes out on the weekends.

Thursdays and Fridays are better, but if you really want to see what the pros do and how they do it, go on a Wednesday. That's practice day. The tournament hasn't started; the pressure's off. On a Wednesday every pro is like Fred Couples: relaxed, convivial, easygoing.

Even better, you can get right up there. It's you, the gallery rope, and, 10 feet away, your favorite pro. You can see how he handles himself, how he sets up, how he swings. And you can watch all this largely unimpeded by the jostlings of unpleasant concentrations of humanity. You can watch Fred, stroll over and see Greg, check out John, wander over to see Davis, and then amble back Fred's way. Wednesdays, now that's the ticket.

Resolved: I check out a Tour event on a Wednesday.

August 23

"There are times when your mind starts going the other way, and you can't do that. You have to get your mind to go the right way and not have those bad thoughts. I have to tell myself, 'Focus, Monica, focus.'"

—Monica Seles

Certainly the bad thoughts that plague Monica Seles are far worse than what troubles most of us. Her mind returns to April 30, 1993, when a lunatic stabbed her on a Hamburg, Germany, tennis court and nearly killed her.

She has thankfully come back from the physical and psychological wounds that threatened to end her championship tennis career. But it was no easy job. It took more than two years before she played competitive tennis again.

Though she is back and playing, Monica says she still "backtracks" and falls into dark moods. She is an upbeat, positive person. But she would have to be superhuman not to think about what happened and the terrifying prospect that lurking in some crowd somewhere is a person who might want to do it again.

But she refuses to dwell. She refuses to let her mind slip backward for long. She has made a commitment to go on with her life. Fear will not stop her. Bad thoughts will not overwhelm her or control her. She will stay focused on the many positive aspects of her life, and go on.

Golfers can learn much from Monica Seles, both by her inspirational example and her ability to cast out negative thoughts and focus, always focus, on her athletic mission.

Resolved: I tell myself "Focus, focus" when my mind starts going the other way.

August 24

"You can get caught up in being too nice and just playing along. You have days when you need to turn it on."

—Nick Faldo

Nick Faldo is one of the world's great golfers and, especially when he was younger, he had one of the world's great tempers.

One English writer tells about running into him on a practice green at Augusta National after Faldo had shot 5 over par in the Masters. The writer asked about his round and Faldo lit into him with a volley of unprintable remarks. Later the golfer apologized to the writer.

Faldo has talked about his temper to other writers. "I know when I've gone too far," he says. "Sometimes I say to myself, 'Oh, shut up.'" We've all heard those nagging voices. Sometimes that's what you have to do: Simply tell them to shut up.

But the issue of anger is more complex than that. It can be a positive. In fact, it works for Faldo as an inspirational tool. "I need [it] to kick myself up the backside to get myself going. Otherwise I mope around and nothing happens."

We all know what that's like too. We've all had those days. Nothing is happening; you're moping around. It's like you've missed your morning coffee. You have no energy, no pep. For Faldo at least, getting really ticked off can bring him out of this low-energy state and charge him up.

There is nothing wrong with an honest display of emotion, even in the stoical world of golf. You *can* be too nice for your own good. Let it all out and see what happens then. It may be just what your game needs.

Resolved: I make my anger work for me.

August 25

"A great victor, in defeat as great. No more, no less, always himself in both."

—Stephen Vincent Benét

Okay, you lost.

You went out, you played. You entered a tournament. You did not do so well, or the other people played better. In any case, you got beat.

It hurts, doesn't it? It's disappointing. Even if you did your best, it's hard to take. *Especially* if you did your best.

Life goes on. That's the first thing. There's always tomorrow. As long as you're still upright and drawing in O_2 you have a chance to come back.

But you don't much feel like platitudes at this point, do you? You keep thinking back on what happened. What went wrong, how it could have been different. You'd like to get right back on the course and try it again. You'd like to have a few of those shots back.

Or maybe you just want to forget it. Look to the future. That's okay too.

Losing is instructional. It teaches hard lessons. But it ultimately only matters if you give in to it and quit. Quitting is the only lesson from losing that fails to teach. Quit, and you really do lose.

What we learn from losing is how much we care. It would not hurt so much if we didn't care so much. In what other activities in our lives do we care as much as we do about golf? We are lucky for our passion, our commitment, our caring. A mere defeat cannot and will not change that.

Resolved: I accept my loss and move on.

August 26

"Hard heads suffer much."

—Albanian proverb

You push and push and push and push. You want to get better. You want to be a good golfer, maybe even a great golfer. So you push and push and push and push.

It's not your day. You know it from the first tee. But you push and push and push and push.

You're tired. Your head's not in it. But you know what you have to do, and damned if you're not going to do it. So you push and push and push and push.

Then you push and push and push some more. Nothing has changed. You're still not with it and you're never going to get with it. So what do you do?

You push and push and push and push. When you come to a wall you push against it. Doesn't matter how tall or wide or thick that wall is. You are going to push and push and push until the wall topples over, or you do. Because that is what you do: You push and push and push.

That is, in fact, what you have been doing all day long. Pushing your drives, pushing your putts, pushing yourself. And what has it gotten you? Very little, especially in relation to the effort expended. The wall is still standing, and your head and arms and legs hurt from all that heavy labor.

Here's a thought: Why not ease up a little? Go easy on yourself. Do not push so hard or so much. It will do wonders for your state of mind and your game.

Resolved: I ease up a little.

August 27

"By logic and reason we die hourly; by imagination we live."
—J. B. Yeats, in a letter to his son, William

This was a test conducted by university researchers (probably paid for by taxpayer money):

A basketball team was divided into two groups of equal free-throw-shooting abilities. One group spent a designated period of time practicing their free throws. They stood at the line and shot baskets.

The other group spent the same time imagining themselves shooting free throws. Not shooting them physically, just sitting in a room and watching the ball go swish in their minds. They did not pick up a basketball or take a shot. They created mental pictures of success.

Then both groups held a contest to test their respective free-throw-shooting skills. The Imagineers versus the Pragmatics in a free-throw-shooting battle to the finish.

Do we need to tell you which team won?

Now or whenever, spend a little time today imagining those three-foot putts going in. One after another, right into the cup. It may be the best thing you've ever done for your putting game.

Resolved: I picture myself on the greens at my course, making putts.

August 28

"Embrace simplicity."

—Lao-tzu

One thought, one club. Embrace simplicity.

One club, one thought. Embrace simplicity.

The experts say we "should"—there's that word again—have a different address for our driver than for our fairway woods, and a different address still for our long irons, and yet another address for a pitch shot, and one more address for our chips.

Those are a lot of addresses to remember. It is easy to see how we get confused. And we haven't even gotten into the placement of the ball, club selection, environmental factors such as the wind, distance to the pin, backswing, downswing, grip, position of the head, follow-through, etc.

The best advice is this: Embrace simplicity.

Dwell on the complications and you are making the game harder than it needs to be. Find a way to reduce those complications into a simple, coherent philosophy and you will play better golf. Here is a way:

One thought, one club.

Step up to the ball with one thought and one thought only. Let your key be the fact that you are hitting with one club.

One club, one thought. Embrace simplicity. Focus on one thing when you hit, and make that thought a successful one.

Resolved: I focus on one thing when I hit.

August 29

"Worry is impatience."

—Austin O'Malley

Worry, worry, worry. Golfers worry about everything. Their clubs, their swing, their grip, the weather, the height of the fairway grass, the condition of the greens, putting, putting, putting, who they're playing with, green fees, blisters, their short game, their long game—on and on and on and on.

Does it ever do any good?

Worry gets you nowhere in golf. Worry leads to obsession over details, and details are like ivy on a brick wall. Gradually the insidious green leaves spread across the wall, subvert its integrity, and pull it down.

If, as the philosopher suggests, worry is a form of impatience, it becomes even more debilitating to the golfer. Impatience causes a person to rush, the worst of all golfing sins. An impatient person is also an intolerant person, and tolerance, in golf and in life, is a thing to be cultivated.

Forget worry (at least for the hours you're playing golf). Forget the niggling details. Life is too short. Just go out and knock the crap out of the ball.

Resolved: I worry less, a lot less, about my game.

August 30

"Your mind works the best when you're the happiest."
—Peter Thomson, five-time British Open winner

Here's a novel approach to shotmaking: Shoot the shot that will make you happiest. Let happiness be your guide.

You are the one who is going to have to live with the shot you make. Let happiness dictate your choice of club and the way you play it.

If you logically think you should lay it up but going for the flag will make you happier, shoot for the flag. If experience tells you to leave your driver in the bag but you want so much to play it anyhow, put your happiness first and grab that big stick.

What, you say going for the flag could get you into trouble? But so could playing it safe. No one knows until you hit. Let your actions be ruled by the happiness they bring you at the time they occur.

Decide to shoot the shot that will make you happiest. Say to yourself, "I am going to put myself first. I am going to choose the club that I want to play, play it in the way I want to play it, and let everything else take care of itself."

Results are impossible to foresee. Nor are they always an accurate measure of performance. Sometimes you can play really well and your score does not reflect it. Focus on the before of a shot, not solely on the after. Play the shot that makes you happiest, and you will always have internal justification for whatever you do in golf. And with *that*, results hold far less meaning.

Resolved: I play the shot that makes me happy.

August 31

"Where Sam Snead excels is in always being able to enjoy the game—in playing it as much for fun as for a living."

—Jack Nicklaus

One can learn much from Samuel Jackson Snead. It was said that he never took a week off when he was active; he always had a game going. He loved to play, because for him it *was* play.

Not a job.

Not solely exercise.

Not even recreation.

Play.

He once played a round using a stick as his golf club. He shot a 68. (This was in homage to his West Virginia roots where, according to legend—a legend he assiduously cultivated—the young Snead learned to play using the branch of a swamp maple tree.) He once played tradition-bound Augusta National in his bare feet.

Snead played well into his old age; and he played *well*, too. He won PGA titles in his 20s, 30s, 40s, and 50s. He won Senior titles in his 60s and 70s. When he wasn't playing for money in a PGA tournament he was playing for money somewhere else. Snead said he lost interest in the game if he did not have a few side bets going. This was another way he always kept the game a game.

Not a job.

Not solely exercise.

Not even recreation.

Play.

Resolved: I play a round in my bare feet.

September 1

"Continuity of purpose is one of the most essential ingredients of happiness."

—Stephen Mackenna

Play golf with a purpose.

Have fun if the purpose is to have fun. Be serious if your goal is to shoot low scores. Maybe you want to have fun *and* shoot low scores. Well, then make *that* your purpose for playing golf.

You will get more out of golf if you are clear what you want from it. Muddled people make for muddled golfers.

The disappointment some people feel with golf comes not from the game but their own unclear intentions. Be straight with yourself and the game will be straight with you.

Do you want to be the next Phil Mickelson or Ernie Els? Go for it.

Or did you take the game up for mainly social reasons? That's great too. Get involved at your club or course. Go out and meet people.

Or are you a recreational-type player who likes the exercise, being outdoors, having a few laughs?

You will be clear about how to reach your desired ends in golf if you are clear what those ends are. Recreational and social players cannot reasonably get too upset with themselves if they do not shoot par golf. That is not why they are in the game. They are in it for other reasons.

Establish your purpose for playing golf. Once that is clear in your mind, everything will fall easily into place.

Resolved: I play golf with a clear purpose.

September 2

"I have always been delighted at the prospect of a new day, a fresh try, one more start, with perhaps a bit of magic waiting somewhere behind the morning."

—J. B. Priestley

The Top Ten reasons why you should get out of bed and play golf this morning:

10. You will never make a birdie from your bed (dreams don't count).
9. Your biorhythms are perkier in the A.M.
8. Fewer cars on the road reduces the likelihood of a tension-inducing traffic jam.
7. You can get out of bed and out of the house before the wife even notices.
6. You can see the sunrise. (What, you'd rather watch the backs of your eyelids?)
5. Fewer golfers on the course reduces the likelihood of your normal six-hour round.
4. You can make up stories about how well you played, and with fewer people around, there is less chance of someone contradicting it.
3. You can feel smugly superior about playing while others are home in bed.
2. The sooner you get out there the sooner you're able to forget what you did yesterday on the course.
1. What better way to start the day than with golf?

Resolved: I get up and go play golf.

September 3

*"I owe much to my friends; but, all things considered, it strikes
me that I owe even more to my enemies. The real person
springs to life under a sting, even better than under a caress."*
—André Gide

It is a cliché of sports when a team unites against an evil
owner (or manager) to win the championship. The team may
even have been floundering in the depths until the blackguard
presented himself, spurring it to previously undreamed
heights.

The competitive golfer can learn from this. Take motivation where you can get it, even if it is a negative. Turn the negative into a positive, such as:

A poor starting time? Those officials are out to get me. I'll
show them.

A player is criticizing my swing. Says he doesn't respect my
game. Here, respect this.

They're counting me out after a bad round? Don't count
me out.

The course setup favors another type of player. Let me give
you all a lesson in adaptability.

It may not make you popular at cocktail parties, but a contrary nature is a valuable asset in athletics. Show a stubborn
resistance to the forces that oppose you.

Show resistance and then turn these forces in your favor,
the way Robin Hood invited Big John to join his band after
outsparring him on the bridge. The people who oppose you
will become your allies once they realize they have met an
insuperable foe.

Resolved: I turn a negative into a positive.

September 4

Be aggressive. Serve humanity. Better still, serve your golf game.

There is a rather indelicate sporting phrase, frequently called upon by Cro-Magnonesque football coaches in their locker-room pep talks, which goes like this:

"LET'S KICK BUTT AND TAKE NO PRISONERS!"

Now, the question for the day is: Does a phrase of this nature have a place in the gentlemanly and gentlewomanly game of golf?

We believe it does, for these reasons:

Match play. The game is not always against the course. Sometimes it is against another player whom you must beat.

Frequently money is at stake. Sometimes some well-channeled aggression can do wonders for your pocketbook.

If it works, use it. You may be one of those who play better when on the attack.

Skeptics will argue that it is impossible to maintain such an aggressive posture over an entire 18 holes. Furthermore, situations and conditions change. While an aggressive approach may be called for in one instance, it is foolish to apply it in all cases.

Well, you know what a football coach would say to these skeptics: "LET'S KICK THEIR BUTTS!"

Resolved: I kick butt and take no prisoners.

September 5

"If you stop struggling, then you stop life."

—Huey Newton

I accept struggle. I push on.

There are days when it is just not happening—when every club is the wrong club, when every shot is the wrong one.

Today may be one of those days. I accept it. I push on.

Or: I may start off great. I may be walking on air the first five holes.

Then . . .

The wings come off. I go down, down, down. Disaster City.

But I accept it. I push on. And work hard at getting airborne again.

There are times when I am having no fun at all. When consistency eludes me. When my swing deserts me. When everything escapes me but the water on 15.

I accept it all. And push on.

I accept it and push on because I know good times are coming. I know I am going to get loose yet. I know I am going to turn it around. I know I am going to start making putts. I know the ball is going to bounce my way.

I struggle because I am not satisfied. I know I am a better player than I am showing. But I push on. I know I will get there yet. And when I do, look out world!

Resolved: I push on.

September 6

"Golf can be a funny thing. Somehow you just hit your stride. You do a couple of little things and out of the blue you're on track."

—Randy Haag, top amateur golfer

Today, take care of the little things and get your game on track.

A little thing can be as simple as keeping your eye on the ball when you swing, staying down with it, and then rising up to watch its flight as you complete your follow-through.

The same for putting. Concentrate on staying down with the ball and keeping your eyes fixed on the ball as you make a firm stroke. That is a little thing.

A little thing can be trusting your reads. A little thing can be sinking a tricky three-foot putt. Bearing down on it and making it and getting a boost from it that carries over into the rest of your game.

Little things can lead to big things. That is how big things are accomplished: through a succession of successfully completed little things. Look at a pro when she's having trouble. She leaves the Tour for a while to consult with her swing guru. What does the guru advise her on? The little things. The little things that make a big difference. Then she returns to the Tour with the little things back in place.

Fix your sights only on the stars and you will stay earthbound. Attend to the million and one little things that go into the building of a rocket ship, and you will soar beyond the Milky Way.

Resolved: I take care of the little things.

September 7

"When lining up a putt, try to envision the path your ball will travel to the hole."

—Pete Nathan, teaching pro

Before you putt today, see the putt. See the path that your ball will travel into the hole.

You may have trouble doing this. You may just see the putting surface as the green expanse between your ball and the hole, as hard to read as the ocean.

But your ball *will* follow a path, there can be no doubt of that. Your job is to put it on the path that will carry it into the hole. It is important to realize that the path already exists. It is right there, on the green. You just have to see it.

A person lining up a putt is not inventing the path to the hole. He or she is simply trying to find something that already exists.

There is no right and wrong in putting. There is only finding the path or not finding the path. Those who find the path make the putt.

Everything starts with this vision of line. Once you see the putt, you can make the putt.

See the putt as a movie unfolding before your eyes. Rewind the tape. See the ball hop out of the hole and watch the line it travels back to where it started.

The line *is* there. See it, then set the ball off on its destined course. That is how you will make your putts today.

Resolved: I see the ball into the hole.

September 8

*"If you realize too acutely how heavenly valuable time is, you
  are too paralyzed to do anything."*

—Katherine Butler Hathaway

Most golfers have precious little time when it comes to the
game they love. Only the lucky few can play it when they
want, for as long as they want, without regard to the clock.
The rest of us struggle to squeeze in as much time on the
course as we can.

As a result, we put a lot of pressure on ourselves. There is
pressure to play well, pressure to have fun. Pressure to get in
a full 18, pressure even to relax. We put pressure on ourselves
not to feel pressured.

All of this is a function of time. Would we feel so harried
if we were schoolkids on summer vacation just playing to
play? Of course not. We feel the pressure because we want to
maximize the time we have.

And this causes frustration. Our golf time is so valuable,
and look at how we spend it! Hitting bogeys and balls all over
the place and playing miserably. We want to play well in the
limited time we have. A bad round disgusts us as much for
our poor play as for the time we have seemingly wasted.

The best way to get the pressure off your golf game is to
make more time for it.

The time we spend on a golf course is never enough. But
it *is* something, and it is enough to enjoy ourselves if we give
ourselves the chance. Feel relaxed about the time you spend
playing golf. And the next time you go out, conclude your day
by making a date to play again.

Resolved: I relax about the time I have to play.

September 9

"He never tried to put me down. He always tried to put me up."
—NBA guard Avery Johnson, on the influence of his dad on his
early basketball career

Be a positive person. Put yourself up, not down. When you play with others, put them up, not down.

Let this philosophy extend to the people you play with.

Think about your normal partners.

Think about your teaching pro.

Think about your spouse, your parents, your children, or other family relations you play with from time to time.

Think about your other golf partners—your colleagues at work, friends, even strangers who may have walked on and rounded out your foursome.

Do they put you up . . . or down?

Why are you playing with them if it's the latter? Do you have to?

Agreed. Sometimes it is unavoidable. Bad partners can stick to you like barnacles to a ship.

Generally, though, this is a good rule: Surround yourself with positive people. Be sure that the people you play with put you up, too.

Resolved: I surround myself on the golf course with positive people.

September 10

"Joy is but the sign that creative emotion is fulfilling its purpose."

—Charles DuBos

What club do you use when seeking liberation from a bunker?

Nine times out of 10—99 times out of 100—golfers will answer, "Sand wedge." But is it always, always, always the right club to play?

"There is nothing about any club that makes its use mandatory," says Tommy Armour. No law decrees that only the sand wedge is suitable for the sand. In a bunker without a lip, a putter may do the job as neatly.

As is commonly known, the putter can also be used for the frog hairs around the green, not just on the putting surface itself. The land of Hogan and Byron Nelson even coined a term for a putter so employed: "the Texas wedge."

The point is, nothing *has* to be in golf. There are no rules saying this or that club must be employed in a given situation. Be creative. Be spontaneous. This is one of the most rewarding parts of this game—and a sure sign that you are enjoying yourself. You're having fun. A person having fun is willing, even eager to experiment, to flout the rules and cobwebby conventions of the game.

Today, use a club in an original way. What the heck? Who knows what happy end may result?

Resolved: I putt my way out of a bunker.

September 11

"A book is like a garden carried in the pocket."

—Chinese proverb

What about carrying a book when you golf, like a garden in your bag?

Colman McCarthy, the writer, likes to bring a book along for those lag times that occur in any golf outing. His golf author of choice: Bobby Jones. Reading Jones, says McCarthy, "is like a conversation with an old friend, one who knows something about the game and is sure to say it well."

This is the best criterion for choosing a links-time author: If you could, would you like to play a round with him or her? If the answer is yes, then you have found a literary golf companion.

If a book distracts you from your game, put it away for another time. Your playing partners may, at first, resent this intrusion and dislike your removing yourself from the group (for that is what a book will do). But in time they will surely relax about it and be peering over your shoulder to see if they can glean something useful to them.

It is not advisable, however, to read an instructional manual while on the course. Your head will be so full of dos and don'ts by the end of the day, you won't know which end of the club is up.

Better to read a book with short, pithy passages stuffed with wisdom. Better to read a book that motivates and inspires, yet contains sound practical advice and a few hearty yuks besides. Better to read a book like this one!

Resolved: I carry *The Golfer's Book of Daily Inspiration* in my bag.

September 12

"Not serious? I'll say it's serious. It means I can't play golf."

—Dwight Eisenhower, after a visiting dignitary commented that the president's injured wrist did not appear serious

Anybody can get hurt, even golfing presidents of the United States.

Sometimes something serious starts small. Left untended, it becomes *very* serious—that is, it stops you from playing golf.

Any nagging aches and pains? In the elbows or wrists or back? Pay attention to your pain if you have any. It is sending you a message as unmistakable as a ringing phone. It is a message worth listening to. Get it checked out before the unthinkable occurs and you have to stop playing.

Resolved: I make that doctor's appointment I've been putting off.

September 13

"Whatever you would make habitual, practice it; and if you would not make a thing habitual, do not practice it, but accustom yourself to something else."

—Epictetus

Most golfers, when they practice their chipping, use a bunch of balls. They chip one after another up to the green.

Harv Penick had a different approach. He asked his students to chip with only one ball. After they chipped they walked up and putted it in.

Not dozens and dozens of balls. Not multiple chances to hit. One ball, one shot. That's golf.

How many times, when you chip a ball off a green, do you hole it? Not many. Even when you have a bagful of balls, the success rate is poor.

But Harv Penick's students always sunk the balls they chipped. They chipped, then putted them in the hole.

Chipping ball after ball after ball is action without consequence, or reward. So what if you hit one off the mark? You'll make it up on your next chip. It is a practice method that devalues the individual stroke, the most precious thing there is in a round of golf.

A person who follows his chip with a putt has a more accurate sense of where that chip put him on the green. He truly knows whether it has succeeded or not, because he understands its relation to the hole. What good is a good chip if the putt that follows it misses the mark?

Practice your putting with your chipping, and teach yourself success.

Resolved: I use one ball when I practice my chipping.

September 14

"Golf is 20 percent talent and 80 percent management."

—Ben Hogan

What are the characteristics of a good manager?

Authority, a sense of command. A manager takes charge.

It is the same for those who wish to manage their golf game. Take charge of it. Get on top of it. You will be the better player for it.

Golf does not control you. You control it. Take control.

This is not to say you can do whatever you want to do, whenever you want to. Golf is not like *that*.

Rather, it is an attitude. I am the boss. I am taking charge. The course is not in charge, the weather is not in charge, my clubs are not in charge. *I am*. The buck stops with me.

As the manager of my golf game, I do what good managers and leaders do. I am consistent, evenhanded, slow to anger. My competence is assured. I am experienced, hardworking. I am battle-tested and cool in a crisis. I know when to step on the throttle, and when to ease up.

And *I* am in control. Make no mistake. I set the goals, make the hard choices. I accept responsibility when things go wrong. But I never let the little things interfere with my overall progress. Toward that end I am indomitable. Always I keep moving forward.

Be the manager of your golf game. Take charge of it.

Resolved: I take charge of my game.

September 15

"I'm apologizing right now for my mistakes that I make today, but this is my last apology. Now let's go out there and do our best."

—Horton Smith, to a playing partner prior to a tournament

Horton Smith was an old-time pro (he won the inaugural Masters in 1934). This was typically what he said to a partner before they started playing together in a pro-am tournament or any type of pairing.

It's a good strategy for all of us. Get the apologies over up front. Then go play golf.

When you play in a pro-am or a Best Ball tournament you are going to screw up now and then. So is every other human being on the course.

Are you doing it deliberately? As a means of sabotaging your team? Because you want to? Of course not. You are doing the best you can. You want to help your team. The last thing on earth you want to do is let your partner down.

Apologies have no place in your game if you are trying as hard as you can. Still, you may feel compelled to do so. Do as Horton did then. Make your apologies before the round begins. Then attend to the business at hand.

An apology may, on some subconscious level, be an attempt to give yourself permission to repeat your mistake. Which, of course, is what you want to avoid. What good does an apology do, anyway? The shot still stands; an apology will not change that.

Mistakes are part of the game. Quit apologizing for them, and move on.

Resolved: I quit apologizing.

September 16

"It is an indescribable feeling, which I have had four or five times in my life—the positive, powerful indeed, certainty that I was going to win the championship."

—Gary Player

Player had this feeling prior to the 1965 U.S. Open, and sure enough he was right: He won it. Though he had to beat Kel Nagle in an 18-hole playoff to do so.

Player also won three Masters, three British Opens, and two PGAs in one of the greatest careers in the history of golf. In his prime he was a member of Golf's Big Three with Nicklaus and Palmer. He first won the Masters in 1961. Seventeen years later he won it for the third time. That is a long time to be competing at the highest levels of professional golf.

Though only 5'7", Player walked into a sand trap as though he was John Wayne. Nicklaus said he was the best sand player he ever saw, adding that he'd rather see Player on grass than in the sand out of fear that the South African would put the ball in the hole.

Player's prowess in the sand was a testament to how hard he worked. He spent more time in the sand than a sun worshiper at the beach. He prepared extensively for a tournament.

Player experienced that positive, powerful feeling—that certainty that he was going to win the championship—only four or five times in a career that continues to this day on the Senior Tour. But he always kept working. He put in the time.

That is what we all must do. Today and every day. Those good feelings will come. The winning will come. The rewards will come. Meanwhile, put in the time.

Resolved: I put in the time, especially on my sand game.

September 17

"To swing with power, you've got to think power."

—Greg Norman

Nice sentiment, that. But how do you do it? How do you think those powerful thoughts?

First, and most important, you eliminate to the extent that you can the thoughts that weaken you, such as:

I'm not a good driver.

I don't hit the ball very well.

I'm not strong enough.

This is the worst part of my game.

Such thoughts will defeat you before you even step onto the tee. Let go of them.

Remember that a well-struck golf ball is more a product of timing than raw power. A brute with power who lacks timing will consistently see his drives fall short of those by a smaller person who makes solid contact with a smoothly coordinated swing.

Look at the women pros. They can really hit it. If muscles are so important, why don't you see the pros in the weight room? In fact, large bulky muscles can hurt you in golf.

You have the tools, right now, to be a good driver. You lack nothing. You are plenty big, plenty strong, plenty tough. Put yourself in a positive frame of mind, and turn those powerful thoughts into powerful drives.

Resolved: I hit powerful drives.

September 18

"I just kept telling myself to play my game, hit the shots, don't try to do anything crazy, and gut it out."

—Hale Irwin

Play your game. Stay within yourself. Hit the shots you know you can make. Play to your strengths. Trust your instincts and your reads. Stick to what you know. Play the way you always do. Maintain your routine, your way of doing things. It has worked before; it will work this time.

Hit the shots. Walk through every opening you see. Take advantage of your opportunities. Assert yourself. You have put yourself into position to win; now seize it. Make every stroke a positive act.

Don't do anything crazy. A negative way of saying "Keep cool." Stay focused. Don't force it; your time will come. When it comes you will be ready. Play one shot at a time; make up one stroke at a time. Be patient. Success comes to those who know how to wait.

Gut it out. You do not always fly with the angels on a golf course; there are times when your feet are made of lead. This may occur several times over a single round. When it happens, there is only one response: Gut it out. Be indomitable. Know in your heart that you will make it through this difficult passage and once more soar on celestial wings.

Play your game. Hit the shots. Stay focused. Gut it out. That is the road to winning golf.

Resolved: I gut it out through the difficult passages.

September 19

"There is something tough inside us which doesn't give way."
—A. C. Benson

Lanny Wadkins, one tough cookie, tells a revealing story about another tough cookie, Seve Ballesteros. They were playing a Ryder Cup against each other, Seve on the European team and Lanny with the United States. Lanny was paired with Larry Nelson in the early matches and Seve's partner was Antonio Garrido. Seve's team was taking a pounding.

The Wadkins-Nelson team beat the Ballesteros-Garrido team in three out of three matches. Each time was worse than the last. The third match wasn't even funny; Wadkins-Nelson just buried them.

Wadkins started this best ball match with five straight birdies. After Nelson's eagle on 8, they were 9 under par and Ballesteros and Garrido were as good as done.

Then came 14. Wadkins's ball was 18 inches from the cup. All he needed to do was make it in two strokes. Two measly strokes, and the match was over. Lanny looked over at Seve to see if he was going to concede.

Now, your grandmother could hole out an 18-inch putt in two strokes. Your grandmother's grandmother could do it. But Seve would not concede. He shook his head. Something tough inside him would not give way. He made Wadkins sink it.

Sometimes competitive golf is like that. Sometimes it demands nothing less. You must show that granitelike toughness that exists inside you and never gives way.

Resolved: I never give way.

September 20

"Beat on it. Beat on it again."

—Huey Lewis, rock singer, offering his philosophy of golf

It's as good a philosophy as any: Beat on it. Beat on it again.

When in doubt, beat on it. Your doubts may not go away, but you will feel better. Beat on it again.

When you step up to the tee, beat on it. That ball will go . . . *somewhere*. Call for a mulligan if it goes too far afield. Then beat on it again.

Henry Cotton, the fine English golfer of the 1930s, had an interesting swing key. He said that he imagined that the ball had tiny legs, and he tried to chop them off with his club.

Chi Chi Rodriguez has said that he thinks of the ball as a clockface. A hit at six o'clock means he wants the ball to go straight. A hook, where he swings more inside the line, is at seven o'clock; and a slice, where he cuts across the ball, is at five o'clock. Younger players who are familiar only with digital clocks may have a hard time with this method.

These are both fascinating swing keys, and they may be useful to some people. Others, however, will prefer to stick with a simple, consistent philosophy of golf that will never let them down. This philosophy will comfort them through the low times as well as the high. This philosophy will never lead them astray and will guide them through every situation. For it is the raw essence of the game distilled into its most elementary form.

Beat on it. Beat on it again.

Resolved: I beat on it. Then I beat on it again.

September 21

*"Golf is different than other games. Pope's lines have a greater
application to it than any other sport I know: 'Hope springs
eternal in the human breast.'"*

—William Howard Taft, 27th president of the United States

You think your case is hopeless? Think of Angelo Spagnola.

Some years back *Golf Digest* held a competition to find
"the worst avid golfer" in the United States. Angelo, from
Fayette City, Pennsylvania, was one of four men selected for
the 18-hole playoff, loser takes all.

Angelo dusted everybody, putting a number on the board
that could not be topped. He shot a 257. Actually Angelo was
going good until 17, when he hit the wall. He took a 66 on
the hole and that locked up the title for him.

A 257 over 18 holes—that is 14-plus strokes per hole.
Throw out the 17th and Angelo's average is a far more
respectable 11 strokes per hole. Good going, Angelo.

So what are we to derive from this?

As bad as you sometimes think you are, you will never be
as bad as Angelo Spagnola.

As terrible as your blowups may occasionally be, you have
never taken a 66 on a single hole and you never will.

It would be nice to find Angelo Spagnola and play a $20
Nassau with him.

There is hope. There is always hope. For Angelo, for all of
us. As much as golf taketh away, it always leaveth hope. Hope
for a brighter bogey-free tomorrow.

Resolved: Hope, hope, hope. I always hang on to hope!

September 22

"How easily we might walk onward onto the opening landscape, absorbed by new pictures and by thoughts fast succeeding each other."

—Ralph Waldo Emerson

Walking is one of the joys of golf. Now that fall is here, it becomes an even greater joy. You put one foot in front of the other. You pause to hit. Then you locomote some more. A day of golf is a day spent walking amid an opening landscape.

When you walk you truly learn a golf course—that is, up through the bottoms of your shoes. Saddle up one of those mechanical contrivances that swarm across the golf courses of this land like locusts and you alter the primary relationship of the game. No longer is the game a dialogue between you and the ball. A third party has intervened. It is like having an intimate conversation with a friend interrupted by a stranger who wants to sit at your table.

After you hit you go not to the ball, but back to the cart. You wind along an asphalt path until you reach a location somewhat near your ball. You walk out to hit, then return joylessly to your cart. The game is reduced to a humdrum repetition of strokes.

Contrast this with people who walk. They hit, and proceed directly to their ball. Their pathway is covered with grass. They take in the content of the sky, absorb the rhythms of the land, working their lungs as they go. Their primary focus remains the ball, always the ball. You know where you stand at every moment, you know where you are going, and you walk straight for it.

Resolved: I walk.

September 23

"Great emergencies and crises show us how much greater our vital resources are than we had supposed."

—Charles Carryl

One year at the Ryder Cup, Ben Crenshaw found himself in a great golf crisis—a crisis of his own making.

He three-putted a hole and, furious at his incompetence, snapped his putter in half. But since Ryder Cup rules forbid the replacement of a broken club, Ben was stuck. He had to putt using a club other than his putter.

Not only that, he had a long, long way to go. He broke it on 6, leaving him with 12 holes of putterless golf.

First he went to his wedge. That worked okay. Then he tried his 1-iron and that worked even better. The more he played with it, the better he got. Ben went on to hole birdie putts of 18 and 6 feet using the 1-iron.

All of which goes to show: the trouble we find on a golf course is often of our own making; because we got ourselves into it, we can get ourselves out of it, and therefore we needn't fear it; and never break your putter as long as you still need it.

Resolved: If I get myself into a jam, I get myself out of it.

September 24

"Study hard, think quietly."

—William Channing

It is easy for a young person to be intoxicated by the "grip it and rip it" style of John Daly.

But there is more to Daly's game than that. One can trace his growth as a player from his 1991 PGA breakthrough to his British Open win at St. Andrews fours year later. That, too, is amazing to watch. It is as if he has learned to see a golf course in a new, more profound way.

Listen to the words of another player who could grip it and rip it:

"The main reason golf appealed to me so much as a kid was that I could do it by myself, without the dependence on other people that most sports involve. From that simple starting point I became more and more intrigued, as my game improved, by the way in which the elements that make up a golf course determine the type and quality of shots a golfer is called upon to play. Seeking to understand each new hole I encountered, I would try to put myself in the mind of the architect. I'd try to figure out why he had done particular things in particular ways."

That is Jack Nicklaus talking. He drove the ball in his time like John Daly. He overpowered a golf course. But that was not his entire game, not by a long shot.

Study hard. Think quietly. Learn why things are the way they are on a golf course. Two of the all-time-greatest rippers advise it for your game.

Resolved: I seek to understand each new golf hole I play.

September 25

"If you are sweating in golf, it had better be 110 degrees outside."

—Instructor, to his golf pupil

One of the biggest clichés in sports is the one about "giving 100 percent." Some even raise the ante, saying "He gave 110 percent all the time"—or even 200 percent.

In this game, if you want to give 100 percent, make it a tax-deductible contribution to a favorite charity.

A better figure for golfers would be in the 80 to 85 percent range. A golfer who is giving 110 percent is overswinging and trying too hard. He is investing too much in a single shot. His swing speeds up and he receives poor return on his investment. He would get better results if he slowed his swing down and relaxed.

You may not have enough left for the back nine if you put it all on the line on the front nine. You might not have enough left for the next hole if you put it all on the line on this hole. Have the attitude of the turtle, as opposed to the hare.

Pace yourself. Never let 'em see you sweat. That's a good rule for deodorants and golf.

Resolved: I play at a steady 85 percent of capacity.

September 26

"I'd like to lie on a beach for a while, no deadlines in front of me, no books that have to be finished and just feel what the sunlight is like all day and try to sharpen up my golf game a bit."

—Tim O'Brien

It's not too late. There's still some good weather left before winter comes. Go feel what the sunlight is like all day and sharpen up your golf game.

Tim O'Brien is an author and Vietnam veteran whose books about the war have won national acclaim. When he was a kid, he fell in love with golf and never fell out.

"I've always loved golf," he has said. "I grew up on a golf course and imagined myself able to shoot consistently in the mid-70s. I think it'd be nice to spend a year or two making my dreams come true, because they're so easy to make true if we give ourselves the space to do it."

It was O'Brien's dream as a kid to play golf. Not just to be an ordinary player, but to shoot in the 70s. To do that takes time. So he conceives of taking some time off, away from the pressure of deadlines, to do exactly that.

Sounds like a fantasy. Playing golf, soaking up the sun. No deadlines to meet. Not just for a couple of weeks, but for one or two *years*. To O'Brien, though, it's not a fantasy. He says he may do it. It's possible, he says. He says dreams can come true if we let them, if we give them a space in our lives in which they can occur.

Hmmm. Now there's a tantalizing thought.

Resolved: I feel what the sun is like today and sharpen up my golf game.

September 27

"I hate to lose. But in golf, everybody loses because it is so hard mentally."

—Tiger Woods

You want to be a player? Make yourself mentally tough.

For all his talent, Tiger Woods will go nowhere in the pros if he cannot withstand the mental rigors of the game. That is why his coach and father, Earl Woods, a Vietnam veteran, stresses mental toughness to his son. He challenges his son by coughing when Tiger draws back the club, or pointing to out-of-bounds areas, or standing so that his shadow falls across Tiger's putting line.

Here are more of Earl's "toughening up" techniques (with a nod to Jaime Diaz for his assistance):

Keep the game in perspective. The game is about more than just winning and scoring. Enjoy yourself, too.

Use negativity as a motivator. Tiger, whose dad is African-American and whose mom is Asian-American, has encountered racial animosity in his still-young career. Do not turn inward in the face of such hostility, his father tells him. Your self-worth has nothing to do with the poisonous negativity of others.

Evaluate your weaknesses. Improvement gets harder as one gets older. Never be content. Always advance, never retreat.

Steel yourself to losing. That is different from accepting it. Nobody wins 'em all. Take your lumps, learn from them, and move on.

Resolved: I make myself mentally tough.

September 28

"Do continue to believe that with your feeling and your work you are taking part in the greatest; the more strongly you cultivate in yourself the belief, the more will reality and the world go forth from it."

—Rainer Maria Rilke

You need confidence to play golf. Courses can be intimidating. Other players can be intimidating. You need a confidence bordering on chutzpah.

Bernard Gallacher had it. The year was 1969. The Scotsman was, in Samuel Johnson's phrase, "towering in the confidence of twenty-one." (Actually he was 20). He was the youngest member of the British Ryder Cup team and the youngest player ever in the biennial event pitting the best golfers of the United States against those of Great Britain.

The American team, as usual, was packed. It included the likes of Nicklaus, Casper, Trevino. The U.S. had won five consecutive Ryder Cups, and most Stateside observers predicted a sixth. But Gallacher wasn't having any of it. His team included British Open champion Tony Jacklin and, not least, him. Asked if he was awed by the powerful team from across the water, he replied, "I'm not awed by the Americans. I think they should be awed by me."

That's telling 'em, Bernard. The faith you show in yourself can set into motion the events you wish to occur and the events that you know in your heart can occur.

Gallacher's Ryder Cup team played the United States to a 16–16 tie that year. The Americans went on to win the next seven Ryder Cups in a row.

Resolved: I am awed by nothing and no one on a golf course.

September 29

"On the golf course I'm like a little kid again."

—Frank Viola

Be a little kid again. Play a game of 21 in your backyard.

You don't have to go to the golf course to play golf. When you were a kid you played touch football on the street. You played basketball in the driveway. You played Rundown on the lawn. Kids don't need a dedicated area to play a game. They start playing, and adjust their play to fit the area.

The putting game 21 is ideal for the backyard (or the practice green, if you'd rather). Set up a minicourse around the yard. Two tees about five inches apart constitute a hole; lay down as many holes as you can reasonably fit. Challenge yourself. Make yours the Augusta National of backyard putting courses.

You can play alone or with others. When you shoot a ball into the hole—i.e., the tees—on one stroke, you earn two points. A two-putt counts for one point; a three-putt earns you *nothing*. A ball that grazes the tees as it goes in is worth a point. Start from your designated opening tee and go through the holes in order, as you would on a regular course. First one to 21 wins. Hit it exactly; otherwise go back to 12.

Another (shorter) version of the game is 7/11. Game is to 11. Anyone who goes over 11 goes back to 7. Enjoy!

Resolved: I play a backyard game of 21 with my kids.

September 30

"My goal is to please myself. If you try to please everybody else, you're going to end up only disappointing them and yourself."

—Keith Clearwater, touring pro

Today, I please myself. I play golf.

Work is important. There is lots of work to do. There always is.

But not today. Today I am taking the day off. I am playing golf.

Family is important. I want to spend as much time as I can with my family. But not today. Today I'm playing golf.

There are things I could be doing around the house. There always are. Those things can wait. Today I please myself. I play golf.

Pleasing myself is not selfish. I love golf. Golf makes me happy. The happier I am, the more productive I am. Without golf I would be a basket case and no use to anybody. By pleasing myself I have a better chance of pleasing others.

Today, I please myself. I play golf.

Resolved: I play today.

October 1

"As a low handicapper you won't drop a lot of strokes with a single chance. That isn't to say you can't improve, but progress for the highly skilled player will come in small increments, by refining techniques."

—Ken Venturi

Ain't that a drag? When you started this game, you cut strokes like a knife through warm butter. What was everybody saying, how hard golf is? For you it was *easy*.

That was then; this is now. And progress is coming very, very slowly. It's like watching grass grow.

But looked at another way, the incremental rate of progress for skilled players is a good thing. Look how close you are. All you need to do is keep doing what you are doing and you will get there. It will take more time, sure, you know that. But you will get there.

This is what it means to refine your game: You are on the right path. You are going in the right direction. You have the tools to get there. You have patience, you have ability, and most important, you are willing to work hard. You have all that you need. You have already shown that by coming as far as you have, on the path you have chosen for yourself. Those small incremental improvements, while they may seem large to you at times, are just baby steps compared to where you have been and where you are going.

Keep going. Great things lie ahead.

Resolved: I keep going.

October 2

"After I started caddying, I really got into golf. It got to be fun and a challenge."

—Jim Dent, Senior Tour pro

You're young and you want to learn the game from the ground up.

Okay, then. Put down your clubs, take up another's, and be a caddie.

Some of the game's greatest masters started out as caddies: Ben Hogan, Arnold Palmer, Seve Ballesteros, to name a few. Senior Tour pro Jim Dent and many others learned the game that way.

The golf cart has largely replaced the caddie in ordinary play. But you can still get on as a caddie in tournaments and at some private clubs.

You take the clubs out of your hands when you're a caddie and put them on your shoulder. The act is liberating. Freed from the pressure of performance, you see the course in a new light. You think your way around the course. You intently note pin placements, distances, obstacles. It is impossible to club a player whom you don't know. But as time goes on you begin to see more of his or her strengths and weaknesses, and you offer advice on the proper club to use.

When you caddie you put your ego in service to another. This may be the best lesson of all. You are saying, in essence, "I am willing to learn. I am willing to serve." And while it may not be popular to say, a young person will learn the game deeply and more thoroughly with an attitude of humility rather than arrogance.

Resolved: I caddy some rounds.

October 3

"There's always a trick to winning any game, and golf is no different. The key is to recognize an opening and then make it work to your advantage."

—Sam Snead

Sam Snead played fair. He recognized an opening and made it work to his advantage. But you may play against people who want to take unfair advantage.

The following are some classic bits of gamesmanship (supplied by the golf writer Don Wade) that you should keep an eye out for:

Playing too fast or too slow. The idea is to upset your rhythm. So if you like to play fast, this person will slow his game to a crawl. Or he will speed up if you are a more deliberate player.

Walking straight to the next tee after holing out. In other words, not waiting for you. A similar tactic is going straight to the green after hitting an approach.

There are several ways to psych out a person on the putting green. One is to stand behind the hole during someone's putt. The person putting cannot help but be distracted. Another trick is stepping over a player's putting line. You're sizing up your putt and the person steps over its line to the hole. He makes a show of stepping over it, not on it, but the effect is the same: It disrupts your concentration.

What do you do when you come up against a player who seems to be trying to take unfair advantage? Maybe you call him on it, maybe you ignore it. But you definitely get more determined, and you beat the pants off him.

Resolved: I take advantage of anyone who tries to take advantage of me.

October 4

"Like a high school prom, golf is one of those things best looked back on. Beers taste colder, friends seem closer, and life feels sweeter with a signed scorecard and the 18th hole behind you."
—Rick Reilly

Reilly, a writer and golfer, has the right idea. He likes to look back on his day at a suitable 19th-hole establishment. Here are his picks for the best golf watering holes in the world:

- The terrace at Pebble Beach Lodge. An outpost of paradise. Looking out across at the 18th green at Pebble and the blue of Carmel Bay while sipping a cocktail—Reilly's choice: a Del Monte Fizz—you will be able to look your children in the face and tell them: "I have well and truly lived."
- The Jigger Inn, St. Andrews, Scotland. How can you go wrong in the ancient birthplace of golf? Reilly's choice of libation: single malt Scotch.
- Mauna Lani Clubhouse, Hawaii. The cool spot on the Big Island.
- Copenhagen Golf Club Bar, Copenhagen, Denmark. Thousands of deer inhabit the park surrounding the course.
- Kawana Hotel, Kawana Golf Resort, Japan. One of the world's most spectacular courses, in golf-mad Japan.

When you discover a new 19th-hole establishment, it means you have discovered a new place to play, which is always an excellent thing. Make a date with your partners. Go out and do some discovering.

Resolved: I discover a new 19th-hole establishment.

October 5

"I believe most sincerely that the impulse to steer, born of anxiety, is accountable for almost every really bad shot."

—Bobby Jones

You want the ball to go a certain direction. You try to steer it that way. Of course, it doesn't work.

What's the impulse behind trying to steer the ball? Jones offers an interesting analysis: anxiety.

The dictionary defines anxiety as "full of mental distress or uneasiness because of apprehension of danger or misfortune." This was the first definition; the second is even more telling. Anxiety, it says, is "solicitous desire; eagerness."

Apprehension, desire, eagerness. Every golfer understands instantly how this relates to them. Every golfer is familiar with the phenomenon of how if you want a thing badly in this game, it almost never occurs—at least not right away, or in the way you expected it. The *absence* of desire seems to produce better golf.

The desire to steer a ball has to do with our desire to control it. Steering equates with control, we think. But that is an illusory idea. Steering, in fact, causes us to *lose* control. We will maintain control better if we let go of the idea of control. It's like a parent keeping close tabs on a teenager. The teenager ultimately rebels if the controls are too strict.

Golfers are like those parents. We cannot ultimately control the flight of the ball; it has its own destiny. We do the best we can, and then we have to let it go. Let go of the urge to control, and you will rid yourself of much anxiety and cure your habit of steering.

Resolved: I let go.

October 6

"The person who gives up accomplishes nothing. The person who does not give up can move mountains."

—Ernest Hello

If golf is a test of character, the test begins on the back nine. In some ways the back nine is the game.

The back nine defines your round. You can sparkle like polished chrome on the front nine, but if you do not play the back nine well your round will lose much of its shine.

Anybody can have a good front nine. Your energy is up, your enthusiasm is up, and you carry that energy onto the back side. You have a reserve to draw from in case you fall upon hard times, a reserve created by your performance on those early holes.

But what if your front nine did not go as planned? What do you do when your enthusiasm is low and there's no reserve to draw from?

You play the back nine the same as someone who is shooting lights-out golf. You focus on the task at hand—what you need to do at this moment. Look ahead and you are lost. Look behind and you are lost.

See the turn as a time for renewal, starting over. Stay positive at the turn. No matter what happened on the front, stay positive. Make your last nine your best nine. Just because a thing is not going well at the moment is no reason to abandon it. It is amazing what can be accomplished when all hope is seemingly lost.

Resolved: I stay positive at the turn.

October 7

"Take more lessons on the short game than on the full swing. Those shots save you and reduce the penalty of hazards."

—Bob Rotella, teaching pro

Doesn't matter who your pro is.

Doesn't matter what swing lessons he teaches.

Every pro in the civilized world agrees on this one universal: The short game is king.

Driving earns you oohs and aahs. But the person who masters the short game is the person who cashes the paychecks.

The short game is what saves you. It is what gets you out of the sand. It is what puts the ball in the hole.

When you stand on the green take a look back at the tee, if you can see it at all. The tee is way far out of the picture when it comes time to score in golf. The tee is an afterthought.

The deed in golf is putting the ball in the hole. The short game is what does the deed.

Make an appointment today. Tune up that swing. Tune up your ability to score and do the deed. Take a lesson on the short game.

Resolved: I take a lesson on the short game.

October 8

"Age is a case of mind over matter. If you don't mind, it doesn't matter."

—Satchel Paige

At 71, Gene Sarazen shot two straight rounds under 80 at the British Open, including a hole in one.

At 70, Paul Runyan could drive the ball farther than he could in the 1930s, when he won two PGAS.

At 54, Ben Hogan shot a 66 in the final round of the Masters tournament.

At 52, Sam Snead won the Greater Greensboro Open on the PGA Tour. Ten years later, he finished third in the PGA Championship. At 67, he shot his age in the first round of the Quad Cities Open, another regular Tour stop. Two days later he shot a 66.

At 50, Harry Vardon struggled valiantly but lost the 1920 U.S. Open by one stroke.

At 46, Jack Nicklaus won his sixth Green Jacket at the Masters tournament.

At 45, Hale Irwin won his third U.S. Open.

These were (and are) extraordinary golfers, playing against younger men on tough, championship-level courses. They did not let their age handicap them. So why should you?

In golf, age is not a barrier to anything. You can whip a 30-year-old if you're 50. You can beat a 20-year-old if you're 40. Experience counts for a lot. Use it (and everything else you can muster) when you play—and show those young whippersnappers a thing or two.

Resolved: I never let my age, or thoughts about my age, beat me.

October 9

"Scottish golf is great, but St. Andrews and Gleneagles have traps where you get in and you're never heard from again."

—Bob Hope

Now that summer is over and most of the tourists have gone home, what about a playing tour of the great golf courses of Scotland?

Carnoustie. Muirfield. Royal Troon. St. Andrews. No golfer's education is complete without a visit to one or more of these historic British Open sites.

They play a different game over there. They invented golf and have been playing it for 500 years or so. Go see it. Take a journey to the ancient roots of golf.

The golf courses of Scotland look different and play different from their cousins in North America. Fairways tend to be harder, greens less forgiving. The bunkers are scary, wind inevitable. Courses are based on "misdirection and blindness," says an admiring Tom Watson. You aim for a different fairway than the one you're on, not knowing where the pin is. Your target may be a church steeple in town. A caddie who knows his way around the maze is a virtual necessity.

These courses were once pasturelands for livestock. Their uses now are more sublime. "They mow some grass and that's your fairway," says Payne Stewart. "They cultivate some nice grass and that's your green. It always takes a lot of patience and imagination."

History, imagination, inspiration, golf. What more could a person ask for?

Resolved: I take a golfing trip to Scotland.

October 10

"It all depends on how we look at things, and not on how they are in themselves."

—Carl Jung

How do you view a bogey? As an accomplishment or a sign of failure?

In America we tend to see it as "the rankest blasphemy," in Robert Browning's phrase. It is perceived as a negative, one over the standard and thus unacceptable, undesirable.

Contrast this attitude with the British view of a bogey. A bogey, for them, is something to crow about. They generally see par as the standard for pros and the very best amateur players. For everyone else, bogey is the goal. Play bogey golf in Britain and you are playing good golf. You have reason to be proud.

If we adopted the bogey standard here in America we would immediately give ourselves an extra 18 strokes. Instead of 72, our goal would be 90. Bet you feel better already.

Of course, it is unreasonable to expect a wholesale change of heart in this country. Traditionalists would see it as yet another sign of falling standards, one more symptom of a nation in decline. Even so, the British perspective on the bogey is worth bearing in mind. It may forestall discouragement and give you a new appreciation of the merits of your own game. "In Britain," you can say, tossing the ball jauntily in the air after going one over on the hole, "that's as good as a par."

Resolved: I shoot bogey golf and feel good about it.

October 11

"The rung of a ladder was never meant to rest upon, but only to hold a man's foot long enough to enable him to put the other somewhat higher."

—Thomas Henry Huxley

Set goals as a golfer. See your goals as a ladder upon which you climb higher.

But stay flexible. Reassess and readjust your goals periodically. Replace the ladder and get a new one if you need to, or change the distance between the rungs to make it easier or harder depending on your situation.

Set your goals in clay, not concrete. Shape them according to changing times and circumstances.

You may be making faster progress than you expected. But you are driving yourself too hard. If so, cut back.

Your goals may have been too ambitious at the start—a familiar predicament. Quit killing yourself; ease up. Scale back an unreasonable expectation to a healthier rate of development. The I'm-in-it-for-the-long-haul approach is a far better way to grow as a golfer anyway.

You may be right on schedule but feel you can do more. Shift into a higher gear if that's the case. Or you may initially have set your sights too low. Amp it up, then. You can always scale back if it gets to be too much.

You may also find that your goals are right in line with the progress you are making. Keep a steady hand on the wheel, Captain, and full steam ahead!

Resolved: I stay flexible about my golfing goals.

October 12

"Never forget that success at stroke play very rarely depends on one shot. Check any impulse to try for miracles short of a do-or-die situation on the final hole."

—Jack Nicklaus

Another way to say this is: Pick your spots.

Some people play the lottery when they play golf. They go for broke on every shot. They look to hit the jackpot every time.

Everybody can understand that. We all get those urges. Throw caution to the wind and all that.

Today, though, we will take Jack's advice. We will be shrewd, canny, patient. We will bide our time. A round of golf consists of 70, 80, 90 shots. It makes no sense to go for it all on one shot just for the sake of going for it.

You want a miracle? Go to Lourdes. Today I am playing good, tough, consistent golf. I am going to wear people down. I am going to pick my spots.

Picking your spots means coolly and calmly assessing each situation for what it is. You know what you can do. How do your strengths match up with the situation you're in? Picking your spots means being a realist. You cannot control every situation you're in, but you can control your response to it.

Be canny. Play under control. Pick your spots.

Resolved: I pick my spots.

October 13

"Everything that enlarges the sphere of human powers, that shows man he could do what he thought he could not do, is valuable."

—Samuel Johnson

Do what you thought you could not do. Play a tough hole better than you have ever played it before.

Andrew Carnegie, the wealthy industrialist and philanthropist, died in 1919. He was one of the richest men of his time and an avid golfer. In 1901 he sold his company, Carnegie Steel Corporation, to U.S. Steel for $250 million. On the day the sale became final, he appeared at a New York City office to sign the papers.

There, he met a friend who had been tipped off about the big deal. The friend greeted him with an enthusiastic handshake, saying he had heard "great things" about Carnegie.

Carnegie was stunned. He had been playing golf earlier that day and had scored a par on a hole that had always given him trouble. "How did you know I had a par on the fifth today?" asked the bewildered millionaire.

That's a golfer for you. Deals—even $250 million deals—come and go. But a par—now, that's something to brag about!

In memory of Andrew Carnegie and his precedent-shattering accomplishment, we set two modest goals for ourselves today:

1. Score a par on a hole that has given us problems in the past.
2. Close a $250 million deal.

Resolved: I play a tough hole better than I ever have before.

October 14

"All the best work is done the way ants do things—by tiny but untiring and regular additions."

—Lafcadio Hearn

A. W. Tillinghast, the designer of Winged Foot, said that "a round of golf should represent 18 inspirations." For many of us, though, golf more represents 18 perspirations. We've got to work at it, plain and simple, to get through.

We make one good shot. Then another. We make a putt or three. We build our game up slowly, by tiny but regular additions, the way ants do things.

But there is something else to do when all your labors seem antlike: Focus on the parts of your golf game that are working.

Some days you just can't buy a putt. Keep working at it, but while you're doing that focus on the other parts of your game that are working for you.

Some days it is your tee game that betrays you. Then focus on your irons or your game around the greens. Some days it is your fairway woods that desert you. Pick it up elsewhere. Focus on what you are doing well.

You can cause problems for yourself by letting one part of your game that is not working poison the other parts that are. Avoid or at least minimize this by shifting the focus onto what you are doing right—the ways in which you are continuing to perform well. This positive outlook will help you get through these periods of stress and hasten the time when all the parts of your game come together.

Resolved: I focus on the parts of my golf game that are working.

October 15

"When I'm in this state everything is pure, vividly clear. I'm in a cocoon of concentration."

—Tony Jacklin

This is a wonderful place to be, this cocoon of concentration. Oh that we could all visit more often! We spin these delicious fibers around ourselves when we are into a hot round. We become encircled and enthralled by the game, and nothing else matters.

Here's how to bring yourself back to reality: Check your score.

Imagine the scenario. You are beating the front nine like a drum. The ball is juiced. You are stroking and scoring, and scoring and stroking.

Then a little voice whispers in your ear: "How ya doin'? Better see. Better check it out." It's only human nature. You want to tote it up, you want to see how well you are doing right this second.

Swat that little voice like a fly. You risk unraveling that precious cocoon—and your accomplishments so far—if you tote your score up prematurely. Totaling your score ahead of time will jump you ahead to a dreamy future that will steal you out of the vivid present. It will lift your vision to a faraway place and distract it from the immediate.

Poof! There went your round.

Wait till the end of nine to total your score, or the end of the round if your hot streak begins on the backside. Think process. Enjoy the act for itself. Run with the moment.

Resolved: I tote up my scores at 9 and 18.

October 16

"I wish I could go back in my head and be 15 again."
—Helen Alfredsson, LPGA touring pro

Alfredsson, a Swedish pro in her 30s, was talking about why golfers get the yips:

"When I was a kid in Sweden, all the girls and boys would just look at the line. We were so happy," she told an interviewer. "But everyone who plays golf keeps gathering so much information, too much information. Deeper and deeper they delve. Too deep. And the very brightest golfers seem to take in the most overload. Until—bap!—they go haywire."

Bap! They go haywire. Sound familiar?

Alfredsson has, like every golfer, suffered from the yips. The yips are the worst form of putting insecurity. Tommy Armour defined them as "that ghastly time when, with the first movement of the putter, the golfer blacks out, loses sight of the ball, and hasn't the remotest idea of what to do with the putter."

Today, let's take a cue from Alfredsson. Let's go back to an age when we had complete and utter confidence in ourselves. For Helen, that was 15. For you, it could be 18 or 27 or 35. Think about the person you were when you were that age.

How would *that* person play golf today? How would he handle himself? How would she respond to the golf challenges and problems that you face? Call up that young man or woman—that utterly confident, full-of-life youngster—the next time you go out on the course and he or she may teach you something.

Resolved: I play like I am 15 again.

October 17

"Make 'em quick."

—Macdonald Smith

This is our favorite piece of putting advice: Make 'em quick.

Be purposeful when your turn comes on the greens today. Be direct, no wasted energy or effort. Sight the line, make a practice stroke, and give it a firm rap. Make 'em quick.

All right, all right. Macdonald Smith didn't exactly say that. What he said was: "Miss 'em quick," but we think that's too negative. We doubt that Smith, a stylish swinger and an excellent putter who always *made* 'em quick, would have objected to the switch.

To make 'em quick does not mean to hurry. Take your time. There is plenty of time. What is the point of rushing when you are just going to have to wait for the party ahead of you to hit on the next tee?

But you do not want to slow to a crawl, either. Find a rhythm that works for you. Going too slowly can be as bad for you as hitting too quickly.

Make 'em quick is a rule that has to do more with efficiency than anything else. Play crisply, sharply, efficiently. Nothing is more efficient on the greens than making your putts.

Forget about speed. Remove all considerations of time. Think efficiency.

Resolved: I make 'em quick.

October 18

"I just played crappy and he played crappy, and I guess he outcrapped me."

   —Wayne Grady, after Greg Norman beat him in match play

That's the way it goes in golf. Sometimes you just have to out-crap 'em.

A golf course is really nothing more than a converted cow pasture. Well, some days there's nothing converted about it. You just roll up the cuffs of your trousers and wade in. The one with the queasiest stomach loses.

Today, if it comes to that on the golf course, just do it. Out-crap 'em.

It ain't pretty, but so what? Let someone else worry about aesthetics. You just outcrap 'em.

This isn't the golf they play at the Masters. This is Skunk Golf, winning ugly. But somebody's got to win at Skunk Golf the same as any other kind of golf, and it might as well be you.

Anybody can play well when they're feeling inspired. But to go out there and maintain your dignity when you're stinking up the joint, now that's a real accomplishment.

Some days are going to be like that. Today may be one of those days. You play crappy and your partners play just as bad.

It comes down to a question of who's going to outlast the others. Why not you? Don't give in just because everyone else is. Remember: An ugly win is always better than a pretty loss.

Resolved: I win ugly.

October 19

"The putt is a funny game. You can't think you have got it for always. You can lose it tomorrow."

—Roberto de Vicenzo

Today, I am struck as if by inspiration. Today I purchase a new putter.

Putters are not like spouses. It is possible to dispose of one that you do not like. It is misplaced loyalty to be faithful to a putter that is not faithful to you.

De Vicenzo changed *his* every week. He constantly scoured pro shops and pawnshops to find a club that met his fancy, if only for a while. He collected putters the way Imelda Marcos collected shoes.

Out with the old, in with the new (or used, if it feels good). A new putter will give you a psychological high. When the high wears off, find another putter and get high again.

Nobody knows in putting. That is the one thing everybody knows.

One day you are a genius, sinking everything in sight. The next day you are an idiot and completely lost. Genius or idiot—there is no middle ground. Some days you don't know which one you'll be until your first stroke.

Hang on to a putter you like. Sooner sell your firstborn child to slave traders than get rid of that putter. But if you don't like the one you're using? Get a new one. Do it today. It may turn out to be a stroke of genius.

☒

Resolved: I buy a new putter today.

October 20

"Weekend golfers underplay breaking putts and tour pros overplay them."

—Tom Watson

Putting, putting, putting, putting. It always comes back to that. Putting is the gasoline that drives your golf engine. Sink a few putts and watch the rest of your game go roaring down the speedway.

Here is something to try: Today, all day, overplay the break on your putts.

It is true what Watson says. The pros seem to inspect every blade of grass before they make a putt. They study it and study it and study it until, as one commentator remarked, you want to invoke "the same-day rule."

Weekend golfers tend to go the opposite way. We look our putts over, but many of us aren't sure exactly what we are looking for. So we hit it up there and hope for the best.

Today, while we will continue to hope for the best, we will go against our usual habit and overplay our putts. We will make a conscious effort to do this, as a means of learning more about how to read greens and how to play the break.

Overplaying your putts at least for today builds awareness. It will help overcome the tendency to underplay the break and enable you to strike a happy medium in which you get your putts just right.

Resolved: I overplay the break on my putts.

October 21

"When I want to hit a long ball, I hit a little easier."

—Macdonald Smith

Step up with the determination to crush that round dimply thing and invariably you will hit a wormy little excuse for a drive that your mother would be ashamed to call her own.

Step up, however, with an attitude of a Southern California beach bum—loosey-goosey; not a care in the world; relaxed, no pressure, you're just out there having a good time—and watch in awe as the ball joins the jet stream and flies into the next state.

Ever wonder why that is?

Millions of golfers have wondered why that is and no one, as yet, has arrived at a suitable answer. Nevertheless, it is true. So why question it? Just go with it, as that beach boy might say.

Swing hard. Ball goes soft.

Swing easy. Ball goes far.

Some mysteries are best left unexplained. Cowabunga, dude.

Resolved: I swing easy.

October 22

"Simplicity, concentration, economy of time and effort."
—Tommy Armour, on what characterizes the best golfers

Simplicity. Probably you are doing something else while you are reading this. Which is typical (and quite okay). All of us like to do two or more things at once these days—drive and talk on the phone, eat lunch and read a magazine, walk and listen to the Walkman, etc. You will play more successful golf, however, if you pare away the nonessential and focus on one thing at a time. Do one thing at a time and you have a better chance of doing it well.

Concentration. "Think what to do," said Tommy Armour. "That's concentration in golf." A focused golfer is one who has eliminated the details, who is thinking of one thing and one thing only and concentrating on doing it right. Think simply and directly, and your golf game will get better.

Economy of Time. A good golfer does not play fast or slow; he plays at his own pace. Therein lies the value of rhythm and routine. He does not rush or tarry. His motions are directed always with one aim: making solid contact with the ball.

Economy of Effort. Armour conducted his lessons while lounging under a sun umbrella at the Boca Raton golf course where he taught. "Educated languor," he joked. "That is the example I want to set for my golfers." And an excellent example it is. The golfer who is trying too hard is probably a tense golfer—struggling, swinging stiffly, forcing his game. Cultivate an attitude of educated languor when you play. You know what to do. You know how to do it. Now do it in your own way, in your own time, and enjoy yourself.

Resolved: I cultivate an attitude of educated languor.

October 23

"It is possible, even desirable, to have sex on a golf course, something you can't say of tennis, bowling, or motocross."

—Rick Reilly

Imagine: You and your partner (preferably of the opposite sex, although, one supposes, this is not mandatory) are playing the back nine on a quiet late-fall day.

It is unseasonably warm and nice. Your game has almost been an afterthought. The two of you are reveling in the fall colors, walking and laughing and basking in each other's company as the late-afternoon shadows form amazing dark shapes on the grass.

No one is around.

"Hmm," you say. "Wanna take a break?"

She's game. That's what you like about this girl. She's always game.

You take a seat on the grass. You're in a pretty secluded spot off the 16th fairway, about halfway down.

"Hmm," you think. "This is nice."

She reads your mind. That's another thing you like about this girl. Her mind works like yours.

You are amazed. You never knew such inspiration on a golf course before. Clothes begin coming off, belts are unbuckled. It is possible, however, to manage it all without removing your Foot-Joys.

It is really happening, it really is. She is making happy sounds; you are in bliss. Now you understand what it truly means to score in golf . . .

. . . and the marshal drives up.

Resolved: I indulge my every golfing fantasy (but keep an eye out for the course marshal).

October 24

"The hard, unglamorous reality is that you play well because your swing is built on a solid foundation. When a pro has problems, it's usually because his basics slip."

—Tom Watson

The most basic basic is the grip. Check your hands. Do you have calluses? You may need to do some rethinking if you do.

The first thing that Harv Penick did with new students is check their hands for calluses. Calluses—the sign of hard work in manual labor—are a sign of misplaced effort in golf. They probably mean that a player is holding the club too firmly.

Penick, ever a believer in the corrective benefits of language, emphasized "placing" the hands on the club rather than grabbing it. "Placing was always a valuable word, since it implies lighter grip pressure," said Ben Crenshaw, one of Penick's greatest pupils.

Too firm a grip may signify even more. It may mean you are simply taking the game too seriously. You are applying too much pressure to yourself and, by extension, your club.

In the rest of your life you may be able to bear down and do a thing that needs to be done, through sheer force of will. You apply yourself. You push. You do it, and it gets done.

You may be bringing this attitude with you onto the golf course. You may be bearing down and just trying to do the thing that needs to be done. And this attitude manifests itself every time you pick up a club.

Lighten up on yourself and your club. You will have far better results.

Resolved: I check my grip.

October 25

"When I said you were an optimist, I didn't mean that you took too rosy a view of matters, but that you were full of the zest of life and confident about the value and the success of what you undertook."

—George Santayana, writing to a friend

A golfing friend we know explained his dilemma thusly:

"I read those tips in the magazines. Who doesn't, right? You try and pick up things. I read one and I think, 'Yeah, that sounds good,' and I go out and try it. Then I pick up another magazine, or maybe even the same magazine, and I read another tip from some other guy and I say, 'Yeah, that sounds good,' and I try that one too. I'll try anything if I think it'll help me.

"I explained this to a buddy of mine, and he said I needed to specialize. You can't jump around from one magazine tip guy to the next. You gotta find one guy and stick with him. Stick with Tom Watson if you like Tom Watson. Or Greg Norman if you like him. Whatever. As long as it's one guy and not a bunch of different guys.

"Anyway, this sounded like pretty good advice to me, so that's what I'm doing. I decided to pick Jack Nicklaus and stick with him. He golfs a lot like me."

Oh well, never hurts to try anyway. There is always the chance that a tip might actually work. In this way, and in so many others, golfers remain perpetual optimists. They believe that enlightenment is always around the next bend in the fairway.

Resolved: I stay optimistic about my game.

October 26

"We are all of us weak at times."

—Lewis Carroll

You are only as strong as your weaknesses.

Every golfer has a club in his bag that he fears. You play around it, or away from it. You substitute a different club because you know what happens when you play the other. Thus, you become even less proficient with the club you fear and your fear grows.

The same holds true for certain golf course conditions or situations, such as sand or wind or even walking up to the first tee. We develop mental blocks about them too.

Today, we step out of that cycle. We look fear in the face. We make a commitment to turn a weakness into a strength.

We learn to play a 2-iron well if it is giving us trouble now.

We become a good sand player if we fear the bunkers.

We calm our nerves and maintain our confidence on the opening tee.

We learn to chip if that is a weakness in our game.

We get better at putting.

What you perceive now as a weakness may become, through effort, a positive attribute. Turn weakness into strength. See weakness only as a latent, as-yet-undeveloped strength. Be fearless. Develop all your capacities and make your game an all-around strong one.

Resolved: I turn a weakness into a strength.

October 27

"The golfer has more enemies than any other athlete. He has 14 clubs in his bag, all of them different; 18 holes to play; and all around him are sand, trees, grass, water, wind. . . ."

—Dan Jenkins

Jenkins left one name off his enemies list: hills.

Hills are brutal on a golf course. They are tough to walk up and hit over. They loom large in the geography of our minds, too. We think about the hill on 5 before we start, and privately figure that if we play it well we will have a good round.

Raise the level of your game when you come to a hill. Bear down. Raise your game to meet the upraised geography.

How do you do this? By seeing a hill for what it is: a lump of dirt. Our problems with hills come when we turn them into mountains and exaggerate their impact. A hill is just one of the factors that we must manage over 18 holes.

Take this clear-eyed approach with the other "enemies" as well: sand, trees, rough, water, wind. Every other player must face these obstacles too. See them for what they are. If you land in sand, you land in sand. Then you get out. If you hit it in water you take a penalty and keep playing. The game goes on.

Look your enemies straight in the eye. See them for what they are and nothing more. This will reduce their power and raise the level of your performance.

Resolved: I see a hill for what it is.

October 28

"No pessimist ever discovered the secrets of the stars, or sailed to an uncharted land, or opened a new heaven to the human spirit."

—Helen Keller

Wage war against pessimism. Come back strong.

Show hope, faith, and love. Come back strong.

When the game throws you for a loop, as inevitably it will, come back strong.

If you play poorly on the front nine, come back strong on the back.

If you play poorly on the first 17 holes, salvage it on 18. Come back strong.

Come back strong today if you played poorly yesterday.

Some days those old, bad voices will return to haunt you. So will those old nasty habits you have been trying so hard to eradicate. In your panic you may fear that all your hours on the golf course have been undone.

One way to put those nagging voices to rest: Come back strong.

Your problems may indicate a lack of self-discipline. You know what to do, you just did not do it. Or perhaps you just need to work harder.

Redouble your efforts then. Come back strong.

Then again, your bad day may be nothing more than that: a bad day. Happened before, it'll happen again. When it happens, put it behind you in the best way imaginable. Come back strong.

Resolved: I come back strong.

October 29

"Friends are necessary to a happy life."

—Harry Emerson Fosdick

John Updike and his regular golf partners take a vote at the end of each round. The vote is to decide who among them hit "The Most Ignominious Shot." There are usually several contenders—the drive that landed two fairways over, the putt that ran across the green and back into the trap, the ball that got stuck in a tree, etc. Voting is always conducted over alcoholic beverages of some type.

Your foursome may also want to cast ballots on who hit the most ignominious shot. Updike says it takes some of the sting out of actually performing the ugly deed.

Sometimes we get so locked into our own skulls during a game of golf that we forget why we are out there in the first place. One reason—the main reason—is the people we are playing with.

For many of us, golf is just an excuse to get together with our friends. You take friends onto the course, and you make friends while you are there. Our friends are as necessary to our golf as a bag and clubs.

Who else to play "The Most Ignominious Shot" with? Who else to buck you up when you're feeling low? Who else to knock you down to size when you're acting uppity? Who else to trade memories with? Who else to hoist beers with at the end of the day? Who else to share a laugh with? Who else but your friends?

Resolved: I enjoy my golfing friends.

October 30

Golfers are, by and large, a well-behaved lot. When we encounter a bloke who is rude or offensive or of a vulgar habit of mind, we generally prefer, as do all well-mannered people, to simply absent ourselves from the situation rather than risk a confrontation.

But circumstances may arise in which it is impossible to walk away. Greg Norman found himself in just such a situation at the 1986 U.S. Open at Shinnecock. It was the third day. Norman started in the lead but watched as his game—and his five-stroke lead—crumbled. After a double bogey on 13 he stepped up to the tee at 14 when, from out of the gallery, a rude honker bleated, "You're choking, Norman!"

The blond and large-of-body Australian did not respond at first. He hit, then responded. "If you have something to say to me, say it after the round when I can do something about it," he told the heckler.

The heckler was slain. St. Greg had slain the dragon. Rendered speechless, it slunk back into the crowd like the low and cowardly beast it was. But the confrontation had quite the opposite effect on Norman. He got a charge from it.

Struggling to lift his game from a trough of depression up to that point, he finished up strong with a 1-under-par 71.

Maybe you would do what Greg did, maybe not. But it is something to consider the next time someone acts like a lout on the golf course.

Resolved: I speak up if somebody is rude or ill-tempered.

October 31

"Know your swing. Most golfers do not know what they look like when they swing the club. They think they look like Jack Nicklaus, but in reality they look like somebody having a spasm."

—Dan Jenkins

Find out what you really look like: Videotape your swing.

A pro can do it as part of a package of lessons. He or she may also be helpful in making sense out of what you are seeing, but it is not mandatory. Nearly everyone these days owns a videocamera or has access to one and can do it themselves.

It is surprising how few golfers have seen themselves in action, considering how easy it is to do. Maybe they are frightened of what they'll see.

Seeing yourself swing a golf club is like trying on a new bathing suit in front of a mirror: "So this is what I look like." You may not be entirely thrilled by what you see. You may think you can do better. This will serve as a motivation to improve.

It might be fun to keep a video record of your swing from year to year. Better still, videotape yourself when you are swinging the club well. Review the tape if your game turns sour and see what you are doing different now than you were then.

If nothing else, it is good for a laugh. You can show it on a night like tonight, and scare the hell out of the neighbors.

Resolved: I videotape my swing.

November 1

"I never found the companion that was so companionable as solitude."

—Henry David Thoreau

As the days grow shorter and winter approaches, steal away on your own for a game of golf.

Ever played solo? Not as a single walking onto a group, but truly alone?

It is not easy to do. Courses generally frown on the practice, if not forbid it. Demand for space is too keen. But there are days in late fall and winter when they might let you on alone, if you get lucky, when twilight time is ending and everybody who wants to has already gone out, and there is no harm in one individual on foot going out on the course while darkness falls.

You have the place to yourself. Others are out playing in the failing light too, but they are up ahead and so it is quiet where you walk.

There is no need to hurry; you go at your own pace. Still, you play quickly because the sun has other business and will not tarry for long.

You can practice if it strikes you as worth doing. Hit two tee balls and play an imaginary game against yourself.

But practice is too much like work today, and work is far from your mind. If you hustle you will get in nine holes, but it hardly matters how many holes you play. All that matters is you are playing, hitting a ball, and giving chase across wide green fields in the rich vibrant dark.

Resolved: I play solo sometime.

November 2

"There is probably not a single man or woman who has not overcome powerful obstacles and accomplished things extremely difficult to undertake."

—Ernest Dimnet

Put yourself in a position to succeed. Do that, and you have done nearly all that you can do as a golfer.

You will not always win. But you will only win unless you first put yourself into a position to succeed.

Play a round of golf with this in mind. Put yourself into a position to succeed. Make this the underpinning of every shot. You will have no problems determining your strategy if you do.

How do you play your tee ball? Put yourself in a position to suceed. How do you play an approach? Put yourself in a position to succeed.

You have an eight-foot putt to win a tournament. That's a tough position, and it could go either way.

But one thing is sure: You have put yourself in a position to succeed. You have done what you needed to do. Of course you want to make the putt, and that is important. What's also important is that you recognize that it took an awful lot of work and hard effort to get where you are, and you *made* it. You have overcome powerful obstacles and undertaken a difficult thing. You deserve credit for that, irrespective of what happens with the putt.

Put yourself in a position to succeed and sooner or later you will.

Resolved: I put myself in a position to succeed.

November 3

This is the hardest thing: putting them away when you are in the lead.

The history of golf is littered with the ruins of golfers who could not finish the kill. The most famous instance occurred at the 1966 U.S. Open at the Olympic Club in San Francisco when Arnold Palmer gave up seven strokes on the back nine and threw away the championship. Billy Casper tied him at the end of 72 holes and beat Arnold in a playoff to claim the crown.

What happened to Arnold? He said that he began thinking about his place in history, about setting a record—not his golf—and this doomed him.

Now, you may not be playing for golf immortality or to set a record. But self-consciousness of this type—any sort of pulling away from the moment—can wreck your golf the same as it did Arnold's.

There is a tendency to ease up when playing well or in the lead. You lose your aggressiveness; you begin to coast. Before you know it, your edge is gone.

Mercy has no place in winning golf. Fight for every hole. Fight on every shot. Give nothing away. Concede nothing. Do what Grandma should have done when she heard the Wolf knocking on the door. Bolt the door shut and walk away.

Resolved: I fight for every hole, and on every shot.

November 4

"I am convinced that we have a degree of delight, and that no small one, in the real misfortunes and pains of others."

—Edmund Burke

Let's get catty, shall we?

Of all the pleasures that golf is heir to, this may be the most sublime: *Everybody gets theirs.* Nicklaus, Watson, Norman, Faldo, Ballesteros—there are no exemptions on *this* tour. No matter how proud the peacock, how brilliant its plumage, golf plucks its feathers.

The Germans have a word for this emotion: *schadenfreude*, or taking delight in the misfortunes of others.

Schadenfreude is a wonderful motivator too, one of the best. Say you play a round with an associate from the office. He is a good player, but not as good as he thinks. But everything goes his way and he sparkles like cheap jewelry in a foursome that includes, much to your displeasure, the president of the company.

You make another date to play. You practice, take a secret lesson from a pro. And count the days.

The day arrives. Your colleague takes a divot on his opening tee shot and the divot travels farther than the ball. Things deteriorate from there. The look of intense suffering on your colleague's face is a delight to behold. Meanwhile, you have a pretty good day and even receive praise from your golf-playing company president, who is again in the foursome.

Everybody gets theirs. No one is spared. Meanwhile, keep practicing.

Resolved: When a rival from work goes down in flames on the golf course, I offer my heartfelt sympathy.

November 5

It is time to put a little felicity in your golf game. It is time to hit a golf ball off a cruise ship.

First, you must book a cruise. It is impossible to hit a golf ball off a 12-foot El Toro. Well, not *impossible*—but the effect is not quite the same as on a luxury ocean liner.

The choice of waters is yours. The Caribbean, South America, South Pacific are all nice. The cruise line must have accommodations for golfers, but why would you want to go on one that didn't?

According to an item in L. M. Boyd's column: "Collagen comes from bone cartilage, tendon tissue. Boil it and it turns to gelatin. Makers of golf gear mix it with ground citrus peel to turn out golf balls for cruise ships. Knocked overboard, they dissolve and feed the fish."

See, you'll even be helping the environment! As opposed to when you normally hit into water, when all the ball does is sink to the bottom in disgrace.

The fairway is as big as the ocean. It *is* the ocean. If only all fairways were this big. The ball sails and sails, and although you do not get the roll you ordinarily would, it hardly matters. You are hitting it in the air 350, 400 yards, *easy*. Who's to contradict you, anyhow?

Then, after you are done, go eat. That is the second-best thing to do on a cruise ship.

Resolved: I hit a golf ball off a cruise ship.

November 6

"By wisdom a house is built, and through understanding it is established; through knowledge its rooms are filled with rare and beautiful treasures."

—Proverbs 24:3–4

Do you judge your day when you get up, before you've had your morning coffee?

Do you judge how the entire year has gone in August?

Do you judge a two-week vacation after the first week?

Do you judge the beauty and sturdiness of a house before it is built?

Well, then. Why do you judge a round of golf before it is over?

Oh. You say you don't. Good for you. Then we're talking to some others here. They have yet to learn the wisdom of waiting till a round is over before assessing its merits.

Many golfers tend to make premature judgments about their round as they are playing it. These judgments are almost always of a negative cast. A person playing well after five holes would never assume that he or she is going to have a record-setting round. But people who are struggling after five holes (or nine or eleven) will frequently bury themselves prematurely and write their round off as a failure.

Stay out of this trap. Wait until the end to evaluate your round. Prejudging your round forecloses the possibility of good things, even great things, occurring later on. Wait until the house is built until you make your walk-through. You may yet discover rooms filled with rare and beautiful treasures.

Resolved: I wait till the end of my round before forming any conclusions.

November 7

"I realized I came into the world with nothing, and I could leave with nothing."

—Paul Azinger, after being diagnosed with cancer

Months after Paul Azinger won his first-ever major golf title, the 1993 PGA Championship, doctors told him he had cancer.

He was still on a high after winning the PGA in August, still contending for the money title and Player of the Year honors. Then came the news: lymphoma in his shoulder. It stunned him to the core. Despite his fame and success, he felt stripped bare. What had once been so meaningful to him, his golf game, was suddenly rendered meaningless.

There was more to his life, though. A wife and family who loved him, the genuine admiration and friendship of his colleagues on the Tour, and a newfound relationship with God. "I realize I am nothing without God," he said.

Azinger left the Tour to devote himself to getting healthy. Chemotherapy lasted six months. He had a goal: play golf on the Tour again. He was lucky. Doctors feel they caught the cancer in time, and in one of the most emotional moments of his life, Azinger rejoined the PGA Tour in early 1995.

"I used to dread my birthday," he said. "Now I can't wait to get to 35 and I can't wait to get to 36 and 37 and 38. I can't wait to celebrate all those birthdays."

Resolved: I refuse to be bothered anymore by the little things—in golf or anyplace else.

November 8

"I am a better putter now, because it doesn't mean so much to me."

—Tommy Armour

This is the infernal catch-22 of golf:

You almost certainly will not get what you want on any given day in golf if you want it too much. "I am going to break 80 today," you tell yourself with steely resolve. Then you struggle to break 100.

A week later you're kinda tired and you think, "I don't care what I shoot today," and you really mean it. That's the day you set a course record.

Want a thing in golf and it will elude you. Not want it and FedEx will deliver it to your door.

So is that the secret to golf? Not caring? Not wanting? No, that's the catch:

Want a thing and you will not get it. Not want and you may. But those who do not want it will only get it if they wanted it in the first place. That's the catch: You must want in order to not want.

And yet there is a way out of this jam: acceptance. Acceptance is not passivity or a form of resignation; you still go out and *do* it. You still whack it around with gusto, chase low scores, and give it your best shot.

Play well? Accept it. Play not so well? Accept it. However it goes, you accept it and move on. Take the game as it comes. This will lift you out of the want–not want cycle and move your game forward.

Resolved: I accept what happens.

November 9

"Certainly there are ways of translating ideas that can be helpful, but the objective is not to swing the club in a specified manner, nor to execute a series of complicated movements in a prescribed sequence, nor to look pretty while doing it, but primarily and essentially to strike the ball with the head of the club so that the ball will perform according to one's wishes."

—Bobby Jones

To be brief, give it the treatment.

This is Ernie Els's term. It may not be as eloquent as Bobby Jones, but it speaks volumes: Give it the treatment.

Ernie Els is one of the best players in the world because he frequently gives the ball "the treatment." He widens his stance. He slows his swing down. And he knocks the cover off the ball.

That's telling 'em, Ern. Give it the treatment.

It is an attitude as much as anything else. When Ernie starts giving the ball the treatment, watch out. Hide the children. Barricade the doors, board the windows. Ever heard a golf ball scream? It does when it gets the treatment.

You can read books and magazine articles. You can watch videos. You can take lessons. You may find ways of translating ideas that are helpful to you.

But this is a pretty good method too: Step up to the ball, and give it the treatment.

Resolved: I give it the treatment.

November 10

"The more you separate performance from self-worth, the better off you'll be."

—Bob Rotella

Question for the day: Do you think you'd be a happier golfer if you were a better golfer?

"Yes, yes, a thousand times yes!" comes the thunderous reply.

No, wait. Think about it a minute. It is a more complicated question than appears on the surface. You would be a better golfer if you trimmed some strokes. But would be you be any happier?

Shaving how many strokes, in your mind, would constitute happiness? Five? Fifteen? Twenty-five? If you shoot 100 now and are miserably unhappy as a golfer, you must face the uncomfortable fact that you will probably be miserably unhappy shooting 85. If you are overly critical of yourself at an 11-handicap, you will likely find just as much to be critical about even at a five.

Consider, too, if suddenly you became a scratch golfer. This would almost assuredly make you more ambitious and more competitive than you are today. These are not qualities that lend themselves to feelings of self-fulfillment.

You are ensuring yourself a lifetime of golfing misery if you equate strokes with happiness or self-worth. Your scores will vary from day to day, sometimes radically. Why let your mood, your whole person, be in thrall to that?

Walk onto a golf course happy and you have a far better chance of walking off happy.

Resolved: I separate self-worth from performance.

November 11

"Pressure is getting shot at while you're running through the jungle. Pressure is when you don't know where the bullets are coming from. Playing golf isn't easy. But pressure? I don't feel the pressure."

—Vietnam War veteran Walter Morgan,
on playing the Senior Tour

Men of great character have played the game of golf. Many of them fought in their nation's wars and served with valor.

On Veterans Day, a partial honor roll of heroes who also played golf:

World War I. Two of the game's greatest teachers, Ernest Jones and Tommy Armour, fought in the War to End All Wars.

World War II. Four-time British Open champion Bobby Locke flew in the RAF. American Bob Sweeny flew for the Eagle Squadron in alliance with the RAF. After the war, Sweeny lost the U.S. Amateur Championship to a young unknown named Arnold Palmer. Tour pro Lloyd Mangrum won two Purple Hearts for his bravery at the Battle of the Bulge. Inveterate amateur golfer Dwight Eisenhower led the Allied Forces in Europe and later served as president of the United States.

Vietnam. Larry Nelson took up golf at the age of 21 after returning from service in Vietnam. He later joined the professional tour. Walter Morgan spent 20 years in the Army, including two tours of duty in Vietnam, before joining the Senior Tour. Buddy Allen won a Bronze Star and two Army commendations for bravery in Vietnam. After leaving the service in 1969, he joined the PGA Tour and won two titles.

Resolved: I do what all these men would do if they could. I play golf.

November 12

"The highest reward for a man's toil is not what he gets for it, but what he becomes by it."

—John Ruskin

Make one last good effort. Men and women, boys and girls: Make one last good effort.

Make one last good effort when you're nearing the end of your round and you're tired.

Make one last good effort when you are struggling on a hole. Get that ball on the green, and get it in the hole.

Make one last good effort when you are on top of your game and everything is going your way. You will need that one last good effort just as surely at this time as any other.

Make one last good effort when you walk onto the 18th tee, and then again when you reach the final green. Finish your round knowing that you gave it all you had, that you made one last good effort.

We are nearing the end of the year. You have set goals for yourself, things you wanted to accomplish in golf and in other areas of your life. Make one last good effort, and another after that, and another after that.

Making one last good effort requires courage, strength, and determination. You have shown that you possess these qualities by the simple fact that you have come as far as you have. Now finish the job. Make one last good effort.

Resolved: I make one last good effort.

November 13

"It's just one of those days when you hit what I would consider perfect putts. I hit edge after edge after edge."

—Tiger Woods, playing in the U.S. Amateur

Have one of those days today: Go for the edge.

Go for the edge of the cup. Roll the ball up; make sure it gets there. Send it up to the edge and watch it disappear.

Go for the edge in other ways—in *every* way. Take the driver out of the bag. We want the edge it gives us. We do not ignore the risks so much as appreciate them. We take that big stick in our paws and go for it all.

The edge is an attitude. We exalt and exclaim this attitude. Today we have it.

We look for any advantage we can find. We play with controlled aggression, willing to explore the limits of what we can do on a golf course. We are fearless.

Others may give away strokes. Others may let events overwhelm them. Others may let opportunities slip through their hands.

Not us. We play on the edge.

In so doing we raise our game to a new level. We find we are capable of things we did not know were possible. We challenge ourselves and rise to meet the challenge. We go for the edge—and make it.

Resolved: I go for the edge.

November 14

"There's nothing wrong with four-putting. It just means you missed the third one."

—Fuzzy Zoeller

Fuzzy is kidding, but he does have a point: A four-putt is not exactly the end of the world.

A four-putt is a banana peel, that's all it is.

How would you react if you took a pratfall on the sidewalk after slipping on a banana peel? Sure, you'd be embarrassed. Your pride would be hurt. Maybe you even skinned your elbow on the pavement.

It is definitely not something you want to repeat, but do you suddenly decide you are a clumsy oaf because of it? That you can't walk? That you need to go to walking school and relearn how to do it? That you need to break your legs?

Naw, you just throw the peel in the trash, laugh or smile good-naturedly along with anyone who may have witnessed the fall, and go on. It was a banana peel, nothing more. There is certainly no reason to indulge in extensive self-analysis that questions your ability to put one foot in front of the other because of it.

A four-putt is only one of the many banana peels in the game of golf. Some might argue that golf is one gigantic banana peel. In any case, forget about it. It is just a lousy banana peel. Pick yourself up, smile about it, go on. The faster you put it behind you, the less likely you are to take any more embarrassing tumbles.

Resolved: I take a four-putt with a smile.

November 15

"When you feel a fool, and a bad golfer to boot, what can you do except to throw the club away?"

—Bobby Jones

All things considered, golfers ought not to throw their clubs. But many of them do anyway.

If you are one of those people (like Bobby Jones as a young man, Arnold Palmer, Tommy Bolt, and many more) who occasionally succumb to the urge, you might want to keep a few things in mind.

First, if you're going to throw it, really do the job. Flipping the club has a certain panache, but it is not nearly as satisfying as an all-out "I can't take this anymore!" heave. A golf club in flight is a beautiful thing to see, like geese migrating south for the winter.

Secondly, keep your promises. Follow through with it if you say you are going to do it. An old-time golfer named Ralph Guldahl once promised to throw his clubs in a lake if he did not win a tournament. When he lost he backed down on his pledge to dunk his clubs and received heavy criticism for it. People wanted to see those clubs take a bath.

Another important club-throwing consideration is this: Have a good reason. Don't throw a club just because you've made a 12 on a par 3; wait until you've done something truly awful. Make every throw count. It's also imperative to have a sense of place. What are you going to do on the back nine if you're tossing clubs left and right on the front? Let your fury build. It will be all the more satisfying when you finally release it.

Resolved: When I throw my club, I get my money's worth and really heave it.

November 16

"Take what God-given talent you have and work with it. Don't work against it."

—Ben Crenshaw

It is fascinating to read Harv Penick's account of teaching Ben Crenshaw as a youngster.

Both Ben and his brother Charles were very talented young golfers. But Ben concentrated on golf while Charles played a variety of sports, and this made the difference.

Ben always had a wondrous touch on the greens, which came, perhaps, from his piano-playing mom. One time Ben was leading three other players on the back nine. He said that he would play the remaining six holes left-handed and challenged the others to beat him. He played left-handed the rest of the round and won.

One characteristic of the young Crenshaw was enthusiasm. He loved to play. He played in the cold. He played when everyone else had gone home. He would win a tournament and afterwards go play another round.

Harv Penick told Ben "to play golf to his heart's content and to practice only when guidance was needed." This is good advice not only for a young prodigy such as Ben Crenshaw, but also for those of us who are neither young nor prodigious.

Play in the cold. Play when everyone else has gone home. Play when it's "crazy" to play. Take what God-given talent you have and give it an outlet for expression. Seek guidance when you need it. But mainly, play, play, play. Play to your heart's content.

Resolved: I play to my heart's content.

November 17

"The game had its instant fascination for me. The difference between a good shot and a bad shot was marvellously large, and yet the difference between a good swing and a bad swing seemed microscopically small."

—John Updike

Every golfer appreciates this fact—the microscopically small yet marvelously large difference between a good shot and a bad shot.

One of the greatest ever, Bobby Jones, said that at most he only struck a half-dozen exactly right shots in a round. The rest were off in some way.

The USGA says that if you move your driver out of line by *one* degree, your ball will go 10 yards off the target. One degree equals 10 yards? It doesn't seem fair somehow.

What do we do, then, with the odds so clearly stacked against us?

Well, we can fix on the many imperfect shots we hit and feel despair about them.

Or:

We can be fascinated and challenged by the razor-thin margin of excellence in this grandest of games. We can focus on the times we do get it exactly right, those times we bring that driver down in line and give the ball a good smacking.

Today, take the latter approach. Do as Rick Reilly advises: "If you hit one well, rejoice, and enjoy the walk down the middle of the fairway."

Resolved: I rejoice, and enjoy the walk down the middle of the fairway.

November 18

"A good person doubles the length of his or her existence. To have lived so as to look back with pleasure on life is to have lived twice."

—Martial

Live golf twice. Look back on it with pleasure.

We golfers are an unusual lot. We can play a marvelous round and hit the ball wonderfully. But when we look back on it all we can talk about is the shot we sclaffed on 14.

Self-criticism has value up to a point. But that is not what we are up to today. Today, look back with pleasure.

Been keeping a golfing diary for the year? Take it out, flip through the pages. Look back with pleasure.

Remember the good bounces, the laughs, the holed putts, the wondrous recoveries, that chip out of the sand that went in on 7, the time you nearly hit an ace on 17, the sun setting behind the trees as you raced the daylight to get in a full 18, the drinks and camaraderie at the end of the day.

Remember the last time you played, whenever that was: last week, last month, six months ago. Let your mind go back to that time and enjoy it once more. What's the harm? Treat your golfing past as you would a good wine. Savor it.

Look back with pleasure. This is another way to focus on the positive in your game. Then go out and make new memories that you can look back on with pleasure in the future.

Resolved: I look back with pleasure.

November 19

"When a friend is in trouble, don't annoy him by asking if there is anything you can do. Think up something appropriate and do it."

—E. W. Howe

When a friend is in trouble on the golf course, think up something appropriate and do it.

Pick up his clubs for him and tote them up to the green. Lend him the new driver out of your bag that he has been admiring for weeks. Leave him alone if he wants to be alone. Let him go out of turn and hit first on the tee, if you think it might change his rhythm and bring him out of his funk. Most certainly, buy drinks after. These simple acts of kindness may help a fellow traveler far more than the advice that golfers usually dispense to those who are struggling.

You may be able to help your friend in another way. Maybe you haven't seen this friend in a while. Maybe he has been struggling in his personal life and that is why he has been out of commission.

Pick up the phone, give him a call. Get him out on the golf course. Don't take no for an answer. Golf is a good way to get away from it all. Your friend may need that.

Heck, you may need it. Life may be pressing in a little bit too hard on you these days. You may need a break too.

What, there's no time? There's time. Go out and *make* the time. Why is there only time for doing things that cause us stress, provide mixed rewards, make us unhappy? Make a grand gesture. Do something nice for yourself and a friend who may need it. Play a round of golf.

Resolved: I play a round of golf with a friend I haven't seen in a while.

November 20

"If there was any reward I treasured most, it was the way the game responded to my inner drives, to the feeling we all have that—in those moments that are so profoundly a challenge, to man himself—he has done his best. That—win or lose—nothing more could have been done."

—Arnold Palmer

Want to be inspired? Want to challenge yourself? Play a great golf course.

Your home course is fine. Nothing wrong with it at all. It is a fine little course.

Now go out and test yourself. Play a course that tests you and everything you know. Play a course that is so beautiful it makes your eyes hurt. Play a course where you can take nothing for granted, that forces you to play your very best.

You know the type of course I'm talking about. Maybe you have even been avoiding it. If it takes an extra dip into the wallet, so be it.

Play a course where you leave it all on the course. Where nothing more could have been done.

Play a course like that and you know what the effect will be? You will be *pumped.* A hit of energy like an electrical current will shoot through your veins. You will realize anew why you got into this game and why you love it so.

And you will want to do it again. As soon as you can. Because you tested yourself against that great golf course and—you'll never guess what happened. You measured up.

Resolved: I play a great golf course.

November 21

*"There are people who rise to certain occasions, and there
are people who back off. Maybe it's a lack of confidence.
But through the years you see the players who have tenacity
to them."*

—Hale Irwin

Be tenacious. Be a player who rises to the occasion.

The official opening of a round of golf is the first tee. But we all know that sometimes our games do not get started until the 2nd or 7th or 15th tees. When your game finally slips from neutral into drive, be ready for it. Push that pedal down. Rise to the occasion.

Except in our dreams, few of us will stand on the 18th green with a chance to win the U.S. Open on our final putt. But we can still rise to the occasion as it presents itself to us in our own lives.

Rising to the occasion means being sensitive to your game and listening to what it is telling you. Your clubs may be acting like spoiled children and refusing to cooperate. Is the best response to get angry and stomp around like a child yourself? Maybe you just need to show more patience with yourself.

Give your game the space it needs to excel. Loosen its leash. It may not want to perform exactly as you are telling it to perform, right at that moment. Expect that. A gentler hand may even speed the time it takes before your game begins to cooperate with you.

Then, when it comes—and it will come—be tenacious. Take the moment in hand and start hitting shots.

Resolved: I rise to the occasion.

November 22

"Nothing is done while something remains to be done. To finish is the mark of the master."

—Henri Frederic Amiel

In the 1600s, Charles I of England was playing golf when a messenger informed him that a civil war had broken out in his kingdom. "Oh, well," he said. "First things first . . ." He finished his round before attending to business.

Good for you, Chuck! Earthquakes, fires, civil war, floods, *whatever*—it can all wait until you finish your round.

It is important to finish what you start in golf no less than in other pursuits. You set out to play 18, then play 18. How do you know how you did unless you play 'em all? You may be walking away from your best golf if you cut out early.

There will always be outside pressures on you, always pressures on you to cut your round short or even to not play at all. Walk away from those pressures. Make a pact with yourself to ignore them, at least while you are on the course.

One year four men were playing Augusta National when suddenly the president of the United States, Dwight Eisenhower, appeared. Ike, who had been in the foursome behind them, was extremely agitated and wanted to know if he could play through.

"Certainly, Mr. President," said one. "But what's the hurry?"

"New York's just been bombed," said Ike.

It's an old joke, but you get the drift. If it's worth doing in the first place, do it all the way.

Resolved: I finish my round.

November 23

"Eventually all golfers suffer a nervous collapse."

—Stephen Baker

Stephen Baker is the author of a classic golf humor book, *How to Play Golf in the Low 120's.* In it he lists a few telltale signs of a golfer who is playing too much:

The golfer can no longer function in his job, and he is about to lose it.

His wife and children no longer recognize him when and if he comes home.

He suffers from acute indigestion, insomnia, heart palpitations, high blood pressure, dizzy spells, a nervous facial tic, stutter.

He talks in his sleep about golf shots he should have made.

Golfers with one or more of these symptoms should consult the expert advice of those versed in emotional problems, such as a psychiatrist or priest. He tells of one golfer who saw an analyst for over a year because he was suffering emotional turmoil from a chronic slice. The analyst sent him home completely cured. "He was told his backswing was too fast," writes Baker.

Baker is kidding, but golf burnout is real. Symptoms include chronic pain and emotional and physical fatigue. Take some time off if the game is starting to wear on you. Take a week off. See how that feels. Take another week off it feels good. Stay away a month or more if you need to.

When you come back, having reacquainted yourself with your family and free of all those nervous facial tics, you can enjoy the game anew.

Resolved: I take some time off to recharge my batteries.

November 24

"As you get older, it is harder to have heroes, but it is sort of necessary."

—Ernest Hemingway

There are lots of heroes in golf, even for those who are older and have a harder time finding them.

There is Paul Azinger, coming back to the tour after a cancer diagnosis.

There is Greg Norman, who handles victory and his occasional stunning defeat with grace and class.

There are the moms of the LPGA Tour, many of whom travel with their children around the country and combine family with the ardent pursuit of golfing excellence.

There are many heroes in golf. We learn by their excellent examples. They model the best of who we are.

Here is another way we learn from them: their faults, their mistakes, their sins, their weaknesses. These can be just as inspiring as their virtues.

Why? Because they remind us that we don't have to be a Superman to be a great champion or an athletic hero. These people are just like you and me. They have faults like you and me. We can achieve greatness and yet still be our imperfect selves. We can still realize our dreams though we have faults.

There is no magic that these men and women possess that we ourselves do not possess. The magic is not exclusively theirs or anyone else's. The gift of the hero is that he or she grabbed for the magic. But you can too. Take it! Grab it! Now! Today!

Resolved: I grab for the magic.

November 25

"I don't think there's any question the game is self-limiting. If you increase length, you lose accuracy. The game is so old that everything's been tried."

—Frank Thomas, technical expert

Golf companies advertise that such and such a player uses their clubs or balls or shoes or whatever. The inference—and sometimes it's a boldly stated outright assertion!—is that if you use these clubs you too will become a better player.

Of course, those companies pay top players to use their equipment. The players sign exclusive contracts and receive huge sums. The players would play a different brand of club or wear a different logo on their hat if their sponsor changed—frequently, this is what happens.

Golf, like life, is a matter of trade-offs. Increase length, lose accuracy. Gain accuracy, lose some length. There are no magic fixes when it comes to golf equipment. Change your shoes and it's still the same pair of feet in those shoes. Change your clubs and it's the same pair of hands holding them, with the same grip.

Place your faith where it belongs: in yourself. Your clubs matter, but only to the degree you think they matter. Give Greg Norman a stick and he will still beat most amateurs playing with the latest that technology can offer. He knows how to wield that stick, and has confidence in his ability to do it. Trust yourself, have faith in your abilities, and you can play with anything.

Resolved: I trust myself and my clubs.

November 26

"I was just trying to tell myself, 'One more good tee ball.'"
—Mike Donald, approaching the 18th tee
of a U.S. Open playoff

Tell yourself when you approach 18: One more good tee ball.

Maybe you have had a good day. Maybe you have struggled. In any case: One more good tee ball.

When your putt goes down on 17, immediately forget about it. Reach down, pick up your ball, and begin thinking: "One more good tee ball."

Eighteen is the final hole. A good final hole can change the hue of a less-than-rosy day. It can chase the clouds away and bring the sun out. A great final hole can turn a good round into a great round. A great final hole can turn a great round into a thing of beauty. It can be the exclamation point on a document of Jeffersonian eloquence.

Start the last hole right. One more good tee ball.

You are no doubt tired. Perhaps you are thinking ahead to the clubhouse. Summon your thoughts back to the moment. Revivify your spirits with a final heroic effort. Think it, and see it in your mind's eye. One more good tee ball.

One more good tee ball leads to one more good approach, which leads to one more good putt. Birdie! Should that blessed event occur, you will most assuredly forget about how tired you were and want to proceed immediately to the first tee. Hold that same thought if you do convince your partners to go out again: One more good tee ball.

Resolved: One more good tee ball on 18.

November 27

"For the long hours and days it has taken from me, golf has given back what Ralph Waldo Emerson would call a new me, a life enhanced, lengthened into a new dimension."

—John Updike

The broadcaster Bernie Ward likes to tell a parable about Cinderella at the ball.

Midnight has arrived. The clock has begun to chime. Cinderella, in a mad dash, bolts from the palace and the arms of her lovestruck but baffled Prince. She races down the steps, her lovely gown beginning to turn to rags even as she loses her slipper. She jumps in her carrriage and the horses make their getaway as the clock strikes twelve.

Dressed once again in rags, her fairy-tale night over, a heartbroken Cinderella confronts her Fairy Godmother. "Why," she asks in tears. "Why did the ball have to end at midnight?"

The Fairy Godmother is a good ole gal who knows more than Cinderella ever will. She sympathizes with the young girl, and in her sympathy shares with her this fundamental truth:

"Dear girl," she says. "You are lucky you got to go at all."

This is true for us golfers, too. We really are a lucky lot, with much to be thankful for. We get to spend at least part of our time ambling around cultivated green pastures under a vast, magnificent sky.

The ball may not last as long as we like. We may not dance as well as we wish. But we are lucky, oh so lucky, to get to go.

Resolved: I count my blessings in golf and life.

November 28

"We live to play: that is my slogan."

—J. B. Yeats

It is the day after Thanksgiving, a virtual holiday in this country. And what is the best thing to do on a holiday, virtual or otherwise? Play golf.

Of course, probably a few million other people have the same idea. Consequently your local pitch 'n' putt is jammed like the Hollywood Freeway at rush hour. What to do? Retreat to the fridge for more leftovers? Nope. You still try to get on. How?

Go early, or late. Sometimes you can get on if you get there first thing in the morning before the masses have descended. Or very late in the day after they've gone home.

Go as a single. You will have a more realistic shot if you go alone and try to catch on with a group that may have had a late dropout.

Be willing to hang. Don't just hop back in the car again when they tell you the course is booked solid with no openings. Hang out awhile.

Schmooze with the pro (or whoever's in charge of starting times). Put on a pitiful face and tell a sob story if nothing else works. The starter may take pity on you or just get sick of looking at you, and cut you a break.

Sneak on. We don't really recommend this, because it's unethical. Besides, you might get caught. But if that's what it takes to get you onto the course—well, just watch out for the marshal. They can be such fuddy-duddies about things like that.

Resolved: I try to get on *somewhere* today.

November 29

*"The beginning and the end reach out their hands to each
  other."*

—Proverb

Make your last shot in practice a good one.

If your last shot is a drive, make solid contact. Make a shot
that fills you with confidence as you gather up your clubs and
approach the first tee.

If you are on the practice green, sink your final putt. Make
it count. Hit it with a firm stroke that puts confidence in your
step as you head off.

See your last shot in practice as the first (uncounted) shot
of your round. Start on a positive note. Start with success.
Success in golf comes from making good shots, and when you
step up to the first tee you will already have one under your
belt.

Make your last shot in practice a place upon which to
build, a starting point, a launch pad for your future golf
exploration.

Resolved: I make my last shot in practice a good one.

November 30

"The amount of satisfaction you get from life depends largely on your own ingenuity, self-sufficiency, and resourcefulness."

—Dr. William Menninger

Today, I take my satisfaction where I can get it.

I can't play at all today. My only contact with the game is reading this passage. All right, then. I will take my satisfaction from *that*.

Satisfaction in golf is such a slippery animal even in the best of circumstances. You must grab hold of it whenever you can.

There are no small victories in golf. Every victory is a big victory if you allow yourself to build upon it. Taking satisfaction in what you do is a kind of victory.

Satisfaction does not equate with complacency. Nor is it smugness. This form of satisfaction originates from a wellspring of good feeling about myself and my abilities.

I have set goals and made progress toward them. I am satisfied about that.

I know I will do better. I know I can do better. I am satisfied about that too.

But I know that I am doing the very best I can. I can do no more than what I am doing right now, and that gives me great satisfaction.

Resolved: I feel satisfied about my game and myself.

December 1 (LEE TREVINO'S BIRTHDAY)

"Golf is like fighting. A guy can beat the hell out of you but you keep getting up. Finally the guy says, 'Man, when is this guy going to lie down?'"

—Lee Trevino

In the case of Lee Trevino the answer is: Never.

The public image of Trevino is that of a happy-go-lucky wisecracking man who enjoys his life and his golf. But you do not win two U.S. Opens, two British Opens, and a PGA by being happy-go-lucky. You do it by being a tough, serious-minded competitor. Lee Trevino is certainly that.

But it is Lee's birthday, and we cannot let it pass without paying tribute to his lighter side too. The Texas-born son (Horizon City, hello!) of a Mexican grave digger, Trevino joked that as soon as he made some money he'd become "a Spaniard instead of a Mexican." He said, "I always thought Manual Labor was a Mexican." About why he plays the fade, he said: "You can talk to a fade, but a hook won't listen." And, on surviving in the PGA: "The two things that don't last are pros putting for bogeys and dogs chasing cars."

At a PGA Championship in Birmingham, Alabama, he was walking down the fairway with his squat black caddie, Herman Mitchell. A voice from the gallery shouted out, "What do you feed him, Lee?" "Rednecks," Trevino replied, "and he's hungry."

Lee Trevino. A man who fought against the odds. Who combines humor with earnestness of purpose.

Resolved: I maintain a sense of humor with a tough-as-nails disposition.

December 2

"Keep playing."

—Sam Snead, asked for one piece of advice for senior golfers

Teaching pro John Geersten Jr. observes this tendency among senior golfers:

"As we get older, we tend to turn our bodies less and lose strength as well. This results in a flatter, shorter, weaker, and less effective swing." To make up for this loss of strength, senior golfers swing harder with their arms, resulting in a "jerky, fast, and usually off-balance swing," says Gersten.

The solution: Make that full extension. Concentrate on taking as full a shoulder turn as you can. Stretching exercises will help in this regard.

Here's another thing that will help: Never retire from golf.

Retire from your job. Retire from your company. Leave a cold northern state and retire to Florida. Retire your debt. Do *all* these things, but never retire from golf.

Never retire from golf—not for a year, not even for a month. You have the time now; you worked hard to earn this time. Now enjoy it. Play in February, play in November, play throughout the year. To make that good full turn you need to be as loose and flexible as your body will permit. A body needs to play regularly to retain its flexibility.

Sometimes arthritis or other physical conditions prevent you from playing as you get older. But play as long as you can and the mental and physical benefits you derive from the game will enable you to play still longer. Playing leads to more playing.

Resolved: I never retire from golf.

December 3

"Desire is the bottom line. You've got to have 100 percent desire. Anything less is complacency."

—Tom Watson

I want it.

I want it so bad I can taste it.

I have 100 percent desire. I cannot and will not conceive of a world in which the thing I want does not occur. It will happen because I will make it happen.

I will do everything in my power to achieve it. I will work very, very hard. No one will outwork me. I will sacrifice. I will do whatever it takes.

I want this in a way I have never wanted anything else in my life. I want it and I am going to get it.

I want it because I have dreamed it. I owe it to my dreams to do it.

Many people have sacrificed for me. Helped me, taught me. My parents, coaches and teachers, friends. I want to do it for them, too.

I believe in God. God comforts, assists, strengthens me. I want it for my God.

I want it for selfish reasons. I want to show those who doubted me that they were wrong. I want to show myself that I was right.

I want it. I deserve it. I am going to get it.

Resolved: I want it and I am going to get it.

December 4

Young? Like the game? Go for it. Hold nothing back.

There is no reason in heaven or on earth why you cannot be a Greg Norman or a Nancy Lopez, if that is what you desire and are willing to work for it.

No. You don't want to be them. Be yourself. Be better than them.

Make no mistake: The game will challenge you as nothing has before. You will get so furious with yourself that you will want to throw down your clubs and quit

Here are the words of an old guy, long dead. Name of Winston Churchill. All he did, in his time, was save the world. This is what he said:

"Never, never, never give up."

Burn these words into your personal data bank. Never give up. Never, never, never quit striving. Keep dreaming. You can do it. If it is only you who believes, you can still do it.

Believe in yourself and your God, and ride this faith like a spaceship toward the stars.

Resolved: I never, never, never give up.

December 5

"Things are in their essence what we choose to make them."

—Oscar Wilde

Athletes frequently alternate hard days with easy days in their training schedules. They work out hard one day, easy the next, then hard, then easy, etc. This reduces the risk of injury and keeps them fresh mentally. Nobody can go all out all the time.

Why not divide a golf course into twos based on this principle? Bear down on one hole, take it easy the next. Easy, hard, easy, hard, etc. Taking an easy-hard tack may help you sustain your concentration longer. You may find you play better when you are taking it easy than when you are bearing down.

A golf course has a physical reality and a conventional logic. But that does not mean we have to submit to them. Turn the course around in your mind. Shake it up and spill out its contents. Divide it in your mind into twos or threes or any way that suits you. Playing 18 holes can seem like climbing a mountain at times. Anything you can do to make the task easier is valuable.

The idea is, keep your attitude fresh. Mental fatigue produces physical fatigue. Keep your mind sharp and you will play sharp.

Resolved: I keep a fresh outlook.

December 6

"You don't go home and talk about the great tennis courts that you played, but you do talk about the golf courses you played."
—Hank Ketcham

Break out of your rut. Play a course you've never played before.

Maybe rut is too negative a word. Call it a "habit," then. Whatever you call it, break out of it today.

Playing the same course most of the time makes sense. You're comfortable there. It's close by. You know the traps. It's like home in a way: familiar, cozy, comfortable. Like that old pair of slippers you can't bear to throw away.

Splurge today. Buy yourself a new pair of slippers—and play a golf course you've never played before. Or one that you haven't played in a while.

Golf is not like baseball or hockey or football or tennis or baseball or any of those other sports. The area of play changes. The game is not the same from course to course. Each course presents new challenges, different challenges. New things to learn, new ways of doing things.

But every golfer knows this. Every golfer loves to take a crack at a new course. It's just a matter of getting off the old duff and doing it.

Maybe it means driving a little farther, rearranging the schedule, finding more time to play. But it's worth it.

Playing a new golf course is like meeting someone new from the opposite sex. It's exciting. There's a hint of mystery to it. It's a turn-on.

Turn on, tune in, and drop into a new course today.

Resolved: I play a course I've never played before.

December 7

"Negative thoughts and carelessness cause more missed short putts than any other factors."

—Harv Penick

Stay positive when you putt the short ones. Stay positive when you putt the long ones too, but especially the short ones.

Short putts are easy to take for granted. You are supposed to make them. So you step up, yawning with boredom, and lip the cup.

You may be thinking about your previous putt, or maybe you have already jumped mentally to the next tee. You may even be chatting with another player, so unconcerned are you with the putt.

Whatever your state of mind, you have lost focus and it can hurt you. It especially stings in this situation, because it is such a makable putt.

It is impossible to sustain your concentration equally over the three or four hours it takes to play a round of golf. You're going to have lapses, times when you are just not *there*. It's inevitable.

One way to snap out of a funk is to concentrate on the little things. Forget your score. Forget the big picture. Concentrate on one or two little things, and do them the best you can.

One of those little things—one of those things that can get you back on track—are your short putts.

Focus on the short putts the same as any other stroke. Use them as a building block for the rest of your game.

Resolved: I focus on the short putts, too.

December 8

"Every day you don't hit balls is one day longer it takes you to get better."

—Ben Hogan

Get better. Hit balls.

What better way to spend your time? Hit balls.

Get away from everybody and everything. Hit balls.

Take out your frustrations. Hit balls.

Work at your game. Spend some time on it. Hit balls.

Think about your game. Think about it without interruption. Hit balls.

Hit balls. Work them from left to right. Work them from right to left. Aim for a yardage marker on the range. Hit balls.

Hitting balls is a very meditative act. You are doing the thing for the thing itself. The way you keep score is through your own satisfaction. You like the way it makes you feel. You like the sound when you really pop one. You like lacing up the spikes and setting to the business at hand.

It's after work. You're on your way home. You're moving from one set of responsibilities to another. You drive past the course. Traffic is terrible. You glance at your watch. You stop, you get out. You buy a bucket.

The driving range is near the freeway. Cars are jammed up on the freeway, hardly moving. You share a private laugh and applaud the wisdom of your move.

You find an empty station. Your bucket is heavy with balls. You set one on the tee and step back. You look around. Life is good.

Then you go to work.

Resolved: I hit balls today.

December 9

"Work out your own salvation. Do not depend on others."
—Buddha

Four-time British Open champion Willie Park Jr. learned to putt on the brick floor of his Scottish home. He said he never faced a putting green that was as hard to play as that floor.

When Chi Chi Rodriguez was a kid in Puerto Rico he used a crushed tin can as his golf ball and a branch of a tree for his club. Then he hit the can around the street with his friends.

Jim Dent, a big hitter on the Senior Tour, grew up in a poor black neighborhood that bordered Augusta National. He and his pals would watch the men play from behind a fence. Then the boys would stage their own makeshift games on the dirt streets in front of their houses. They dug holes in the dirt and passed a putter between them, playing for a quarter apiece, winner take all.

The history of golf is peopled by men and women who broke the mold, who refused to let their circumstances tell them what they could and could not do with their lives. They did not belong to a country club or in some cases even have access to a golf course. They loved the game. They let their love for the game lead them to success. Their will and desire overpowered all other considerations.

Make the best of your situation. Work out your own golfing salvation—wherever you are, whatever your circumstances. Let your love for the game lead you. Make your will and desire overpower all other considerations.

Resolved: I work out my own golfing salvation.

December 10

"I think my game has improved. Experience is a huge factor, maturity is a huge factor, and you know you are kind of getting into that thing of playing against Nick Price or Greg Norman or Jack Nicklaus or whoever. But you are playing against the golf course."

—Tom Lehman

It is the oldest and sagest snippet of wisdom in the Book of Golf: Play the course.

You laugh with your pals, you tee off with them, you hit with them, you commiserate with them. But you do not play against them, or anyone else for that matter. Play the course.

They post scoresheets at tournaments listing the players and how they are faring against one another. But they fail to list the most steadfast opponent of them all. Play the course.

The same is true at professional tournaments. Leader boards around the course tell us the positions of the players. But the most important player does not rate a mention. Play the course.

Question: If this knowledge is such a banal golfing commonplace, why did it take Tom Lehman and so many other pro golfers so long to learn it?

Answer: Because it is right there for them to see. They take it for granted, and ignore it.

Edgar Allan Poe said that the safest place to hide a thing was in the most obvious spot. Playing the course is so obvious, so easy. There must be more to golf than that.

Let others look past the obvious. Play the course.

Resolved: I play the course.

December 11

"A bad cornerback needs a bad memory and an awful lot of confidence."

—John Madden

John Madden, the ex-coach and TV commentator, was talking about defensive backs in the NFL and the attitude they need to survive.

A cornerback is the loneliest man in football (apart from field-goal kickers with the game on the line). He stands apart from the cluster of players grouped around the ball. He often performs his job by himself, without help from his teammates. He faces a receiver who is usually the fastest man on the field. When a cornerback fails in his job and the receiver makes a big gain or even a touchdown, everybody in the stadium knows instantly who is at fault.

Every golfer is like a defensive cornerback.

He stands apart. All alone, with no teammates to assist him.

When a golfer makes a mistake, everyone knows who did it, including—and most especially—the golfer himself. There is no hiding from your errors in golf, no assigning blame to others.

Today, play golf with the arrogance of a defensive back. Believe in yourself. Know that you cannot be beat. And if you get beat? Forget it. Cultivate a bad memory—or more precisely, a selective memory. Remember the good, forget the bad. That is all you can do. You make problems for yourself if you internalize yesterday's defeat and carry it over to today. That was yesterday; today is today, and the difference is everything.

Resolved: I keep my confidence up.

December 12

"Wonder is essentially an 'opening' attitude—an awareness that there is more to life than one has yet fathomed, an experience of new vistas in life to be explored."

—Rollo May

Open with wonder. Close with wonder. This afternoon, amaze yourself with the way you play golf.

Sometimes in high-stress situations you ask yourself to do things that you have never done before. Do it today, in that 7,000-yard high-stress environment known as a golf course.

Today, ask yourself to do something you have never done before. And see how you respond.

You play a certain way most of the time and most of the time it is fine. You're all right for what you do.

But in today's round, dig deep. Dig a little deeper than normal. Venture into unexplored areas. Just let it happen. Leave the analyzing for later.

What you will find, when you do, is that your old order has disappeared. You faced a high-stress situation. You asked yourself to respond, and you did. And now, the world is made new.

New possibilities, new vistas, new avenues of exploration have suddenly appeared. Or maybe they were there all the time, and you just couldn't see them before. But now you have. You have reached the farthest edge of what you once thought were your abilities and you have found, to your profound wonderment, that you are capable of so much more.

Resolved: I amaze myself on the golf course today.

December 13

"I'm not going to change my life for anybody. I just want to be the best and do it in my own little way. Drink a few beers and have fun."

—Ian Woosnam

Drink a few beers. Have fun. Is there a better motto for a golfer?

Woosie made this remark after winning the Masters several years ago, after which he went out, drank a few beers, and had some fun. You ought to do the same.

Play well today? Good show. Drink a few beers and have fun. You're entitled.

Oh, you didn't play so well? Oh, well. Better luck next time. Now go drink a few beers and have some fun. You're even more entitled.

Golf is a pleasurable activity, and part of the pleasure is in what we do after. We get together with our partners, we drink a few beers, we have fun.

You may not be in the mood because your performance was less than sublime. But that is no reason to deprive yourself of some good wholesome postround pleasure. Will abstinence from either alcohol or fun make you play better the next time out? Not likely.

When you play well, drink a few beers and have fun. When you play not so well, drink a few beers and have fun.

You are out there, giving it your all. Bully for you. Afterward drink a few beers, have fun.

Resolved: I drink a few beers today after golf and have some fun.

December 14

"None goes his way alone; all that we send into the lives of others comes back into our own."

—Edwin Markham

Eight out of 10 golfers were introduced to the game by a member of their own family. That seems logical. We are around these people so much, why not play golf with them?

So that is your charge today. Invite a member of your family for a round of golf. Ask your wife or husband. Ask your son or daughter. Ask a parent. Call on a brother or sister or an uncle or aunt. Call on a father-in-law. Call on a third cousin twice removed if you think she might be interested. Make golf a family affair.

There is certain to be much grumbling about this: "I can barely stand some of these people when I see them once a year at Thanksgiving," you say, "and now you want me to play golf with them?"

"And," you continue, "you want me to invite my in-laws too? I'd rather stick my fingers in a vise."

Easy. You are only playing golf with them. You are not inviting them to come stay with you for a week (although, it is true, you must be aware of the potential danger). Besides, you might even like it. You might discover a side of Uncle Jack or Sister-in-Law Jill that you never knew existed. Golf is like that. You can find out a lot about people when you take them out of their normal environment and put them on a golf course. Sometimes they find out a lot about themselves, too.

Resolved: I invite a family member to play golf.

December 15

"A good golf course makes you want to play so badly that you hardly have the time to change your shoes."

—Ben Crenshaw

First rule when playing a good golf course: Change your shoes. Enthusiasm will only carry you so far in your loafers. Better to wear spikes.

Second rule when playing a good course: Be suspicious of the obvious.

The enthusiastic Mr. Crenshaw explains, "When playing any classic course, my first piece of advice is to be suspicious of the obvious. If a hole has a bunker in the landing area that can easily be carried, it's a good idea to know what is behind that bunker before you hit your tee shot."

Try to get into the head of the architect who designed the course. Why did he put *that* there? What's the reasoning *here*? Tap in to his thought processes. This will help you negotiate your way around the course even as it challenges your shot-making abilities.

The best golf courses give you choices on how to play a shot. Some of these apparent avenues of approach are nothing more than a ruse. Playing golf on a challenging course is like solving a mystery. There are clues that you must decipher and evaluate. The architect seeks to cloak the mystery with disguise and deception.

Be like Sam Spade. Outthink that mastermind architect. Be always one step ahead. Don't fall for his ruses. Be suspicious of the obvious, and you will recover the missing falcon.

Resolved: I suspect the obvious on a good golf course.

December 16

"All that matters in golf is the next shot."

—Ralph Guldahl

This shot, this moment, this swing. This is all that matters in golf, and this is all that will ever matter.

The reason you hit this shot is to set up your next shot. This is golf strategy boiled down to its essence and the heart of Guldahl's message.

This shot. Next shot.

This shot establishes the conditions for your next shot, just as the present establishes the conditions upon which the future will unfold. Take command of the present and you control the future. You create the conditions for success for your next shot by focusing on and executing this shot.

Your drive sets up your second shot. Your second shot sets up your approach. Your approach sets up your position on the green. Each shot sets up the next. It is a simple, logical sequence of events.

This shot. Next shot.

You court disaster if you disrupt this elemental sequence. It's like splitting the atom. Hit the next shot before *this* shot, and kaboom!

You render yourself vulnerable to the present by jumping ahead to the future. The future is a whimsy, a cloud, a puff of smoke. Invest in the concrete and material present.

You will be considering your next shot if you think solely in terms of this shot. Control the present, and you control the future.

Resolved: This shot, this moment, this swing.

December 17

Find what works for you. This is the secret of success in putting and golf.

Try the cross-handed grip.

Try a new putter.

Return to a putter that you once used.

Putt one-handed.

Putt with a pool cue (actually, no, that's against the rules).

Develop your own grip à la Bernhard Langer.

Try the croquet-style approach of an aging Sam Snead.

Coddle your putter and give it a name, such as Ben Crenshaw's "Little Ben."

Try an extra-long putter.

Look at the hole, not the ball, when you putt.

Putt with your eyes closed.

Try anything, try everything. Try things that have never been tried before. Become the Orville and Wilbur Wright of putting. Let your putting green be a Kitty Hawk of experimentation.

Just remember this: It could work.

This is the thing never to forget. Your experiments will go nowhere with a defeatist attitude.

It could work. It really could.

You could be making a change for the better. You could be making the change that really does improve your putting. Enter into your experiments with a spirit of optimism, and your putting game truly could take flight.

Resolved: I view my putting experiments with optimism.

December 18

"Knowledge is power."

—Francis Bacon

Ever ranked your game through your bag?

No doubt you have a favorite club. You love that 5-wood and would sleep with it if your wife let you. But how about the other woods in your bag? How do they rate?

Same with the irons. Nobody except for Jack Nicklaus can play a 1-iron; you may not even have one in your bag. You may have warm thoughts about your 5- and 7-irons. What about the others?

Take a few minutes to rate your clubs, even if you have a good general idea already. Develop specific knowledge about your game, and figure out how to apply it on a golf course.

How can you build on your strengths unless you truly know what they are? How can you make your "weaknesses" into strengths? Evaluate your relationship with each club. How have you used it in the past? What do you like about it? Dislike? In what situations can you apply it successfully in the future?

This is a form of mental preparation. The more you know about your clubs, the better you *will* use them. Knowledge is power. You will deliberate less when you choose a club before a shot, and you will have more confidence in the choices you make.

Resolved: I rank my game through my bag.

December 19

Have power over yourself. Take power over your game. Walk onto the green in command.

This is the purpose of every approach shot: Walk onto the green in command.

This is the purpose of every iron shot or fairway wood: Walk onto the green in command.

This is the purpose of every tee ball you hit: Walk onto the green in command.

This is your strategy at the start of every hole: Walk onto the green in command.

Your choice of club becomes clear. How to play the shot becomes clear. Once you are clear on your purpose: Walk onto the green in command.

Think of Tom Watson or Greg Norman walking onto the final green of a tournament, receiving the applause of the gallery. Look at their bearing, how they carry themselves. They are walking onto the green in command.

Walk onto the green in command, and you have done everything you can do up to that point. You have put yourself into a position to get good results on the green, and to score. Even if you have had trouble on the hole up till then, you can still obtain good results if you walk onto the green with the right attitude and sense of internal command.

The specifics do not matter. How you get there does not matter.

What matters is this: Walk onto the green in command.

Resolved: I walk onto the green in command.

December 20

"The work will teach you how to do it."

—Estonian proverb

Your job today: Get better.

Somehow, some way, get better. Learn something that will help you get better. Do something that will help you get better. Just get better.

Listen to somebody who really knows your game. Listen hard, put it in your game, and get better.

When you hit your tee ball, learn from it. Get better.

Go to school on your putting. All day long, learn from what you do and get better.

This is your job. Take it seriously. Do it like you mean it. Get better.

Get better with an iron today. Get better with a wood. Get better with at least one club today.

You play pretty well. You can play even better. Be determined to get better.

Learn something during practice and put it into play during your round. Learn something during your round and work on it some more in practice.

Learn something on the first tee. Put it into play by the 18th tee or sooner.

Learn something on the 18th green. Put it into play the next time you go out.

Be a sponge when it comes to learning on a golf course. Sop up everything that helps you get better.

The game will show you how. With the commitment you will find the way. Get better.

Resolved: I get better.

December 21

"If one has not learned enough of golf by the time he steps onto the first tee, then he has run out of time."

—Bobby Jones

Today is the official beginning of winter, the shortest day of the year.

But winter started long before today. It arrived in the chill of the late-afternoon air. It arrived on a cold, cold morning in early December. Maybe it even trumpeted its arrival with a big snowstorm. Winter arrived in a thousand different ways regardless of its official start date, independent of the calendar's reckoning.

Similarly, your golf game does not begin at its "official" beginning.

The start of every round of golf is the first tee, but your success will be determined by all the things you have done up to that point.

You must be physically and mentally prepared to play. You must put yourself in a frame of mind that allows you to implement the physical tools at your disposal.

A well-prepared person is a person who has taken the care and time. It is a sign of desire.

Prepare to play. Prepare to succeed. Make this the reason for your preparations: success. And make these preparations every day of the year, all year long.

Make that commitment today, but also for tomorrow and the day after that. Prepare to succeed.

Resolved: I prepare to succeed.

December 22

"Making solid contact is by far the most important key to hitting great chips and pitches."

—Scott Davenport, teaching pro

Let this be your swing key for the day: Make solid contact.

Make solid contact when you hit your chips and pitches. They will be great chips and pitches when you do.

Make solid contact when you hit your tee ball. You will hit great tee balls when you do. Think about the clubface striking the surface of the ball flush. Make solid contact, and watch the ball bounce down the fairway.

Make solid contact on the greens. The ball will only go into the hole if you get it there first. Make solid contact. Get it to the hole.

Don't get cheated. Take your cuts. Make solid contact.

You will always get respect for your golf if you make solid contact. A golfer who makes solid contact is a golfer who hits fairways and greens.

When you make solid contact, you are not overswinging or trying to do much. You are not slicing or spraying the ball. The ball is following the dictates of the club swung smoothly on line. When you make solid contact, you do not need to worry about your score. The score takes care of itself.

You can always feel comfortable about the way you played when you make solid contact. When you make solid contact, you are playing well with an opportunity to play even better.

Play solid golf. Make solid contact.

Resolved: I make solid contact.

December 23

"The happiness that is genuinely satisfying is accompanied by the fullest exercise of our faculties, and the fullest realization of the world in which we live."

—Bertrand Russell

Germany's Bernhard Langer stood on the final green of the 1991 Ryder Cup, and the whole world was watching.

Langer had fought hard—as hard as he could fight—to get into this position. Down by one hole with three holes left to play, he sunk a six-footer for par to halve 16 with his opponent, three-time U.S. Open champion Hale Irwin. Then, on the next hole, he made par to Irwin's bogey and tied the match. He stood only five feet away from beating Irwin and the United States.

He missed the putt.

Langer was crushed. The United States won, Europe lost. He felt he had let his teammates down, even as his putter had let him down all day long. Considering the intense pressure, there is probably not a person alive who could have sunk that putt on 18.

Langer did everything he could short of making that putt. He gave it his all. That is all anyone could ask of him—and all that you can ask of yourself. The results we seek may not be the results we obtain. But if there is happiness to be found in this life, it is in the fact of giving to a task everything we have, and leaving nothing wanting.

Empty the tank. Leave nothing in reserve. Give it your all.

Resolved: I give it my all.

December 24

"There are two things keeping me out here. Faith in God and faith in myself. I'll never quit."

—Bobby Clampett

Place your faith in the unseen. Place your faith in what is yet to come.

Most people will judge you by your past. This is understandable to a degree. The best indication of what a person will do today is what he or she has done in the past.

But this is a very limiting view. You will never achieve all that you can achieve in golf or life if you accept the definitions of yourself imposed from without by other people. Those people define you in order to keep you in your place and protect theirs.

Why let the past, or the views that people hold of your past, limit your future?

Hang on to your dreams. Dreams are the best part of you. Hang on to your view of the future. Your view of the future is interwoven with your dreams, and you need to fight for them both.

Everything in the physical world obeys limits. Even the vast universe has boundaries. But the spirit inside you—the best part of you—has no limits. And certainly no limits that can be defined by other human beings.

Listen to what your heart tells you. People may let you down from time to time. But your dream never will. Place your faith in what is to come, what is unseen, what cannot be grasped by the human hand. Believe, believe, believe with all your being in the truth of your vision.

Resolved: I put my faith in what is to come.

December 25

"Were I a philosopher, I should write a philosophy of toys,
showing that nothing else in life needs to be taken seriously."
—Robert Lynd

Today is a day for giving gifts (among other things). Give yourself some new golf toys.

Buy a membership in a club. Buy a new set of sticks. Treat yourself to a round at an expensive course where you have always wanted to play. Make arrangements for that golf vacation to Kaanapali.

What's that you say, isn't that being selfish? This is a day in which we give unto others.

Listen. The kids have their Nintendo; they're happy. So is the spouse. The family's taken care of. You're going to church a little later, and afterward you and the family are working at a community soup kitchen. You've got it covered.

What, more grumbling? These are just toys, you say. Mere playthings. Unserious and therefore unimportant.

We beg to differ. Nothing is more serious than your toys. Toys are what explains you to yourself. You have to work; that's not *you*. What's you is what you do in your free time, when you can truly be yourself. Your toys are what you turn to when you want to be you. They reflect who you are better than a mirror.

It is not that you have too many toys, it is that you do not have enough of them. It is not that you play with toys, it is that you do not play enough.

Rectify that today. Grab your kids and your toys, and go play.

Resolved: I play with my golf toys.

December 26

"When a man's capacity is fully engaged, he is really living, even though it be but for a day."

—Joseph Odell

Engage yourself fully. Rise to the challenge that the game of golf presents.

Playing a course for the first time? Rise to the challenge.

Playing the course you always play? Play the back nine better than you ever have before. Make a par on a tough hole. Two-putt all the greens. The challenges may be harder to find in the commonplace. But they are there. Find them and rise up to meet them.

If you do not see an immediate challenge, make one up. The challenge may be as simple as putting a little money down. The fact is, though, there are plenty of challenges in golf without having to go hunt for them. They confront us at every turn.

There is a challenge to driving the ball, a challenge to putting, a challenge to escaping from sand, a challenge to maintaining one's concentration, a challenge to avoid being frustrated. The challenges are both physical and mental. If you are a person who is shy of facing challenges, you chose the wrong game.

Expect to be challenged, then, when you go out on the golf course. Look forward to it. It is, in part, why we play.

Relish the game. Relish its challenges. Look forward to golf's challenges and meet them head-on.

Resolved: I look forward to the challenges I will face today.

December 27

"Before enlightenment, a woodcutter chops wood. After enlightenment, a woodcutter chops wood."

—Zen saying

Congratulations. You did it. You made it to the top of the mountain.

You set goals for yourself this year and you reached them. You set a high target and you made a bull's-eye. Now what?

Play, play.

What you do now is what you did before: Play, play.

Set new goals for yourself and go after them. Set the target higher this time. Plant your flag at the top of a taller mountain.

The key to the treasure was never the treasure anyway. The key to the treasure is the key.

What you can expect to find at the end of a long journey is what you set out with at the start. There is nothing that you will find at journey's end that you do not already possess and indeed possessed every step of the way. You probably instinctively realized this a long time ago.

Were you having fun playing golf? Did you enjoy yourself? Was the process of playing and learning and working and practicing giving you what you wanted while you were doing it, while you were pursuing your goals? If the answers to these questions are yes, then you will be happy to hear this news: Your future looks as bright as your past.

Before enlightenment, play golf. After enlightenment, play golf.

Resolved: I play.

December 28

"As long as there's a bit of a laugh going, things are all right. As soon as this infernal seriousness, like a greasy sea, heaves up, everything is lost."

—D. H. Lawrence

Here is a challenge for you:

Go down to your TV room—you know, the one with the sliding glass door that opens onto the patio. Get some balls and take out an iron of your choice. Open the door about a foot. Then try to hit the balls through the opening in the door.

PGA Tour pro Ken Green, an enemy of all types of infernal seriousness, has been known to do that. It is not known how his glass doors have fared in the process.

Here is another of Green's practice methods, certainly superior to the first because it does not put your personal property at risk.

Park a rental car in the driveway. Open the trunk of the car and see how many balls you can chip into it. Give yourself a point for each successful chip. More advanced players can roll down the windows and chip into the car, or better yet, *through* it. Explain innocently to the rental-car people that you don't know how the dings got there.

Of course, you could set up a target in your backyard and practice your chipping in a more conventional fashion. But what would be the fun in that?

Resolved: I practice chipping into the trunk of a rental car.

December 29

"It's like anything else, you don't lose it as fast if you keep at it. It's when you stop playing and then try to go back that you've lost it."

—Sam Snead

Make a commitment to the game as you would a spouse. For a lifetime.

You will have a hard time getting started again if you stop. It is a law of physics and golf. A body at rest tends to remain at rest, especially if parked on the couch with a channel changer.

Hang with it. If you cannot play today, play tomorrow. If not tomorrow, then next week. If not next week, next month. Never give up the game for good. Just put it on hiatus if you must.

But if you feel like quitting, there probably is something wrong. Not with the game, but with your attitude toward it. Are you still *playing* golf, as opposed to working at it or striving toward betterment? Are you having fun? Has it become some sort of grim-faced test of character?

Perhaps a break is in order. But keep it short and sweet. The game will reward you for your loyalty. It always gives back. Remain loyal to golf, and in this way remain loyal to yourself.

Resolved: I stay loyal to golf—today, tomorrow, forever.

December 30

*"It is nothing new or original to say that golf is played one
stroke at a time. But it took me many years to realize it."*

—Bobby Jones

One stroke at a time.

This sentiment is not even new or original in this book.
We have been saying it throughout the year in various forms
and disguises.

One stroke at a time.

This fundamental truth of golf equates with a fundamental truth of life: one day at a time, one moment at a time.

The very best golfers know how precious strokes are. They
never want to waste a one. Why should it be any different for
lesser players? Perhaps that is why they are lesser, because
they place such a low value on their strokes.

Another truth of life is to live fully, as fully as you can while
you are able. Again, this rings true for golfers: Grab for everything you can out of the game.

One stroke at a time.

Fully commit to what you are doing, right now, this
moment. One stroke at a time.

Play with passion. Play with zeal. One stroke at a time.

Realize the present fully. Give everything you've got, everything you can muster, to your game, your life. One stroke at
a time.

Resolved: One stroke at a time.

December 31

"In my beginning is my end."

—T. S. Eliot

The year ends. But there is no end really. Golf is a lifetime endeavor that transcends calendar boundaries.

The beginning foreshadows the end. The end refers back to the beginning. In between it all is golf.

Going out tonight? No? Staying home? Whatever you do, wherever you are, celebrate in some fashion. You deserve it. We have a certain number of years allotted to us. When one goes out it is worth celebrating.

And how is your golf? How'd you do this year? Accomplish the goals you set for yourself?

What, you say you could have done better? Sure you could have. We all could have. And we will.

On second thought, we did just fine. In taking stock we sometimes focus overmuch on what is missing from the cupboard, not on what is actually there. We have an abundance, most of us, if we would but recognize it.

Today, squeeze in a game of golf. It is practically a national holiday anyway. Then go out and get drunk. Golf and a good drunk: the perfect way to end the year, the perfect way to live a life.

Feel lucky, because you are. Be optimistic, because the world needs people of faith and heart. Be positive, because the opposite gets you nowhere. Be happy, because life is grand and time is short.

And know that next year—*next year!*—will be the best year of our golfing lives.

Resolved: I make next year the best year of my golfing life.

About the Author

Kevin Nelson's previous book on golf is *The Greatest Golf Shot Ever Made, and Other Lively & Entertaining Tales from the Lore and History of Golf.* This is his 10th book. He lives in the San Francisco Bay Area.

Index